Diverse Narratives of Legal Objectivity

Dia-Logos

Schriften zu Philosophie und Sozialwissenschaften
Studies in Philosophy and Social Sciences

Herausgegeben von / Edited by
Tadeusz Buksiński / Piotr W. Juchacz

Bd. /vol. 19

PETER LANG
EDITION

Vito Breda / Lidia Rodak (eds.)

Diverse Narratives of Legal Objectivity

An Interdisciplinary Perspective

PETER LANG
EDITION

Bibliographic Information published by the Deutsche Nationalbibliothek
The Deutsche Nationalbibliothek lists this publication in the Deutsche Nationalbibliografie; detailed bibliographic data is available in the internet at http://dnb.d-nb.de.

Library of Congress Cataloging-in-Publication Data
Names: Breda, Vito, 1971- editor. | Rodak, Lidia, 1979- editor.
Title: Diverse narratives of legal objectivity : an interdisciplinary perspective / Vito Breda, Lidia Rodak (eds.).
Description: Frankfurt am Main : Peter Lang, 2016. | Series: Dia-logos ; 19 | Includes bibliographical references.
Identifiers: LCCN 2015047206 | ISBN 9783631653432
Subjects: LCSH: Law--Language. | Law--Philosophy. | Objectivity. | Jurisprudence.
Classification: LCC K213 .D575 2016 | DDC 340/.14--dc23 LC record available at http://lccn.loc.gov/2015047206

This publication was supported by the University of Silesia.

ISSN 1619-005X
ISBN 978-3-631-65343-2 (Print)
ISBN 978-3-653-04533-8 (E-Book)
DOI 10.3726/ 978-3-653-04533-8

Peter Lang Edition is an Imprint of Peter Lang GmbH.

Peter Lang – Frankfurt am Main · Berlin · Bruxelles · New York · Oxford · Warszawa · Wien

This publication has been peer reviewed.

www.peterlang.com

Table of Contents

Introduction

Objectivity is an inherently complex philosophical concept and, as such, it is a continually recurring theme in philosophical and jurisprudential debates. One of the fundamental questions, still surrounded in controversy, is whether objectivity is a "self-generated" universal concept that transcends local discourse. If so, how can it be philosophically justifiable, and what part, if any, does the jurisprudential debate play in such a discourse? Although these questions may appear a bit naive nowadays, they express the ambitions and power of the concept of objectivity. On one hand, it represents the desire for truth, akin to Kant's "things in themselves", something fixed and eternal. On the more negative side, objectivity interpreted as the narration of a timeless universal truth is associated with its power to impose authority from above.

In "*The Structure of Scientific Revolution*", Thomas Kuhn claimed: "that there is no representation of facts without an observatory language, and there is no observatory language which is "theory free"". Under this system, a rejection of objectivity in its strong sense seems inevitable. In line with this way of thinking, social sciences have adopted the concept of intersubjectivity in place of objectivity, which seems better suited to humanities in general. Law and legal discourse, however, which play central roles in organizing human society, remain strongly committed to the notion of objectivity, despite all the controversy that surrounds it. The rationale behind this is far from straightforward. It is not at all clear whether law has a distinctive type of objectivity, separate from scientific epistemic methods, or whether legal discourse has its own specificity that influences legal objectivity. If either of these are true, we have to ask what it is for law to be objective and whether objectivity is suitable for law, given its contested and changeable nature. If objectivity is somehow necessary for law, we also need to ascertain whether there is just one type of objectivity or different types of objectivity that meet its requirements. These questions are all addressed in the book.

The main aim of this edited collection of essays is to contribute to the debate on legal objectivity. The authors address the debates on the status of law and judicial discourse separately and the papers can be roughly divided into two categories. Articles in the first category focus on the general debate over metaphysical objectivity (by Pazdziora, Berdisova, Pichlak and Rodak). Articles in the second category form part of the debate over the possibility of epistemologically objective procedures (by Pieniazek, Denaro, Sena, Cercel, Marrani, Breda, and Szerletcs).

Taking into account the specific character of practical legal discourse, which has a strong commitment to both objectivity and subjectivity, it can be questioned whether objectivity is suitable for legal discourse at all. In order to understand the scope of the papers in this collection, it is helpful to look briefly at some of the criticisms of objectivity in this respect. Sir Neil MacCormick has written extensively on the practice of legal reasoning and objectivity and, on several occasions, he admitted to his doctoral students that he considered the concept of objectivity in judicial discourse as an unhelpful idea. In MacCormick's later renderings, objectivity in judicial discourse is a contested concept for two different sets of reasons. The first set relates to the failure of objectivity in judicial discourse to eliminate the subjective; the second set focuses on ideological bias.

The first set of critiques is based on the law's inability to evaluate complex data. For example, MacCormick argues that, in an ideal scenario, the numbers of variables and infinite number of possible commutations that the court would have to consider as part of its judicial activity make a judgement based on subjective opinions inevitable. So, by definition, this is antithetical to the idea of objectivity. However, these types of critical engagements, which focus on the objectivity of legal narrative, are drawn from a misguided representation of what can be expected from judicial reasoning and they are seldom mentioned in this book. Most contemporary legal authors accept that few complex scientific activities can deliver an absolutely objective result. It is reasonable to expect judges to act in a similar way to scientists and normalise the results of their studies after having considered all the variables. Normalising the results may sound 'dodgy' and, to some extent, it is. For example, judges may prefer certain epistemic practices to others, and this may be exploited by lawyers who seek to bias the judgement. However, the practice of reducing relevant variables, evaluating narratives, and assessing results is axiomatic of most complex scientific activities. Over the centuries, these epistemic activities have delivered reasonably consistent results and progressively increased the precision of legal studies. In other words, scientific methods have delivered the 'goods'. As Richard Rorty argues, judicial opinions based on a series of intersubjective evaluations have, over the years, been perceived as objective by a community of experts. Objectivity *of legal discourse,* as in any other branch of science, cannot be constructed in absolute terms.

In comparison to MacCormick's epistemic critiques that deny the possibility of judicial objectivity, his ideological critiques suggest that objectivity *in law* is a pernicious concept and that judges are instruments of power, making use of their positions to protect ideological assumptions, reactionary ideas, and even discriminatory practices against minorities and women. The Critical Legal Studies, Critical Gender Studies and Critical Race Theories movements have been instrumental in exposing the effects of discriminatory judicial practices, judicial paternalism and xenophobia.

This set of critiques is well represented in this collection of essays. However, the contributors substantiate their narratives with different types of scholarship, employing philosophical, analytical, historical and architectural perspectives, along with empirical studies and in-depth comparative analyses of the legal systems researched. This process was aided by a series of workshops (including those organised at the biennial IVR World Congress of Legal Philosophy, and at the University of Palermo). The results of these activities matured over a long period to form the present collection.

From the meetings that preceded the completion of this collection, it emerged that law has a strong demand for objectivity, yet it might be approached from many different perspectives. The papers in this volume all conform to this view, each revealing its own perspective and employed theory. As a consequence, objectivity, as analyzed in this volume, avoids any claims to universality.

The complexity of the issues will become apparent by reading this volume, but the reader may find it helpful to first have a brief overview of each of the articles, outlining the author's chosen aspects of legal objectivity.

The first set of articles, representing the philosophical and analytical approaches, refer mainly to the metaphysical aspect of legal objectivity. Papers by Michal Pazdziora, Lucia Berdisova, Maciej Pichlak and Lidia Rodak all address the question of what type of objectivity is suitable for law. Each of the authors proposes their own solution.

Michał Paździora, author of "*What rationality? Whose objectivity?*" (1), poses the question of who or what is the subject of objectivity and rationality in law. Reflecting on the significance of the objectivity of law for lawyers, he points out that it is possible to identify an ideological bias under the surface of legal discourse. He introduces the importance of legal reality, which necessarily involves the perspective of subjects, even if this is in an "invisible way". His arguments for a "subjectively underpinned objectivity" sketch out the background for the other papers, revealing the participants of objective legal discourse.

Lucia Berdisova, in her paper "*Objectivity and arbitrariness of a blind rule-following or what it means to follow a (legal) rule blindly?*" (2), seeks a normative justification for procedural objectivity. Through her discussion of the "Kripkenstein" argument on the impossibility of following rules, she poses fundamental questions on the concept of law and its objectivity. By refuting the arguments of rule scepticism, the author defends objectivity of law and reaches the conclusion that objectivity is created, not discovered. She continues the discussion by looking at the human agency involved in creating objectivity, leading neatly into the question posed by the next contributor of who is responsible for creating objectivity of law. Through the interpretative debate on "whether or how is it possible to follow rules", she shows how the epistemological and metaphysical perspectives are tightly connected.

Maciej Pichlak (4) discusses the interplay between objectivity and institutional reflexivity in law. His essay aims to answer the question of how objectivity is possible within law. It focuses on two notions of objectivity that can be observed in legal practice: objectivity as a social fact, and objectivity as a moral ideal of legal practice. Employing an institutional perspective on social sciences, he claims not only that these two dimensions of objectivity may be plausibly explained, but also that they concur within social institutions. Concurrence does not mean conflation though: the relation between the factual and ideal aspects of objectivity is dialectical in nature and they need to be distinguished clearly. After explicating the weaknesses of other theoretical perspectives that fall into the fallacy of conflating the factual and the ideal, the paper subsequently develops an institutional concept of objectivity. Adopting the notion of institutional reflexivity as characterizing contemporary institutions, the author outlines the idea of "reflexive objectivity" in law.

Lidia Rodak (5) continues the discussion on what kind of objectivity is suitable for law. Through her analysis of debates from the different schools of Feminist Jurisprudence on the limitations of essentialist and anti-essentialism positions, she proposes "essentialism of a kind" as the ideal model for objectivity of law. Such a position recognises the role of subjectivity in protecting the rights of citizens, while admitting that law necessarily needs "objectivity of a kind". The next group of papers addresses the question of how, if at all, it is possible to apply objectivity in practical legal discourse. The authors investigate the internal procedures and mechanisms of practical legal discourse to trace the involvement of human agency in legal objectivity. This debate is divided in four discussions, from analytical, philosophical and empirical, and historical perspectives, providing a full interdisciplinary picture of legal objectivity.

Marcin Pieniążek, (6.) comments on Paul Ricœur's theory of semantic autonomy of texts and the perspective of the legislator. The objective meaning of legal texts is, *inter alia,* of deep interest for the jurisprudence in the context of both the interpretation and the application of law. Pieniążek proposes Ricœur's views as the foundation for "the third way" of thinking about the objectivity of legal texts. The author manages to interpret semantic autonomy as a form of understanding the objectivity of legal texts, whilst retaining their autonomy in the context of the legislator's intention and still conforming to the hermeneutical model of the application of law.

Taking a philosophical perspective, Pietro Denaro (3) continues the discussion on human agency involved in legal discourse by sketching out the key arguments for defending a theory whereby both actions and omissions have a causal role. In the first part of his essay, he criticizes those views which deny the causal role of omissions. In the second part, he presents a rapid overview of some of the problems relating to metaphysical objectivity in theories of human agency in order to affirm that we do make a difference by omitting as well as by acting.

Finally, Jaqueline Sena (7), discusses the possibility of neutrality in legal science and judicial activity by reviewing the works of Luis Alberto Warat. She postulates that neutrality is not possible within a judicial activity, making reference to contemporary democracies that have lost their power to represent the people. Her conclusion is that the idea of neutrality of judges is nothing more than a harmful fiction.

Papers in the historical perspective section discuss whether historical and architectural perspectives could provide a justification for current judicial procedures.

Cosmin Sebastian Cercel (8) explores the dark partnership between authoritarianism and law. His paper aims to further complicate the articulate the question of objectivity within legal and historical discourse by exploring the theoretical intricacies raised by the historiography of totalitarianism. His focus is on the ambiguous status of law within authoritarian settings, one marked by thorough complicity between ideology and "legal" normativity. The paper addresses three core questions, namely: the role of the theory of totalitarianism in historical and memorial discourses in structuring the law within authoritarian contexts; the historiographical and jurisprudential implications of examining the past through the chosen framework; and the construction of meaning through a historical recollection marked by the paradox of evil law. By underlining the pivotal role of the theory of totalitarianism in politics for representing the past, he attempts, through a genealogical reading informed by the works of Giorgio Agamben and Lacan's psychoanalysis, to explore the potentialities of a different rendering of totalitarian law as part of legal modernity. In this way, the author critically examines the limits of representation of law and totalitarianism in both historiographical and jurisprudential settings.

David Marrani (9) focuses on the institution of the "Palaces of Justice". Empirical evidence shows that there is a link between the architecture of the courts of justice and respect for the law. Court architecture may influence the efficiency of the law in terms of individual case resolution, which in turn has an impact on the cohesion of society. Law courts operate like microcosms of social organisation In the past, the myth of authority was represented by neoclassical architecture in civil law countries, such as France, or Gothic revival architecture in common law countries, such as the UK; the "palaces of justice". In more recent years, we have witnessed a radical shift in courthouse design with wide scale use of glass. The use of transparency, or what the author terms the new opacity, can be seen as in tune with postmodern idea of objectivity as an empty form. This fascinating article studies the relation between the architecture of the courts and types of objectivity.

The empirical debate reflects on how procedural objectivity affects the decision process in current legal practice.

Vito Breda (10) reports on the results of his hermeneutical research project entitled "*Objectivity in UK Judicial Discourse*". The research focuses on mapping out the cluster of interpretations of objectivity (and arguments derived there from) made by common law judges in the UK, with a particular emphasis on judgements made by the House of Lords and the UK Supreme Court.

Antal Szerletics (11) postulates a connection between paternalism and "objective" best interests. He examines the paternalistic character of the English Mental Capacity Act (2005). It is argued that, although the system of surrogate decision-making in the EMCA seems to fit well within a liberal political framework, there are certain value-driven background assumptions that influence the way mentally incapacitated people are paternalised'. This is so both with respect to the construction of the concept of mental capacity (i.e. the statutory "threshold" for paternalistic interventions) and the determination of best interests. The best interest standard is explored in the second part of the paper through an analysis of relevant case law of the Court of Protection.

Overall, this collection of essays explores the connection, and the pretence of such a connection, between transparency and objectivity in legal narratives. Through discussing the involvement of human agency and the analysis of legal discourse from different perspectives, the debate on objectivity in law is transformed into one about an objectivity that is co-created by its participants. The essays reveal the inevitable intersections between the epistemological and metaphysical foundations of law, where a set of epistemic techniques permanently verify the status of legal objectivity from the bottom of the legal discourse rather than from the top. It is more about many types of objectivity suitable for law, rather than just one legal objective narration.

PART I Philosophical Perspectives

Michal Pazdziora,

University of Wroclaw, Poland

1. What rationality? Whose objectivity?

> "To become a lawyer, or even a teacher of law, has meant to enter an exterior world, to engage in a distinct vocation, to learn an art that is distant from the self. […] it is written, it legislates, it is an exterior fate, a foreign of institutional will inscribed on the soul."[1]

The quotation above from the introduction to P. Goodrich's and D. G. Carlson's "Law and the Postmodern Mind" testifies to the connection between the modernistic concept of law and the categories of external reality and objectivity. What is more, for lawyers themselves, i.e. the actors viewing the institution of law from inside, this connection seems constitutive. Therefore, in the legal practice law and jurisprudence appear as an external and objective reality. While subscribing to the view that any discussion of objectivity in law can not disregard legal practice, I would like to focus on two issues, emphasised by K. Marx in the Theses on Feuerbach.

> "The question whether objective truth can be attributed to human thinking is not a question of theory but is a practical question. Man must prove the truth — i.e. the reality and power, the this-sidedness of his thinking in practice. The dispute over the reality or non-reality of thinking that is isolated from practice is a purely *scholastic* question"[2].

Even though Marx never elaborated on his theory of practice, his analyses of the relationship between the theory and practice may be quite enlightening despite their limited scope. However, unlike Marx, we have to reject the belief in "theoretical certainty or revolutionary self-confidence"[3] and we are forced to relinquish any theology of reason or the logic of history. Yet, despite the weak points indicated,

---

1 Peter Goodrich (ed*), Law and the Postmodern Mind: Essays on Psychoanalysis and Jurisprudence* (Univ of Michigan Press 1998) 1.

2 2nd Karl Marx Thesis on Feuerbach Friedrich Engels, *Ludwig Feuerbach and the End of Classical German Philosophy* (Electric Book Co 2001) 61–65 <http://site.ebrary.com/id/2001676> accessed 19 April 2015.

3 Richard J Bernstein, *Beyond Objectivism and Relativism: Science, Hermeneutics, and Praxis* (4 pr, Univ of Pennsylvania Press 1991) 230.

Marx's theses raise two important issues. Firstly, the question of "objectivity" must be seen as a practical issue rather than a purely theoretical one. Consequently, the category of objectivity becomes a practical issue of how reality emerges and is perceived in the lawyers' awareness. Secondly, all theoretical models of objectivity disregarding universally established practice of creating reality inevitably become scholastic. In the *Theses on Feuerbach* theory becomes theoretical practice which perceives the relationship between the determinants and their results not as an expressive relation, i.e. static inevitability which may be identified, but as a relationship of creation, i.e. dynamic contingency of the inevitable[4]. To alter the practice it is not sufficient to provide theoretical arguments in support of a definite concept of objectivity; it is necessary to alter theoretical practice. We are well aware that our consciousness is a product of conditioning and educating, while we tend to forget that people alter the conditions and that the educators themselves must be educated first[5].

In this article, I will primarily focus on the reality seen from the epistemological perspective. Objectivity related to epistemology manifests itself in the endeavour to be independent from the factors which may distort the cognitive process. In this sense, objectivity has routinely been contrasted with subjectivity. Especially in law this claim of objectivity is particularly emphasised both in the doctrine and case-law.

> "(…) the demand to be objective is the demand to be free of bias or other factors that distort judgment, that prevent the things we are judging from presenting themselves clearly and accurately. This, then, is a demand for epistemic objectivity: that the cognitive processes and mechanisms by which we form beliefs about the world be constituted in such a way that they at least tend toward the production of accurate representations of how things are."[6]

The relationship between objectivity and subjectivity brings about three concepts of objectivity: strong objectivity as completely independent of the subject, modest version of objectivity as minimisation of the subject's intervention and minimal version of objectivity which is based on the acceptance of majority in a certain group[7]. The article's central aim is to provide arguments not only proving that it is impossible to eliminate subjectivity in the process of interpretation and application

4 Louis Althusser and Etienne Balibar, *Czytanie 'Kapitału'* [Reading Capital] (Wiktor Dłuski tr, 1st edn, Państwowy Insytut Wydawniczy 1975) 75.

5 3rd Karl Marx Thesis on Feuerbach Engels (n 2) 61–65.

6 Brian Leiter (ed), *Objectivity in Law and Mor*als (Cambridge University Press 2001) 1.

7 Lidka Rodak, 'Objective Interpretation as Conforming Interpretation' (2011) 1 Oñati Socio-Legal Series 4.

of law, but primarily to emphasise its constitutive and creative role in the process of establishing objectivity. For this purpose (I) I am going to present the way in which modern philosophy enables connecting objectivity with the category of rationality in order to indicate, in accordance with Marx's theses, how the issue of objectivity may be constructed and reconstructed in connection with practice. Then, (II) I am going to discuss the category of hard cases in law in order to assess the consequences of the adopted view of objectivity in legal practice. Although questioning the legitimacy of the search for objectivity, both in theory and practice, seems to have recently become fashionable while emphasising the subjective element in law, I am not going to deprecate the need for objectivity. To the contrary, I am convinced that objectivity by all means needs to be cultivated. The article also aims at proving that objectivity in law cannot be treated in absolute terms. Considering subjectivity as a necessary condition for objectivisation enables the rethinking of the concept of objectivity in law.

I

Bogdan Baran points out that the history of philosophy employs two meanings of the notion[8]. The first – stemming from the notion of rationalism – refers to the theoretical-methodological view, connected with the process of explaining the reality and justification of statements describing it by putting it under the spell of the system of concepts. By and large, rationality is simply equated here with a scientific method. Rationality in the other meaning is an existential category referring to individual and particular decisions. To act rationally is thus to make conscious choices in accordance with what is imposed by the current circumstances. Actions of an individual "thrown into a situation" are qualified as rational if they are justified by his or her way of understanding the reality. The rationality thus defined is not used in the logical sense, in the former meaning, but in the psychological and sociological sense, placing it not so much within the supraindividual criteria of choice, but within the understanding of the surrounding reality, particular situations and events affected by a multiplicity of factors, characteristic for an individual.

Supported by the methodological construction developed by Marek Siemek, the discussion concerning reality may be conducted at the epistemic or epistemological level.

---

8 Bogdan Baran, 'Przyczynek Do Krytyki Bieżących Badań Nad Racjonalnością' [Contribution to the Critique of Current Research on Rationality] (1980) 2 Studia Filozoficzne 109–16.

"Epistemology – as ontology of knowledge – must then 'carve' its object from the onset; it will not be the 'cognition' as the part of epistemic field separated from the 'object', but precisely the relation between cognition and object – thus the area itself in its comprehensive structure."[9]

Siemek defines the epistemic form of knowledge as *the state of direct reflection of a certain ontic reality*. The area constituting knowledge, dichotomically divided into ontic sphere of the "object" and logically cognitive sphere of the "subject", is defined as epistemic level. Cognitive action is mainly focused here on the "objective" level and accumulates in the form of independent "objective" knowledge about the reality itself – *episteme*. The question about *episteme* is a question exceeding the status and cognitive functions of the theory of the epistemic level as it is the level of questions concerning the structural whole and the determinants enabling the perception of something as objective[10]. Enquiring about rationality at the epistemic level, we are in fact enquiring about the cohesion of the subjectively perceived system of possible meanings, but also non-meanings, which are always invisible within the functioning view. By enquiring about rationality at the epistemological level, we are enquiring about the conditions of the possibility of knowledge, perceiving the epistemic field as comprehensively conditioned by them, thus enabling the articulation of the senses which can not appear within the determined paradigm and revealing its problematic and non-apparent character. According to Siemek, new theoretical instruments escaping any doctrinal restrictions that emerged in the second half of the 20th century operate at the epistemological level. Not only does it formulate a new kind of theory, but – confronted by a new kind of theoretical objects – it thus discovers another sphere of reality. "It thus discovers that 'the subject' always is an inherent element of each instance of its 'objectivity'".[11] Thus, the created epistemic level loses its ontological innocence – by constituting one of the determinants of human experience, it determines the scope of human action.

---

9 Marek J. Siemek, *Idea Transcendentalizmu U Fichtego I Kanta: Studium Z Dziejów Filozoficznej Problematyki* Wiedzy [The Idea of Transcendentalism in Fichte and Kant. The Study of the History of Philosophical Problems of Knowledge] (1st edn, Państwowe Wydawn Naukowe 1977) 43.

10 Marek J Siemek, *Drogi Współczesnej Filozo*fii [The Ways of contemporary philosophy] (1st edn, Czytelnik 1978); see also: Marek J Siemek, *Filozofia, Dialektyka, Rzeczywistość* [Philosophy, Dialectic, Reality] (1st edn, Państwowy Insytut Wydawniczy 1982) 62–3.

11 Robert Kwaśnica, *Dwie racjonalności : Od filozofii sensu ku pedagogice ogólnej ogólne*j, [Two of Rationality. From Philosophy of Sense to General Pedagogy] (2nd edn, Wydawnictwo Naukowe Dolnośląskiej Szkoły Wyższej Edukacji TWP 2007) 38.

> "Historicity, socialisation, culture; these are various terms – and possibly various dimensions – of new objectivity (...)."[12]

The horizon of an epistemological question does not have to be understood as Kantian transcendentalism, even though it obviously is rooted in Kantian philosophy. In the sense of the research area characteristic for philosophy Siemek included Gadamer's and Ricouer's hermeneutics, trends in Sartre's and Merlau-Pounty's phenomenological epistemology, the representatives of the Frankfurt School (Adorno, Horkheimer, Marcuse, Fromm), their heir and creator of the universal pragmatics J. Habermas, a representative of transcendental pragmatics K. O. Appel, representatives of structuralism and semiology (Barthes and Eco) and representatives of reflexively-oriented sociology. The argumentation of the Polish philosopher may be illustrated with Ch. S. Peirce's metaphor of the cable. This new philosophical instrumentarium should not form a chain which is no stronger than its weakest link, but a cable whose fibres may be ever so slender, provided they are sufficiently numerous and intimately connected.

To summarise: human reality is the existence of sense; enquiring about it, one should be guided by the question about sense-making determinants, which enabled and preceded experience[13]. After rationality becomes established in experience, it determines categories, assumptions and interpretation procedures, thus not only creating the human living space but also organising the manner of acquiring new experience. R. Kwaśnica clarifies this relation in the following way:

> "(...) while the source of rationality is everything which surrounds us, which we encounter in our lives and which we experience as the determinants of our actions, yet these determinants do not constitute a complex of "pure" facts, i.e. the facts that have not been commented on by the generations preceding ours and by our contemporaries, but they are a structure of sense. This denotes that what we experience as the determinants of our actions has been identified before us and equipped with the meaning corresponding to the human way of experiencing the world, while we – undertaking to interpret these meanings, decrypting and modifying their content – transfer them and establish within the structure of our experience, constructing our own rationality."[14]

If rationality is understood as a sense-making structure, it results in two types of organisation of experience, relative to the axiological orientation established and dominating in our experience: adaptive rationality based on instrumental values and emancipation rationality based on non-instrumental axiological orientation.

12 ibid 45.
13 ibid 22.
14 ibid 35.

If the world is the world of sense, rationality decides on the manner of attributing it with sense, i.e. objectivising it in one's own experience. In the following pages, I am going to prove that each of the discussed types of rationality constructs disparate pictures of objectivity.

Instrumental values impose the relation between the means and the ends. The basic model to which adaptive rationality refers is the model of instrumental action. Equating human action with the type of instrumental action reduces the function of rationality to the efficiency in the selection of means for the ends determined beforehand. The action is appropriate if it results in notable effects. Effects (aims of the action) are then reduced to certain data and thus they may be empirically verified. The view of objectivity created in this way is based on the assumption of obviousness, order and unquestioned reality of culturally defined world, typicality of situations, motivation, means and rationality of other people. These interpretation assumptions result in failure to perceive subjectivity of one's own knowledge and "suspension of doubts". This naturally does not mean that adaptive rationality excludes doubts, as they always appear despite the effort to avoid them; from the point of view of this discussion it is the way of rejecting them that is vital.

If, in accordance with Marx's remarks, we focus on the very practice of creating reality, the procedures responsible for sustaining its particular view gain in importance. The procedures basically consist in: the manner of justifying knowledge, the manner of reacting to alternative patterns of competences, the manner of introducing changes in one's own view of the world. In practice dominated by instrumental values the sole justification of knowledge is its source and effects which may be attained on its basis. "The more trustworthy the source of knowledge is (i.e. the more universal acceptance of this knowledge is and the more authoritative the people using it are), the more effective the action based on this knowledge is, the better it is justified."[15] In other words, we attribute accidental social practices with the characteristics of strong objectivity, as we best function within the structure which may be attributed with features of obviousness, the structure which is totally predictable and unchanging. The complex of truths and indisputable assessments functioning in a given group, which in practice are perceived as a reflection of the natural order of things, is the source of cognitive fundamentalism. Any departure from the accepted cognitive rules is tantamount to their negation and rejection, actions transgressing against the functioning patterns of behaviour are perceived as incomprehensible and senseless. This results in cognitive reactivity totally eliminating the subjective factor in constructing the

15 ibid 95.

objectivity. Interestingly, R. Kwaśnica remarks here that the changes in one's own view of the world are constrained. "An individual accepts them under the pressure of inevitability, treating them, as it were, as a compromise which must be reached if one wants to sustain one's own view of the world as a whole."[16]

Differences between the structure of sense determined by adaptive rationality and the structure of sense determined by emancipation rationality are primarily seen in disparate axiological perspective – the remaining differences are solely the consequences of disparate axiological assumptions. To present the structure of emancipation rationality, it is best to begin with the reconstruction of the axiological perspective, different than that in adaptive rationality, and go on to contrast both rationalities. Emancipation rationality is based on the values which perceive life not in terms of possessions but in terms of widely conceived change and self-improvement. In the perspective of emancipation rationality the ultimate value is the ability to be the subject of one's own action. In other words, the possibility of deciding on the directions of one's action is expressed in the freedom to determine its ends[17]. The categories of description and interpretative assumptions determined by emancipation values enable treating the social reality as a set of variable interpretations. The knowledge of reality does not display the characteristics of objectivity in the strong sense, as our knowledge of the reality is constantly being communally determined, interactively confirmed and reviewed. Culture ceases to be a set of the regulations conceived beforehand, which must be taken into consideration at each instance of a particular action under the threat of its failure, but it is rather a set of intersubjectively adopted convictions (objectivity in the weaker sense), which require justification and are subject to criticism, constant change and review.

The implemented interpretative procedures are based on universality of justifications. Contrary as in the case of instrumentality of justification of one's actions and their results, whose only criterion is their effectiveness, justification is correct not due to its result but due to the respect of the rules of discourse. Contrary to cognitive fundamentalism, which interpreted the set of rules functioning within a particular group as a reflection of natural, "objective" order of things thus resulting in negation and rejection of each departure from the pattern, cognitive anti-fundamentalism, as perceived in the manner of reacting to alternative models of competences, manifests itself in the awareness of its provisional character. Other people are never cast in the role of means or resources at our disposal to be used

16 ibid 93.

17 ibid 97–100.

to accomplish tasks entrusted to us, but they are partners in the dialogue, partners whose alternative points of view enrich our experience. Contrary to cognitive interventionism, which focuses on sustaining one's own view of the world by rejecting reactively these elements which interfere with it, cognitive intentionality manifests itself in the awareness of the shortcomings of one's own knowledge, searching for them and going beyond them. Changes in one's own view of reality are not extorted by external factors but are intentionally created.

Both types of rationality offer two different ways of objectivising reality. The structures creating objectivity based on instrumental values result in the fact that our reality loses its lucidity. Knowledge of reality is unable to comprise its own constitutive rules with its cognition, as the logic of instrumental action is a self-confirmatory structure. Effectiveness of action in each instance confirms the accuracy of the adopted view of the world. Therefore, departure from the current ways of interpreting reality is perceived as a transgression against the "objective" order and it is equated with excessive subjectivity, i.e. the error of arbitrariness. Domination of instrumental values prevents the interpretation of objectivity as a practical manner of emergence of reality and its perception. Thus, objectivity becomes a static category – objectivity exists or it does not. Theoretical practice remains at the epistemic level and adopts the view of objectivity created within it as static inevitability.

In the structure of emancipation rationality the manner of acquiring experience is mainly determined by universal values (in the formal meaning), procedural and communicative perception of reality and the assumption of uniqueness of situations, means and other people's rationality. Contrary to adaptive rationality, results of the action undertaken on the basis of emancipation rationality do not guarantee anything. Emancipation rationality encourages reflection not so much on the results of undertaken action as on the manner of executing it. Reality perceived from this perspective does not display the characteristics of unquestioned reality, as emancipation is a process which may be implemented only when questions are asked, doubts and problems seen and appreciated. Freedom involves continuous attempts at achieving self-fulfilment and self-awareness, it is not a manipulative unrestricted choice of means to attain ends. The aim of emancipation is to be the subject of one's own action. Therefore, we can not speak of objectivity in the static sense but of the process of objectivisation. Objectivisation is a characteristic of the process of creation of knowledge. Thus objectivity is not rooted in preceding data or coherence of logical theory but in the basis of human intersubjectivity. It is not a static necessity of the created determinants, but due to the fact that the structure of emancipation reality is able to comprise its own determinants of creation, objectivity is perceived in dynamic terms as an accidental necessity.

II

The occurrence of hard cases in law is now associated with R. Dworkin's integrity of law philosophy. In very general terms, a hard case is a case where we are not confronted with a mechanical (syllogistic) application of law; it is a situation in which a judge has no unambiguous legal norms at his or her disposal. The rules of legal methodology in hard cases do not unequivocally result in an unambiguous result. I suggest that the following definition of a hard case be adopted: a hard case in law is a situation when a routine action (mechanical, syllogistic application of law) is not possible[18]. The action may be disrupted by numerous factors. The problem disrupting the action does not result – although most of the time it is probably the case – from an ambiguity of a legal text. A problematic situation may just as well arise when law "meets" other normative systems such as morality, customs, culture or science. Continuously emerging new problems with the application of law in the ever-changing reality. For instance the cases concerning bioethics, distinctly point out to the potential for the emergence of hard cases in the process of law-making and its binding force in application. I aim to reveal the correlations between the deeply rooted manner of action and the ways of objectivising the knowledge of law by a way to which they seem so obvious because of the sets of practical solutions they escape any attempt of reflection. Let us repeat: a hard case is a problematic situation which interferes with a lawyer's smoothly developing practice in the multidimensional space of law.

The adopted concept of hard cases on a non-teleological constituting the basis of pragmatism according to which:

> "The alternative to a teleological interpretation of action, with its inherited dependence on Cartesian dualism, is to conceive of perception and cognition not as preceding action but as a phase of action by which action is directed and redirected in its situational contexts. According to this alternative view, goal-setting does not take place by an act of the intellect *prior to* the actual action, but is instead the result of reflection on aspirations and tendencies that are prereflective and have *already always* been operative. In this act of reflection, we thematize aspirations which are normal at work without our being actively aware of them [...]. According to this view, our perception of the word appears to be structured by our capacities for, and experiences of, action. Even when we are not pursuing any immediate intention of action, the world exists not simply as an external counterpart to our internal self, but in the form of possible actions."[19]

18 Neil MacCormick, *Legal Reasoning and Legal Theory* (Clarendon Press; Oxford University Press 1978) 197.
19 Hans Joas, *The Creativity of Action* (The University of Chicago Press 1996) 158.

Hard cases do not exist beyond the context of an individual action. They are not inherent elements of the legal system and of its functioning, because difficulties cannot be perceived and can not be overcome if they do not constitute an obstacle that is interfering with the action of an individual. An encounter with a hard case exposes the fact that the existing habits do not bring about an expected result. Routine interpretative efforts, tested and reliable (so far) fail. Emerging interferences render reality, or at least its certain fragments, problematic. The emerging problematic situation within the current practice provisionally hinders action. The only solution is the reconstruction of the disrupted context. The solution to the problem is a selective and differentiating behaviour and not the action aiming at externally set ends, since the solution of a particular problematic situation always involves ambiguity, numerous determinants and aspects. Hard cases in law draw attention to conventionality of current premises of action, unquestioned until the problem arose. Confronting the problem reveals the hypothetical character of the reality, conventionality and diversity of the habits functioning within the practice of law.

> 'For the pragmatists, the setting of ends is not an act of consciousness that takes place outside of context of action. Rather, the setting of an end can only be a result of a reflection on resistances encountered by the variously oriented behavior of a life form whose world is already schematized in a practical manner prior to all reflection.'[20]

Thus, the action aiming at solving a hard case can not be based on the pattern proposed by analytical philosophy, where reflectiveness becomes the point of departure for interpreting action. In the proposed concept of hard cases the action develops in the opposite direction. At the beginning, there is action based on habit and only when it is disrupted, is reflection possible. The basic pattern in a hard case is not reflection followed by action but action followed by reflection on the practice preceding the reflection, within which the hard case has emerged. Rationality in the case of action aiming at the solution of a hard case in law thus consists in self-criticism, as the disrupted action requires reorganisation of the current patterns and their readaptation. John Dewey formulated it in the following way:

> 'While the content of knowledge is what has happened, what is taken as finished and hence settled and sure, the reference of knowledge is future or prospective. For knowledge furnishes the means of understanding or giving meaning to what is still going on and what is to be done.'[21]

---

20 Hans Joas, *Pragmatism and Social Theory* (University of Chicago Press 1993) 248.
21 John Dewey, *Democracy and Education* (Dover ed, Dover Publications 2004) 366.

A hard case has a twofold character; on the one hand it is always subjective and individual as it appears and is solved in the consciousness of an individual, on the other hand, its solution, if it is to become an element of cognition, must have supraindividual legal validity.[22] The adopted perspective testifies to the constitutive role of subjectivity in objectivisation of knowledge. Even though a hard case is a problem experienced solely subjectively, its solution must be presented in general terms reflecting the perspective of the whole group, i.e. it must acquire intersubjective validity. Focusing attention on the practical and creative role of knowledge of law in solving legal problems testifies to cognitive openness of legal practice, self-criticism and intersubjective character.[23]

When two different views of objectivity determined by the two defined types of rationality are recalled, their relation to the problem of hard cases in law becomes distinct. The concept of objectivity dominated by instrumental values is expressed in registering and consolidating primarily these circumstances accompanying the practice of law which support the established structure of thinking and are contained within it. The facts questioning the structure are confronted with the whole system of thinking of an individual, ignored or – finally – invalidated and rejected. In other words, the so-called strong objectivity results in the fact that theoretical knowledge of the way in which objectivity emerges in practice comprises solely the circumstances which confirm it. If effectiveness is a factor decisive for truthfulness of knowledge of law, all forms of awareness must be adapted to it. If the role of lawyers is reduced to the freedom of selection of means to attain the ends independent of the practice, this determines the technical character of the practice of law. This attitude performs an ideological function in justifying legal positivism. Legal positivism stems from positivistic methodological awareness based on the separation of the sphere of observable facts from the sphere of values. The object of cognition exists independently of the subject, it is, in its own way, already given. Positivism causes undesirable neutralisation of objectivity equating legitimisation of knowledge with a particular research method – equating epistemology with methodology, while the ignored epistemological issues result in a number of ontological solutions; unquestioned ontology becomes metaphysics.[24]

---

22 Leszek Koczanowicz, *G.H. Mead* (1992 edn, Wydawnictwo Uniwersytetu Wrocławskiego) 32.

23 Sanne Taekema, 'Beyond Common Sense: Philosophical Pragmatism's Relevance to Law' (2006) 29 Nordisk Juridisk Tidsskrift 22.

24 Dorota Wolska, *Odzyskać Doświadczenie : Sporny Temat Humanistyki Współczes*nej [Recover Experience. Controversial Topic of Contemporary Humanities] (Universitas 2012) 169–170.

The assumption that reality is a sphere of facts independent of human cognition is aptly described by Habermas as "ontology of reality". Consistently ignored epistemological problems in cognition of law lead to its secondary ontologisation by equating analytical theory of interpretation of law dominating in legal positivism with law as such. Understanding law as objective reality independent of subjective determinants results in ignoring the role of legal interpretation in cognition of law. The desire of objectivity is satisfied with the passivity of cognition of law.

Meanwhile, the relation of means (methods of interpretation) to ends (content of law) is never neutral.

> 'Only when we recognize the certain means are available to us do we discover goals which had not occurred to us before. Thus, means not only specify goals, but they also expand the scope for possible goal-setting.'[25]

The wider the choice of interpretative and argumentative tools is, the greater is the possibility of objectivisation of law. The impulse for reinterpretation of current results of interpretation of law is the axiological discomfort, the feeling that all previous interpretations of a legal text may cause gross injustice. Appreciation of interpretative problems is connected with a lawyer's subjective determinants. Although such subjectivity can not constitute the grounds for legitimisation of the proposed solution, it is a condition for objectivisation of law. Adherence to the letter of law should not be equated with the adherence to the current interpretative routine. Selection of interpretative tools enables emergence of new ends, while the necessity to persuade a group to change current interpretation of law inevitably results in intersubjective evaluation and legitimisation. Intersubjectivity constitutes the basis for developing the understanding of objectivity appropriate for legal sciences, which does not come from empirical sciences as is the case of positivism. Objectivity understood as objectivisation places time over place, change over possessing, dynamism over stagnation. What is individual and unique in a hard case becomes an impulse to impart law with new content. Objectivisation of law is a process which consists in creative reconstruction of methods of interpretation and not in reactive adjustment of the content to the method, it is a process in which subjective qualities of lawyers are of epistemic significance. Dewey claimed that assessment of institutions ought to be based on the personality type which they favour. The concept of objectivity dominated by instrumental values causes one to view legal culture as a set of accepted patterns of behaviour as well as tried and tested work directives. Difficult cases are seen as a threat to self-evident truths and unquestionable opinions functioning within a given group. A

25 Joas (n 19) 154.

novel experience brings about a "defensive reflex" taking the form of a cognitive reaction aiming at preserving the integrity of a world view. In a problematic situation the particular and the unique becomes removed and hidden. Any change in an existing pattern of legislation is regarded as a forced compromise which one must accept in order to ensure security and peace of mind. Unlike the objectivity based on instrumental values the intersubjective interpretation of objectivity views legal culture as a practice of continuous renegotiating of conventions. Any modifications of routine interpretations resulting from dealing with difficult cases are intentional rather than imposed.

Lucia Berdisova

Faculty of Law, Trnava University in Trnava, Slovakia

2. Objectivity and arbitrariness of blind rule-following or what it means to follow a (legal) rule blindly

> *However, imagine that everything that you had written by your right side so far would have been written by your left side. Try to see what is going on in here in such a way.*
>
> *Juan José Millás, Two women in Prague*

In 1982 Saul Kripke published his influential study *Wittgenstein on rules and private language*[1], which enhanced his citation index enormously. The replies and other reactions were mostly of a critical kind, but this does not mean that the study is not worth analysis; quite the contrary. Many "applications" of Ludwig Wittgenstein's ideas on (in) the domain of legal theory rely on Kripke's study; they are inspired by it or they engage in argument against it. Many of them then lead to the thesis about the specific indeterminacy of law. My aim in this paper is to refute the argument of the impossibility of following rules, i.e. the so-called rule scepticism in the version proposed by Kripke that is transferred into the discussion on the concept of law. Following this I will also refute the argument made against Kripke provided by G. Baker and P.M.S Hacker in *Scepticism, Rules and Language*. Subsequently I strive to provide an argument on the objectivity of law that is crucially based on Dennis Patterson's approach, although Patterson's final "finding" is thereby modified. This will be done based on (de)limitation of the application of Wittgenstein's reminders on legal theory.

In order to achieve these aims I firstly sum up Kripke's argument (part I); secondly I show how he misunderstood Wittgenstein, how Baker and Hacker replied to Kripke and why they even are partially wrong (part II); thirdly I provide some examples of misunderstandings or misuses of Wittgenstein's ideas about the field of law in favour of rule scepticism that stem from Kripke's fallacy or fallacies of a similar kind, and I explain their roots (part III); and finally (part IV)

1 Saul A Kripke, *Wittgenstein on Rules and Private Language* (8th edn, Harvard University Press 1995).

I follow Patterson's new analogy provided in *Normativity and Objectivity in Law*, which sheds new light on the objectivism-subjectivism dispute. However, I revise Patterson's concept of the forms of argument that serves as the background for his stipulation of objectivity as relative to a domain.

The issue of ontological objectivity of law as determinate correctness[2] is at stake in the background of this paper, because of two problems identified by Kripke. Firstly, what we believe we do according to a rule might not correspond to what the rule *really* required us to do. So we believe we have obeyed the rule while *in fact* we have not. Secondly, how then do rules guide us? Moreover, if the law is not sufficiently determinate, the space for epistemic subjectivity of law (e.g. in the sense of lack of impartiality) opens up too. Moreover, the question of law as being epistemically objective in the sense of being "open" to discovery of correct answers is at stake in connection with legal interpretation.[3] Here, Wittgenstein's ideas have been used to defend quite opposite views.[4] I provide an example of such opposite views in the third part of this paper in the writings of J. Boyle and A. Marmor, whereby I criticise both of them. The idea is this: if legal rules may be followed without the need of their interpretation, hence without "subjective" contamination by agents, they are in this way objective.[5] On the other hand, if there is always a need for interpretation, there exists space for contamination by agents all the time.[6]

---

2 For types of objectivity cf. e.g. Matthew Kramer, *Objectivity and the Rule of Law* (CUP 2007). Kramer distinguishes ontological, epistemic and semantic objectivity (genus of objectivity). The ontological type has dimensions of mind-independence, determinate correctness and uniform applicability. Epistemic objectivity has dimensions of transindividual discernibility and impartiality. Truth aptitude is a species of semantic objectivity. The topic of in/determinacy of law falls within the discussions regarding determinate correctness as a species of ontological objectivity.

3 Cf. dimensions of objectivity in Brian Leiter (ed.), *Objectivity in Law and Morals* (CUP 2001) 3.

4 S. Bertea provides argumentation to refute the use of Wittgenstein by some positivists whose aim is to rebut the thesis of the need of interpretation every time we are about to determine what the law requires. Bertea argues that Wittgenstein understood interpretation as pertaining to the theoretical sphere and rule-following as an activity, while positivists (just as interpretativists) understand both as forms of reasoning. See: Stefano Bertea, 'Remarks on a Legal Positivist Misuse of Wittgenstein's Later Philosophy' (2003) 22 Law and Philosophy 513.

5 It is surely possible to argue that the need for interpretation of law does not mean the loss of objectivity.

6 Moreover, the issue of semantic objectivity may arise if one treats Wittgenstein's writings as criteria for semantic objectivity that are determined based on concept of language we accept.

I. Kripkenstein

Saul Kripke interprets Wittgenstein's *Philosophical investigations*[7] (hereinafter "the *Investigations*") in such a way that he formulates a paradox of rule-following which he calls the "Wittgensteinian paradox"[8]. Kripke's Wittgenstein, as his ideas are explained in the respective study, has produced the ironical name – Kripkenstein.[9]

Kripke encourages us to think about the way we have grasped the rule of addition which is denoted by the word 'plus' or by the symbol '+'. The key to grasping a rule, for him, is that the rule determines my answer for indefinitely many sums (ones I have never even considered before) even if I myself have done only a finite number of sums in the past.[10] Let us then imagine that '68 + 57' is a computation I have never performed before.[11] When I perform the computation the answer is of course '125'. This answer, for Kripke, is correct not only in the arithmetical sense but also in the metalinguistic sense (i.e. in the sense that the word 'plus' as I wanted to use it in the past, denoted such a function which if applied to the numbers 68 and 57 'provided' the answer '125').[12] However, then the voice of the bizarre sceptic, as Kripke calls it, comes into play. The bizarre sceptic contests the correctness of my answer and my certainty about the answer in a *metalinguistic sense*. This sceptic claims for instance that I might have used the word 'plus' in such a way that answer which I intended for '68+57' was '5'. This is possible because the sceptic could say that I used the word 'plus' in such a way that it denoted the function 'quus'. Now when performing quaddition with numbers smaller than 57 the answer is the same as performing addition. But when performing quaddition

---

7 The *Investigations* were first published in 1952. This paper uses quotations from Ludwig Wittgenstein, *Philosophical Investigations*, (3rd edn, Blackwell Publishers 2001).

8 Kripke considers this paradox to be fundamental for the Investigations, and it is supposed to create the basis for the so-called private language argument. See: Saul A Kripke, *Wittgenstein on Rules and Private Language* (8th edn, Harvard University Press 1995) 2ff.

9 See: Jaroslav Peregrin, 'Wittgensteinstein a pravidla našich jazykových her' [Eng. 'Wittgenstein and Rules of Our Language Games'] in R Kišoňová and V Vitálošová and A Démuth (eds.), *Wittgensteinovské skúmania* [Eng. *Wittgensteinian Investigations*] (Schola Philosophica 2008) 77.

10 Saul A Kripke, *Wittgenstein on Rules and Private Language* (8th edn, Harvard University Press 1995) 7.

11 Ibid, 8. Kripke chooses this example, but in trying to grasp this point we might do better by imagining a more complex computation (e.g. 7 665 034 plus 622 135).

12 Ibid.

with numbers equal or bigger than 57 the answer is always '5'.[13] According to Kripke the sceptic is hence asking whether there is any *fact* that I meant the term 'plus' in the past such and such which would answer the sceptic's challenge.[14] In other words, whether there is any fact I can point to that shows what I meant by the word 'plus' in the past and hence 'prove' to the sceptic that his scepticism is unjustified, because I indeed meant it in such a way that it denoted the function 'plus', and not 'quus' or any other function. Kripke's sceptic does not end here. He also questions whether I have any *reason* to be sure that I must provide the answer '125' and not '5' for '68+57'.[15] The problem is therefore not how I know that 68 plus 57 equals 125 (arithmetical problem) but how I know that 68 plus 57 as I meant 'plus' in the past denotes 125 (metalinguistic problem).[16]

This puzzle is formulated on an example of arithmetic, but Kripke believes that the sceptical problem which is its core applies to any use of language and any use of rules.[17]

Just to make this clearer for lawyers I can perhaps reformulate this paradox in the following way: if I used some rule in the past and based on it I now act in a certain way, how do I know how I meant this rule in the past (i.e. how do I know what rule I have followed)? Then how can the rule 'guide' me when I apply it in a new case? And moreover, what justifies the use of the specific rule in the present, if everything I have done in the past was also in conformity with different rules?

Following his reading of Wittgenstein, Kripke thinks of more than one answer to his bizarre sceptic. One of them is that I would just point to my previous interpretation of the rule. But according to Kripke such a reference would not satisfy the sceptic. This is so because interpretation is in a way a rule of interpretation of the rule and because even such a rule might be interpreted in more than one way, and hence there is a need to point to a further (more basic) rule of interpretation of the rule which supposed to interpret a previous rule, etc. *ad infinitum*. There, the sceptical challenge is not resolved and for the sceptic the application of a rule is still only a leap in dark.[18] If my *interpretation* of the rule does not justify the application of the rule, what else can do so? Another answer which is considered by Kripke is a *disposition* to apply a certain rule and not another rule. According to dispositive theory (as described by Kripke) we have the disposition to answer

13 Ibid, 8–9.
14 Ibid, 11.
15 Ibid.
16 Ibid, 12.
17 Ibid, 7, 58 or 110.
18 Ibid, 17 and following.

'125' not '5' as the members of a certain community. But not even this would satisfy the sceptic, because not only I but also the whole community may be wrong. That would lead dispositive theory into a blind alley, because whatever I or the community *consider* to be correct (right answer, correct application of the proper rule) merges with what *is* correct. And if there is no incorrect use of the rule there is no correct use of the rule.[19]

The conclusion is that it is not possible to mean something with words or use them according to the rules, because each use of a rule is a leap in the dark. Kripkenstein is hence the creator of a new form of scepticism that is supposed to produce 'the most radical and original sceptical problem that philosophy has seen to date'.[20] But this is not the end of Kripkenstein's extraordinariness. Wittgenstein in Kripke's reading was able to provide a so-called sceptical solution to the sceptical paradox.[21]

This solution is supposed to consist 'in such a description of the game of concept attribution' which provides (i) 'the conditions under which we are justified in attributing concepts to others'[22] and also (ii) 'an account of the utility of this game in our lives'.[23] Kripke speaks of game/games and so he speaks about a community which plays the games. This is so because Kripke understands the so-called private language argument in such a way that a rule may not be followed privately (in isolation from the community, as in the case of Friday on Lonesome Island). That does not mean physical isolation of the person who should follow the rule, but one who is not a member of any community.[24] But let us get back to the description of the game which Kripke provides. This description is based on the clarification of three concepts, namely of agreement, form of life and criteria. Agreement in reactions, in what we do, or how we respond, is essential for the game because it creates the background on which it is possible generally to attribute the grasp of ideas to any member of the community.[25] So we can attribute the concept of rule-following to

19 Ibid, 22ff. There are other objections against dispositive theory provided by the sceptic. Kripke also replies to the sceptic using the 'philosophy of mind' argument (i.e. the argument that a certain act of meaning of a rule belongs among qualia as an irreducible experience perceptible only by introspection). In any case, Kripke does not consider any answer to the sceptic to be sufficient until he provides his own (or Kripkenstein's one).

20 Ibid, 60.

21 Kripke speaks about a sceptical solution because according to him it is not a direct solution of the problem. Ibid, 69.

22 I.e. even the concepts of rule or rule-following, as I understand Kripke.

23 Ibid, 95.

24 Ibid, 110.

25 Ibid, 96.

a person only if this person acts in sufficient conformity with the actions and reactions of the community. Moreover, '[t]he set of responses in which we agree, and the way they interweave with our activities, is our *form of life*'[26]. Then those who respond as if they perform quaddition not addition would share a different form of life.[27] For Kripke, the traditional explanation of our shared form of life is not possible. What justifies us in claiming that by '+' we meant addition is part of our language game that is maintained by the fact that we generally agree.[28] Kripkenstein's idea of the concept of criteria may be briefly summed up thus: the criterion of rule-following is the community itself, the others. So someone 'who claims to be following a rule can be checked by others'.[29]

Let me recall that Kripke's example '68+57' is of such a kind that anyone who is at least mediocre at addition would have no doubt about the answer s/he should provide. For this reason Kripke is in a better position (comparing our intuition and general skills) to state that we answer *unhesitatingly*. Our situation regarding this example of computation does not belong among the situations when we hesitate as to *what rule* to follow/use (which rule 'fits' the case) or *how to follow the rule* (how to use it in this case). But aren't the latter cases the most interesting ones for legal practitioners and especially academics? Is it not a task for legal philosophy to explain[30] disagreement rather than agreement that is why we do not agree on one single answer, and what such an answer (correct response) should consist of?[31]

---

26 Ibid.

27 Ibid.

28 Ibid, 97.

29 Ibid, 101.

30 Following Wittgenstein's method we must not *explain* disagreement but describe it. Wittgenstein's philosophical activity is a descriptive activity; it does not lead to creation of theories, it reminds us of what we already know but did not see clearly. For this reason we should mostly classify our existing knowledge, not seek to gain new. Cf. § 124 *Investigations*: 'Philosophy may in no way interfere with the actual use of language; it can in the end only describe it. For it cannot give it any foundation either. It leaves everything the way it is. (…).' Cf. also § 126 *Investigations:* 'Philosophy simply puts everything before us, and neither explains nor deduces anything.—Since everything lies open to view there is nothing to explain. For what is hidden, for example, is of no interest of use. One might also give the name "philosophy": to what is possible before all new discoveries and inventions'.

31 See: Brian Bix, 'Cautions and Caveats for the Application of Wittgenstein to Legal Theory' in Joseph K Campbell and Michael O'Rourke and David Shier (eds), *Topics in Contemporary Philosophy* (MIT Press 2005, 217–229) 221.

II. Kripkenstein versus Wittgenstein

I have outlined Kripkenstein's sceptical challenge and his reply to the bizarre sceptic. In this part I proceed to the identification of the key difference between Kripkenstein, i.e. Wittgenstein as read by Kripke, and Wittgenstein as I understand him. The task is to realise in which way Kripke misreads Wittgenstein and hence what is misinterpreted in works of scholars who follow or rely on Kripke's interpretation. I focus mainly on the misunderstandings connected with Wittgenstein's philosophical method and its use. I would also comment on one of the most famous critiques of Kripke's study provided by G. Baker and P.M.S. Hacker in the collection of their essays *Scepticism, rules and language.*[32]

My first critical remark: the sceptic in the first place did not question what I meant by the term such and such in the past, but he questioned the *existence of the fact* that I meant the term such and such *as a state of mind.* But later on the sceptic claimed that if there is no such *fact,* then there is no meaning. Does any one of us doubt that it is possible to mean something with words? Why would Wittgenstein question the very possibility of meaning something with words? I believe he did not. Wittgenstein 'only' commented on the effort of philosophers to look for answers to questions like '*What* is it to mean something with words?' or '*What* is the meaning of a word?'. Answers to such questions cannot be provided, and looking for such answers is the result of our captivation with the modality that there *must* exist *something* that *is* "to mean" in a word, or something that *is* the meaning of a/the word in the sense of some object or fact.[33] Again, the undertaking to answer such questions results from the captivation with our grammar[34], and it is a symptom of our craving for generality. For example the grammar of the word 'to measure' in the expression 'to measure length' is different from grammar of this word in the expression 'to measure time'. And an analogy of structures in the language lead us to the question: 'What is time?' or 'How we can measure time?'. The past has already happened so it's gone and we cannot measure it, the future

32 There is a great number of papers and books that analyse Kripkenstein and compare him to the 'real' Wittgenstein. There is no need to name the basic sources to achieve our aims. But obviously the frequency of critique shows that Kripke's reading is the controversial one.

33 Cf. § 115 of *Investigations,* and the preceding and following paragraphs. Subsequently Wittgenstein even criticised his own image theory of language from the *Tractatus logico-philosophicus.*

34 Let me remind that Wittgenstein uses the word 'grammar' in specific way. See e.g. Gordon P Baker, *Wittgenstein's Method. Neglected Aspects* (Blackwell Publishing 2004) 24, 42, 85.

is only about to come, it is not here now, so we cannot measure it yet, and the present does not have dimensions so we cannot measure it either. But if we take a look at the rules of the use of the word 'time' in the language, we realise that they just differ. In our common language we do not have any problems with the use of the word 'time', apart from keeping deadlines of course (to make a little joke), but still no definition fits all the cases or instances of its use. Definition hence cannot explain what we wanted to explain when we surrendered the analogy.[35] By the description of different language games in the *Investigations,* Wittgenstein shows us that we use language in many ways and that the meaning of a word does not need to be (even if it can be) the object it 'represents' or denotes. As words are used in many ways we could say that their meaning consists in their use. But even the word 'meaning' has different uses, and so it is *impossible* to create a theory of meaning (of words). I believe that exactly this is overlooked by some philosophers and lawyers when they conclude that in § 43 of the *Investigations* Wittgenstein claims that the meaning of a word *is* its use.[36] Wittgenstein in fact writes that '[f]or a *large* class of cases – though not for all – in which we employ the word "meaning" it can be defined thus: the meaning of a word is its use in the language'.[37] Hence Wittgenstein did not claim or argue that it is impossible to mean something with words, but he pointed out that to look for the *fact* of meaning or to look for something that is *a* meaning (even if *the* meaning of the word may be in some cases its use) is to surrender to the tendencies Wittgenstein warned us against.

Secondly, Kripkenstein's sceptic said that I follow the rule blindly and so I make a leap in the dark. But Kripkenstein and Wittgenstein crucially differ even here.[38] Wittgenstein stated *for a specific purpose* that I (can) follow the rule blindly, but not that I make a leap in the dark. What is that specific purpose? As a matter of fact, we would need to focus here and be more patient, as this part of the paper

35 Cf. Ludwig Wittgenstein, *The Blue and Brown Books* (Harper Torchbooks 1965) 26.

36 E.g. Stefano Bertea, 'Remarks on a Legal Positivist Misuse of Wittgenstein's Later Philosophy' (2003) 22 Law and Philosophy 513, 531. In any case, most of Bertea's insights are very valuable.

37 *Investigations*, § 43. Gordon Baker reads the use of italics by Wittgenstein in various ways. He does not believe that Wittgenstein always intends only to stress some words. Baker in this case considers the use of italics for the word 'large' to be an effort by Wittgenstein to point out the negative outcomes of the word 'large'. If I understand Baker properly, Wittgenstein here strives to lead the reader to focus and rethink even the class of cases where we use the word 'meaning' differently. See: Gordon P Baker, *Wittgenstein's Method. Neglected Aspects* (Blackwell Publishing 2004) 228.

38 I had already argued that there is no big sceptical challenge or paradox that Wittgenstein was about to solve. Let's keep that in mind here too.

does not only strive to interpret the *Investigations* according to the blind rule-following statement of Kripke. It will also provide the background for discussion in the third part of the paper. In fact, proper understanding of the rule-following part of the *Investigations* calls for clarification of Wittgenstein's method and hence also for an outline of the context of the rule-following part.[39]

In § 219 of the *Investigations* Wittgenstein provides only a "mythological" description of a rule with the aim of disentangling a certain puzzle. To disentangle the puzzle is the specific purpose. Paragraph 219 states:

> "All the steps are really already taken" means: I no longer have any choice. The rule, once stamped with a particular meaning, traces the lines along which it is to be followed though the whole of space.—But if something of this sort really were the case, how would it help?
>
> No; my description only made sense if it was to be understood symbolically.—I should have said: *This is how it strikes me.*
>
> When I obey a rule, I do not choose.
>
> I obey the rule *blindly.*

To find the puzzle we need to go back to the preceding paragraphs of the *Investigations.* The "problem" to "solve" was the nature of language, its relation to the world, or the meaning of words. Wittgenstein criticised many views on language including his own in the *Tractatus,* where the image he was reduced to was in fact that operating language is like calculus according to definite rules. He also criticized similar efforts as being (among others) based on speculation that captivated us in the picture[40] that something *must be* like this or that[41], or as being in a muddle[42] also because of the confusion which overcomes us 'when language is like an engine idling, not when it is doing work'[43]. In order to see things more clearly, to see more clearly the use of words, there is a need to make our grammar more perspicuous, which can be done through perspicuous representations so that we can see connections.[44] And in order to see how it really is, with a view that the use of words may be compared to games and to calculi with fixed rules, we must try to see the concepts of understanding, meaning or thinking more

39 Cf. e.g. Gordon P Baker, *Wittgenstein's Method. Neglected Aspects* (Blackwell Publishing 2004).
40 *Investigations,* § 115.
41 Ibid, § 112.
42 Ibid, § 153.
43 Ibid, § 132.
44 Ibid, § 122.

clearly.[45] Granted, at some point we could say that to understand a word is to know how to use it, and the meaning consists in the use of the word.[46] But then, is the use of a word clearly prescribed? If so, it is so in normal cases, but there are also abnormal cases.[47] Where is the standard? Is understanding a state which is the source of correct use?[48] And if so, when do you know the application? When do you understand?[49] What does it mean to say that I understand the system/the rule? Wittgenstein says that it can mean many things, and to say that understanding is a state would itself be an improper simplification, as many things can go on in fact. So Wittgenstein gave us a new analogy: look at meaning as the way of use of words, and then he disentangles the puzzles which emerge with this new analogy. The new puzzles may arise in connection with (i) understanding a rule, (ii) performing the correct step/action according to the rule, (iii) the criterion of how we mean the rule, (iv) the interpretation of the rule and (v) justifications for following the rule in a certain way – just like this.

There are many ways of teaching somebody to follow rules, e.g. to write or count. We can for instance draw the original letters and then make a pupil draw

---

45 *Investigations*, § 81:

F. P. Ramsey once emphasized in conversation with me that logic was a 'normative science'. I do not know exactly what he had in mind, but it was doubtless closely related to what only dawned on me later: namely, that in philosophy we often *compare* the use of words with games and calculi which have fixed rules, but cannot say that someone who is using language *must* be playing such a game. –But if you say that our languages only *approximate* to such calculi you are standing on the very brink of a misunderstanding. For then it may look as if what we were talking about were an *ideal* language. As if our logic were, so to speak, a logic for a vacuum. –Whereas logic does not treat of language – or of thought – in the sense in which a natural science treats of a natural phenomenon, and the most that can be said is that we *construct* ideal languages. But here the word "ideal" is liable to mislead, for it sounds as if these languages were better, more perfect, than our everyday language; and as if it took the logician to shew people at last what a proper sentence looked like.

All this, however, can only appear in the right light when one has attained greater clarity about the concepts of understanding, meaning, and thinking. For it will then also become clear what can lead us (and did lead me) to think that if anyone utters a sentence and *means* or *understands* it he is operating a calculus according to definite rules.

46 *Investigations*, § 138. In fact Wittgenstein claims that it might be the case, but it does not have to be.

47 Ibid., § 141 and § 142.

48 Ibid, § 146.

49 Ibid, § 148.

shapes so as to match the original shapes. So we have influence and guiding here. But how does that work? Is there something going on in me? Does this following consist in my feeling as I draw the line following the shape of the original?[50] How is it decided that I have taken the right step in following the rule, e.g. at some point, or at some stage?[51] The answer may be that the right step is the one that accords with the order/rule as it was meant.[52] But how was it meant? Are all the steps somehow taken already? If so, what is the criterion for the way the rule was meant?[53] How am I to follow the rule if anything I do might accord with some interpretation of that rule? Wittgenstein responds that this is a misunderstanding in § 198 (part one):

> "But how can a rule shew me what I have to do at *this* point? Whatever I do is, on some interpretation, in accord with the rule." – That is not what we ought to say, but rather: any interpretation still hangs in the air along with what it interprets, and cannot give it any support. Interpretations by themselves do not determine meaning.

So Wittgenstein's answer to the preceding question is in fact a new question, a new view, a new analogy (§ 198, part two):

> "Then can whatever I do be brought into accord with the rule?"–Let me ask this: what has the expression of a rule–say a sign-post–got to do with my actions? What sort of connection is there here? –Well, perhaps this one: I have been trained to react to this sign in a particular way, and now I do so to react to it.

Another objection that Wittgenstein formulates could be: 'But this is only to give a causal connection; to tell how it has come about that we now go by the sign-post; not what this going-by-the-sign really consists in.' Wittgenstein's answer is the following (§ 198, last part):

> On the contrary; I have further indicated that a person goes by a sign-post only in so far as there exists a regular use of the sign-posts, a custom.

How are we to understand these reminders? Interpretations themselves do not determine meaning. So besides interpretations we need something else. But this does not mean that under some circumstances the interpretation would not help me. One of the possibilities is that we are trained and so we just act in this way or that. The question "can a rule determine what I shall do here?" is recognised as a puzzle, and it is deepened in § 201:

---

50 Ibid, § 177.
51 Ibid, § 186.
52 Ibid.
53 Ibid., § 190.

> This was our paradox: no course of action could be determined by a rule, because any course of action can be made out to accord with the rule. The answer was: if *any* action can be made out to accord with the rule, then it can also be made out to conflict with it. And so there would be neither accord nor conflict here.
>
> It can be seen that there is a misunderstanding here from the mere fact that in the course of our argument we give one interpretation after another; as if each one contended us at least for a moment, until we thought of yet another standing behind it. What this shews is that there is a way of grasping a rule which is *not* an *interpretation*, but which is exhibited in what we call "obeying the rule" and "going against it" in actual cases.
>
> Hence there is an inclination to say: any action according to the rule is an interpretation. But we ought to restrict the term "interpretation" to the substitution of one expression of the rule for another.

Then § 202 of the *Investigations* states:

> And hence also 'obeying a rule' is a practice. And to *think* one is obeying a rule is not to obey a rule. Hence it is not possible to obey a rule 'privately': otherwise thinking one was obeying a rule would be the same thing as obeying it.

This means we are trained to follow this rule like this, and the practice of rule-following connects the rule, expression of the rule and the action of rule-following. But does it mean that there is never a need for interpretation? No. This becomes clear in the third part of this paper: Wittgenstein's reminders show agreement in language but they do not explain disagreement in law. Then do I need a justification to follow this rule like this? No, 'if I have exhausted the justifications I have reached bedrock, and my spade is turned. Then I am inclined to say: "This is simply what I do."'[54] In my opinion this reminder about the bedrock of reasoning led Wittgenstein to the symbolical description of a rule which leads us to a new analogy, because we think that the meaning of the rule bridges the gap between the rule and its application, or that we need to *decide* how to use it in every step we make. And this new analogy can be found in § 219. However, it is a new analogy only. It is the picture that dissolves the puzzle that I always need the interpretation of a rule to follow it. We shall not generalise it and claim that we always follow any rule blindly, so that only rules determine every correct and incorrect reaction. Then language would be like logic (see § 81). Language is part of our form of life. Just to reiterate, the sentence 'I obey the rule *blindly*' from the reminder in § 219 of the *Investigations* should not be interpreted in such a way that I always obey all the rules, and so even legal rules, blindly (i.e. I do not choose). This reminder elucidates the grammar of the word 'rule' in the context of following

54 Ibid, § 217.

the rules of language games, *also* by pointing out the difference between causal determination (i.e. the cause of my following the rules of the game like that) and logical determination (i.e. the reason I follow the rules of the game like that), i.e. it points *even* to the "fact" that the justification of why I follow the rules *in this way* ends somewhere.[55]

Hence, in Wittgenstein's mythological description (I follow the rule blindly), if I shoot at a target with my eyes covered, and I just hit the target, I am trained, I do not need to look around, I do not need to see, I do not need to aim, I just act. I have done it (shot and hit) many times before. However, Kripkenstein's sceptical archer does not have covered eyes; he actually shoots into the darkness. But Wittgenstein never claimed that rules cannot guide us, so he never claimed that if we were to train Kripkenstein's sceptical archer, he would be able to hit the target. There is no possibility of a target in darkness. So Kripkenstein's archer *cannot aim at all*. Wittgenstein's reminders are in a way about the reflexivity of the action of rule-following as repeated practice, and about the fact that the justification of why I follow a rule just *like this* ends somewhere.

Thirdly, the reason why in Kripke's reading Wittgenstein was supposed to have produced the paradox is that Kripke generalised Wittgenstein's reminders on rule-following, although they originally served the purpose of clarification (on the utterance) of (the concept of) meaning via *language* games. Kripke's sceptic thus created a theory of rule-following in terms of the impossibility of rule-following, which was then challenged by Kripkenstein's new theory of rule-following that was supposed to refute the sceptical challenge.[56] I would also add that Kripke mixes up the question of how I meant a certain rule in the past (what rule had I used before?) with the question of how to apply the rule in a new case. But if I am certain about the rule I used in the past (May I normally not know it except for the cases I have simply forgotten?), then in my opinion the second question is not challenged or touched by the sceptic.

G. Baker and P.M.S. Hacker replied to Kripke in *Scepticism, Rules and Language*[57]. In the first part of this collection of essays they state that they believe it to be obvious that Kripke's interpretation contradicts Wittgenstein's intentions in the rule-following part of the *Investigations*. In connection with this they claim that Kripke wrongly reconstructed its meaning and he incorrectly identified the

55 See also § 220ff of the *Investigations*.

56 See previous footnotes.

57 Gordon P Baker and PMS Hacker, *Scepticism, Rules and Language* (Basil Blackwell 1984).

aim of Wittgenstein's reminders.[58] Their framework objection is that Wittgenstein considered scepticism to be *nonsensical*[59], so it would be very surprising to make it a central feature of his own work as Kripke claims.[60] What is considered to be the sceptical paradox in the eyes of Kripke, leading to the conclusion that language is impossible as there is no meaning of words, Baker and Hacker consider to be conceptual nihilism. Granted, it may be interesting to find out what led to it, but it is certain that it is incorrect.[61] Baker and Hacker remark that Wittgenstein would surely not refute what everybody else ordinarily believes, and he would not advance theses hence he would not advance scepticism.[62] According to them, if we search the archaeology of § 201 we will realise that it is not the *ratio* of the *Investigations*. It in fact deepens and evolves § 198 and so it does *not* speak about rule-following as community practice, but that 'to follow a rule' is an activity which manifests the grasp of the rule.[63] It has nothing to do with the fact that we are a communal species and that rule-following is in general also community practice.[64]

Baker and Hacker do not only object that the sceptical paradox emerges from misreading of Wittgenstein; they also aim their criticism at the alleged sceptical solution. They offer their own interpretation of the "rule-following" parts of the *Investigations* and they conclude, referring to Wittgenstein's MS 165, that 'it is not the interpretation that builds the bridge between the sign and what is signified or meant; only the practise does that'[65]. This is why the rules themselves do not determine the meanings, but the way we use them in what we do, in our activities, does so. We are taught and trained in what is in accordance with the rules, and

---

58 Ibid, vii.

59 Baker and Hacker explicitly refer to the passages of Wittgenstein's diaries, and to his unfinished remarks published as *On Certainty*.

60 Gordon P Baker and PMS Hacker, *Scepticism, Rules and Language* (Basil Blackwell 1984) 5. Even McGuinness claims that 'we should not look in him [Wittgenstein – author's note] for theories and for ingenious scepticism, as the bad habits of his profession led Saul Kripke to do'. Brian McGuinness, *Approaches to Wittgenstein* (Routledge 2002) 4.

61 Gordon P Baker and PMS Hacker, *Scepticism, Rules and Language* (Basil Blackwell 1984) 6.

62 Ibid, 9. I have already mentioned something similar in my objections.

63 Gordon P Baker and PMS Hacker, *Scepticism, Rules and Language* (Basil Blackwell 1984) 14–16, 20. See also my own objection against Kripke connecting § 219 to § 81 and interpreting it in the light of the effort to make clear what made us hold onto the wrong picture.

64 Ibid, 21.

65 Ibid, 52.

what is not. We are checked, corrected and criticised in our behaviour (in the use of rules).[66] 'It is *acting* according to a rule, a *practise* of normative behaviour that lies at the bottom of our language-games. Language, far from being a reflection of thought, is a form of behaviour.'[67]

Baker and Hacker also focus on the problem of how a rule determines the action that is in accordance with it. They criticise both the concept of community fixation of application of rules through community view, and the dispositive theory.[68] Their objection to the dispositive theory is that it ignores the fact that:

> [T]o understand a rule is to grasp an internal relation between the rule and its (potential) extension. This is something *stipulated*, not discovered, a *fortiori* not a matter of dispositions, either public or private. Whether a person is following a rule, or only thinks incorrectly that he is following a rule, does not depend on what others are or might be doing.[69]

That is to say, if we ask how the rule determines the action which accords with it and we are looking for something that is between the rule and its application, Baker and Hacker answer that there is *nothing* of the kind. The question of what is between them makes no sense because there is an inner relation between the rule and its application and so they are not independent.[70] According to them 'to grasp a rule is to be able to say what accords with it'.[71]

But even if there is nothing between the rule and its application as Baker and Hacker claim, that does not mean that the "text allows the text only", as they are interpreted by Procházka when he discusses the issue of grasping a rule and interpretation.[72] The reason is that there is a difference between the rule and the

---

66 Ibid.

67 Ibid, 53.

68 Ibid, 70ff.

69 Ibid, 76. By 'extension' Baker and Hacker de facto mean 'application'.

70 Ibid, 96.

71 Ibid. See also 83–84:
What *justifies* calling rubies 'red'? Red is this ↑ colour; and rubies are this ↑ colour; i.e. red! Saying 'rubies are red' is a correct application of this rule for the use of 'red'. What *makes* it correct? Nothing. That is what we call 'applying "red" correctly'. There is no room for justification. And as there is no room for justification, so too there is no room for genuine doubt.'.

72 See Radoslav Procházka, *Dobrá vôľa, spravodlivý rozum: Hodnoty a princípy v súdnej praxi* [eng. *Goodness of Will, Fairness of Reason*] (Kalligram 2005) 198. Procházka is here probably tempted by the interpretation of Baker and Hacker provided by Dennis Patterson (in Law's Pragmatism: Law as Practise and Narative) as Procházka builds his argument on Patterson's paper. Moreover, Bix argues that Patterson is over-reading

expression of the rule in language. The latter aspect does not have key importance for Baker and Hacker here, but it is crucial for Procházka's book. Moreover I believe that such interpretation of Baker and Hacker is simply not in conformity with their interpretation of Wittgenstein, and it is so because the rules themselves do not determine their meaning.

I believe that Baker and Hacker wrote about the rules of *language* in order to recognise the sceptic's challenge as nonsensical. They did not state that every time I know/understand a rule (let us say a legal rule), I must automatically know how to apply it. In fact, they explicitly state that I can understand a rule but I may not be able to apply it. These cases they called hard cases.[73]

The conclusion from these two parts of this paper is that Wittgenstein did not create the sceptical paradox, and hence he did not provide its solution. But still, some legal scholars have used Wittgenstein's reminders as being in favour of indeterminacy of law through indeterminacy of language (which might be partially correct under some circumstances), as well as the impossibility of fixing the *application* of rules by rules themselves. This is supposed to undermine the ideal of Rule of Law, not rule of man, because rules cannot rule.

III. Legal scepticism on rule-following

In this part of the paper I analyse some applications of Wittgenstein's later philosophy, or to put it more properly, his late philosophising, on legal science, which led to legal rule-following scepticism. There are many examples that could have been chosen, however I have selected those that seem to be exemplary for us to show typical offences against Wittgenstein's method that also replicate Kripke's fallacy.

Discussions over Wittgenstein's reminders on rule-following seem to have become a quite stable part of writings on the indeterminacy of law. In fact, they are used to argue in favour of quite contradictory views, as I have mentioned above.

Sceptical reading of Wittgenstein may be found mostly in the writings of legal scholars in the eighties and nineties.[74] I believe that they were crucially influenced by Kripkenstein or, what is more, even by incautious reading of Kripkenstein.

Wittgenstein. See: Brian Bix, 'Cautions and Caveats for the Application of Wittgenstein to Legal Theory' in Joseph K Campbell and Michael O'Rourke and David Shier (eds), *Topics in Contemporary Philosophy* (MIT Press 2005, 217–229).

73 Gordon P Baker and PMS Hacker, *Scepticism, Rules and Language* (Basil Blackwell 1984) 72.

74 It seems to me that even though philosophers' interest in Wittgenstein has slightly decreased, the interest of legal scholars appears to be increasing. The same is claimed in Andrew Halpin, *Reasoning with Law* (Hart Publishing 2001) 107.

One of those philosophers is James Boyle.[75] Boyle applies Wittgenstein's ideas in the context of methods and enterprises of the types of theory within Critical Legal Studies ("CLS"). Just to put CLS into context, he is focusing on legal realism[76] and he reproduces one of the realists' claims: language is not neutral and in the application of law there is a need for interpretation, which is in fact a subjective and political act.[77] Boyle further writes that there is good reason for legal scholars' interest in language and meaning as long as the post-Wittgensteinian view on language spreads in the field of law. According to him, this view could be summed up in four forms:

> (i) words do not have "essences", (ii) words do not have "core meanings", (iii) language is, or *can* be, used in an infinite number of ways: it is a malleable instrument for communication, (iv) that a word is most commonly used to mean X does not mean that X is the "core," or "plain," or "essential" meaning of that word. To look to the "plain meaning" of a word as its "real meaning" is a special type of reification, since it ignores the purpose for which the word is actually being used.[78]

This view then must have concrete implications in law, whereby one of them is that it undermines the vision of a judiciary which neutrally interprets the law.[79] Wittgenstein's view on language is then relativistic, according to Boyle.[80]

My objection to Boyle's interpretation of Wittgenstein is that according to Wittgenstein words can be used in many ways, but the uses are however still normative, they are guided by rules, which is why there might appear correct and incorrect uses or normal and abnormal uses; there is a correct and incorrect reaction. It is not like Feyerabend's "Anything goes!". Surely, the rules of language games may

---

75 James Boyle, 'The Politics of Reason: Critical Legal Theory and Local Social Thought' (1985) 133 University of Pennsylvania Law Review 685.

76 The realists' approach differs from Wittgenstein's at the first sight, as claimed by Halpin in Andrew Halpin, *Reasoning with Law* (Hart Publishing 2001) 143. This is so because: If the approach of Wittgenstein is characterised as refining our understanding by seeking to clarify the meaning of words through a more acute grasp of the social practices which those words express, realism appears to stand this process on its head. We are supposed to refine our understanding of our social practices (and anything else besides) by clarifying our meaning of words in relation to a reality that may not be fully evident in the social practices we observe.

77 James Boyle, 'The Politics of Reason: Critical Legal Theory and Local Social Thought' (1985) 133 University of Pennsylvania Law Review 685, 695.

78 Ibid, 708–709.

79 Ibid, 709–710.

80 Ibid, 732, footnote 142.

change, and while speaking – use of language – is our form of life[81], our form of life (or perhaps rather: the content of our form of life) could have been different. But this is far from meaning that the use of language is indeterminate and that language is relativistic *in the way* Boyle claims. Everything could have been different, but it is not. Is it really true that people would not recognize if a judge used the words, even the wording of the law, differently from how it should have been used, or how the legal text should have been interpreted in some specific context, in some specific situation? Even when we accept the view that language is not neutral in *the sense* that it is not a calculus operating on definite rules, and the applications of words do not stem from rules as if they come out of a calculating machine, it would still not mean that normally we do not know what to say; it would not mean that we normally have doubts as to how we should react; or it would not mean that a judge can interpret words in the way s/he (subjectively) pleases in order to favour his or her (possibly political) goals. And it would certainly not mean that 'objectivity' of law was lost either, as the judge is simply not able, even if he or she

81 Wittgenstein wrote that language is part of our form of life, and the reminders that surround the often-quoted § 241 of the *Investigations* ('"So you are saying that human agreement decides what is true and what is false?"—It is what human beings say that is true and false; and they agree in the *language* they use. That is not agreement in opinions but in form of life.') justify, as I believe, the interpretation that language belongs among the (foundations of) human *activities* in which people agree, so discussion on what is or should be correct on this fundamental level is simply not possible. Can we imagine *reasonable* discussion on whether a certain colour is indeed blue? Whether it is truly blue? What if it is in fact hdiuhfs (or any other line of random letters)? How can I justify my calling this colour 'blue'? There is no way. It is the way it is. (Granted, we can think about the 'causal' reason, the word somehow emerged, somebody used it 'for the first time', but this is not what we were asking about. Surely, there is something we could call the 'causal' reason, but that would be a different question, on a different level.) In the *form of life* there is no place for justification and hence no (reasonable) doubt so there is no need for agreement in opinions. Let me return to the example with blue colour one more time. I might point to the (blue) sky and say: "The sky is blue." How shall I justify my assertion if somebody reacts and says: "No, the sky is brown!" This is not a matter of opinion(s); matters of opinion are for instance the decriminalisation of drugs, gay marriage, the limits of democracy while defending against terrorism, or the actual importance or need for legal philosophers. I simply call this colour blue. Wittgenstein made clearer the basic agreement in language (even though language is not a calculus working to definite rules), and his intention was not to analyse the situation where we do not agree what the legal text means and how we should interpret the legal text. Such interpretation would in fact be a matter of opinion.

tried as hard as possible, to interpret or better to say understand the wording of the law without the need to employ his or her 'subjective' (possibly political) views.

Surely, since language is not a calculus of rules, in some cases we have doubts as to how to understand some utterance, legal provision or legal text. But then we are able to argue reasonably in favour of interpretation X, interpretation Y or even interpretation Z. But in such cases (usually called hard ones) the interpretation is a matter of *opinion*, and there may well be a lack of consensus as to the right answer.[82] In the interpretation of law we sometimes have struggles, different opinions on how to interpret the law[83] and how to apply the legal rules[84] – but what does Wittgenstein have to do with that?

Scepticism about language as exposed by legal realists is also refuted in the concise study by Zapf and Moglen.[85] In their view, scepticism as to rule-following, even in the case of judicial decision-making, is in fact only a political argument in favour of wider judicial discretion.[86] Such scepticism is based on looking for problems where there are no problems really, as Wittgenstein suggested in stating that the 'logical relation between words and applications that we read off them is unproblematic'[87]. According to Zapf and Moglen, if the meaning of a word lies in its use, then to know the meaning means to know the use of the word. Hence there is no need to justify our use of words while using language; we can follow the rules of language blindly. But in the sphere of law it is quite different, as they claim, and I have presented a similar objection above. What is expected of those who apply the law, e.g. judges, is really to justify the use and provide reasons for the application of legal rules in particular cases specifically when there is a dispute

82 L. E. Wolcher distinguishes consensus of use, consensus of opinion and consensus of interpretation. See: Louis E. Wolcher, 'Ronald Dworkin's Right Answers Thesis Through the Lens of Wittgenstein' (1997) 29 Rutgers Law Journal 43, 51.

83 What does this text mean? What is the rule?

84 How to follow the rule in this situation?

85 Christian Zapf and Eben Moglen, 'Linguistic Indeterminacy and the Rule of Law: On the Perils of Misunderstanding Wittgenstein' (1996) 84 Georgetown Law Journal 485.

86 Ibid, 486.

87 Ibid, 485.

about their application. So judges decide which application is the "right" one.[88] Then '[j]ustice may be blind, but only if it is not mute'.[89]

Referring to Wittgenstein, even Andrei Marmor strives to show that judges do not need to reach for extra-textual evidence in order to apply rules in specific cases.[90] Marmor applies Wittgenstein on the background of the Hart – Fuller discussion. His aim is to show that to distinguish easy cases and hard cases, as positivists do, is not arbitrary. Marmor defines easy cases as cases where the law may be applied straightforwardly. In contrast, in hard cases 'the issue is not determined by the existing legal standards'.[91] The Hart – Fuller discussion has implications as to whether judges create the law or just apply it.[92]

So let me briefly sum up Marmor's undertaking which led him to the application of Wittgenstein's ideas. Marmor investigates the difference between easy cases and hard cases based on Hart's core of certainty v. penumbra of doubt cases of the use of terms which, as I mentioned above, Boyle in fact denies.[93] There is no need to remind readers of the famous "no vehicles in the park". Marmor seeks

---

88 Zapf and Moglen slightly avoid the problem of identification of legal rules in which the "only" difficulty the judge may have is to select the applicable rule (if there is more than one) and to justify the selection. So I believe there are many situations that may occur while deciding a case. For example, I can have trouble finding out what the rule expressed in the sentence "Unusual punishment is prohibited" requires me to do when imposing a sanction on a criminal. Is capital punishment unusual? It is not that I do not understand the sentence. I know what it means; I have grasped the rule in it. I am just hesitating whether it is applicable tocapital punishment. Or does this hesitation mean that I have not grasped the legal rule? I would probably have had no problem understanding and applying the rule about unusual punishment if I had been a judge living in the USA in 1900. My point is a very simple one: judicial decision-making, and in fact the whole of legal practice, is much more colourful or much richer than it might seem when we look at it as the simple application of rules. So even though using language is normative activity, activity in which we somehow apply and use the rules of language, it cannot simply be stated that what is said about language as normative activity can also be always properly claimed about the practice of law, just because it is normative too and language is somehow involved as well.

89 Christian Zapf and Eben Moglen, 'Linguistic Indeterminacy and the Rule of Law: On the Perils of Misunderstanding Wittgenstein' (1996) 84 Georgetown Law Journal 485, 519.

90 Andrei Marmor, 'No Easy Cases?' in Andrei Marmor, *Interpretation and Legal Theory* (Clarendon Press 1992, pp. 124–154).

91 Ibid, 124.

92 Ibid.

93 See: Herbert L A Hart, *The Concept of Law* (2nd edn, Clarendon Press 1994) 131.

to defend Hart's position against objections by Fuller. He does so by referring to Wittgenstein, while arguing against the scepticism consisting in the claim that the sole expression of the rule in the language cannot guide a judge in deciding a case by the sole application of the legal rule, excluding the need to seek its purpose. Marmor formulates Fuller's critique of Hart thus: '[U]nderstanding a rule must always involve an understanding of its particular purposes'.[94] The judge then according to Fuller needs something more than knowledge of the language, i.e. understanding the language and words in which the legal rules are expressed.

And here Marmor applies Wittgenstein. He asks whether it makes sense to claim that to understand the rule means always to understand its purpose, which is meant to be achieved through its application.[95] Marmor transforms this question into at the first sight Wittgenstein's question whether to understand the rule and to follow the rule consists in interpretation.[96] Marmor then exposes the problem of the alleged gap between the rule and its use that needs to be bridged, and this bridge should be interpretation. Wittgenstein in Marmor's reading repudiates this idea, and he dedicates to it quite a large part of the *Investigations*.[97] Here, as I believe, Marmor made a key mistake as he did not bear in mind Wittgenstein's method, and he did not apply it as (i) he used Wittgenstein's reminders on rule-following as theory, as theses, and moved them to the field of law; (ii) he ignored the aim of those reminders; and (iii) he made a generalisation. Moreover, Marmor relies on interpretation by Baker and Hacker in the above-mentioned study, emphasising that between a rule and its application there is an inner (grammatical) relation and hence it does not make sense to say that somebody can understand a rule and at the same time not be able to apply it.[98] But Marmor took Baker's and Hacker's claim out of context, and he probably overlooked what they mentioned in the brackets. *In concreto*, they stated that based on their aims they would not deal with hard cases.[99] Right, the reader may say, however this is enough for Marmor to show that easy cases in law are possible, and in these cases we do not

---

94 Andrei Marmor, 'No Easy Cases?' in Andrei Marmor, *Interpretation and Legal Theory* (Clarendon Press 1992, pp. 124–154) 336.

95 Ibid, 146.

96 Ibid.

97 Ibid, 147, 148.

98 Ibid, 148.

99 See: Gordon P Baker and PMS Hacker, *Scepticism, Rules and Language* (Basil Blackwell 1984) 72. In footnote 88 I tried to show that perhaps in hard cases I indeed understand the legal rule because I understand the normative text, but I am still not sure how to decide the specific case based on it.

need interpretation encompassing understanding of purposes which should be employed in order to understand the rule and apply it. With this I would agree, but my aim was not to show that there are no easy cases in law, or that in order to follow a legal rule there is always a need for interpretation as substitution of one expression of a rule for another. My aim is to show how Marmor misunderstands Wittgenstein, so his argument would not work based solely on Wittgenstein's reminders. I also intend to show that Marmor mixes rules of language with legal rules, as they are both rules and so what Wittgenstein wrote about rules works for both. I believe this is a mistake. We must bear in mind that legal rules are *often* formulated in language but they are distinct from the rules of language. When the concept of rule-following is elucidated in the *Investigations,* it is done in order to make clear something about language which was improperly understood before (for instance by Wittgenstein in his *Tractatus*), not something about law. It is true that it elucidates something about our activities and that law may be seen as an activity, but which of the puzzles of lawyers or legal scholars are resolved by the rule-following reminders in the *Investigations*? Which was the puzzle that supposedly led Fuller into claiming the need for purpose in the application of legal rules? Does Wittgenstein have anything to say about that?

When Marmor interprets § 201 and § 198 of the *Investigations* just like Baker and Hacker, he claims that Wittgenstein states that interpretation as substitution of one expression of a rule for another cannot determine the correct application. I can agree with that to some extent, however for the first part of § 201 I propose a different interpretation. This is that 'interpretation' in the first part of § 201 is a rule for interpretation of a rule, or a rule for the use of the rule in this step. It is not the substitution of one expression of the rule for another, which is the case of the second part of § 201. And this is of some relevance because then the space for interpretation as engagement of purposes or principles is open. In fact, even Marmor leaves that space open, as we will see later.

Let me just note here that there is one more difference between the rules of language (games) and legal rules. When I formulate/explicate a legal rule, e.g. some customary rule, I do not need to follow this rule at the same time. However, when I formulate the rule of a language game (e.g. we are in a café and I tell the waiter "When I say 'coffee', I want you to bring me ristretto and Pepsi, which is what I always drink here.") I follow the rules of the language and this language game at the same time.

Now let us focus on what Marmor believes Wittgenstein meant about normal and abnormal uses of words, and how this might be useful for legal theory. I believe that Marmor is correct here. It is possible to use words normally and abnormally (in the latter case it is not clear whether the term 'fits', whether it is used correctly). This is a statement about language hence it is a statement about legal language too. The law is vague in this way, because the language which communicates legal rules is sometimes vague.[100] And as the language is vague there is sometimes doubt about the applicability of some legal rule. And there we need interpretation, which Marmor claims Wittgenstein intended as the substitution of one expression of the rule for another. And in such interpretation the purpose of the rule plays a role.[101] But according to Marmor such interpretation does not involve grasping the rule because 'there is nothing more to explain or understand about its meaning'[102], it is just a translation of the expression of the rule. And if judicial decision-making should be an activity of translating it would really be a strange activity. This is why Marmor concludes that '[i]nterpretation is required only when the formulation of the rule leaves doubts as to its applicability in a given set of circumstances'[103]. For Marmor therefore, legal positivism must be rescued, supposedly because legal positivism and interpretativism are said to be incompatible, and interpretativism has been refuted by Marmor thanks to his application of Wittgenstein.[104]

Marmor replicates some of Kripke's fallacies in his violations of Wittgenstein's method. Marmor uses some of the latter's reminder as theses and applies them in the sphere of law. They then lead him to claim that there is an inner relation between *legal* rules and the application of these rules. Moreover, he takes one more step and he extends this thesis to judicial decision-making when he claims that when judges *apply legal* rules there is no need for their interpretation.

Marmor's fallacy, his "leap", may perhaps become clearer when I provide an example. Let us image a game which has two rules only: R1 and R2.

R1 states: It is prohibited to smoke in public places.

R2 states: Judge Dredd decides upon violation of R1.[105]

Now let's try to disentangle Marmor's puzzle using Wittgenstein's reminders (questions). How do the players follow rule R1? How does Judge Dredd follow rule R1 when deciding upon violation of the rule or compliance with it?

---

100 Andrei Marmor, 'No Easy Cases?' in Andrei Marmor, *Interpretation and Legal Theory* (Clarendon Press 1992, pp. 124–154) 152.

101 Ibid, 153.

102 Ibid.

103 Ibid, 154.

104 S. Bertea shows us why this is not in fact the case. See: Stefano Bertea, 'Remarks on a Legal Positivist Misuse of Wittgenstein's Later Philosophy' (2003) 22 Law and Philosophy 513.

105 For our purposes there is no need for sanction.

Marmor ignores single cases. When R1 is applied by a player who smokes or does not smoke in public places, this application is different from the application of R1 when Dredd decides upon violation or compliance in a specific case.[106] Applying the rule when deciding upon its non/violation is different from following or breaking this rule, even though this is also an application of the rule.

As a matter of fact, Marmor ultimately generalises Wittgenstein's reminder from § 201 and creates an apparent definition: interpretation *is* translation.

But this makes the issue of interpretation of law even more confusing. If there is any doubt as to what rule is expressed in a legal text as the legal text is vague, can translation that I myself perform ever help me to understand the rule? In order to translate, I already need to understand. Could interpretation in the form of translation really be helpful?[107] Or does Marmor have in mind cases in which there is some doubt about the expression of the legal rule? As if a judge could possibly

---

106 In this sentence I use the word 'application' in the manner it was used by Wittgenstein. However, I am aware of the fact that in the first case jurisprudential discourse would say that the player simply follows the rule, i.e obeys or disobeys the rule. The difference between the uses of the words by Wittgenstein and by legal scholars might constitute the misunderstandings pointed by S. Bertea in BERTEA, S.: Remarks on a Legal Positivist Misuse of Wittgenstein's Later Philosophy. Law and Philosophy, 22: 513–535.

107 P. Bobbitt in Philip C Bobbitt, 'What it Means to Follow a Rule of Law?' in Linda Meyer (ed), *Rules and Reasoning: Essays in Honor of Fred Schauer* (Hart Publishing 1999, 55–60) 58 formulates this "problem" thus:

Following a rule does not depend upon placing an interpretation on it. To interpret is simply to translate and translation cannot by itself invest understanding because the new formulation must itself be understood. We translate—or interpret—in order to shift to a new decisional pattern for reasons that have nothing to do with understanding. If we did not understand the original statement we could not translate it. And to say that interpretation enables rule-following presupposes that the rule-following in the translated matter is already enabled.

It seems to me that Marmor's study collapses on this very paradox, and this is so because on the one hand he claims that nothing stands between a (legal) rule and its application, so when I understand the rule I know how to apply it, while on the other hand he maintains that interpretation as translation is not the way to grasp the rule as there is nothing more to explain about its meaning. Does he mean here a legal rule or a language game rule? If he has the first in mind, it would not certainly fit. Secondly, Marmor's study would appear to collapse also because he seems to consider all the rules, whether rules of language or legal rules, to be explicable using language itself. So he does not see the difference between rules of language and legal rules which I have mentioned above.

think of three ways of reading which would lead to three different readings of the rule, and then the judge would need to select one of them? If so, what role would translation play? Would it be the process or only the result of judicial activity here?

In this part of the paper I have shown some examples of the use of Wittgenstein's reminder on rule-following that I believe to be improper. Hence arguments on objectivity in law founded on them are erroneous too. In the last part of the paper I follow Dennis Patterson's ideas, which should disentangle the puzzle that requires us to take either the position of objectivism or the position of subjectivism.

IV. Objectivity, rules, Patterson

Dennis Patterson tried to disentangle the puzzle or the question of whether objectivism or subjectivism is right in his *Normativity and Objectivity in Law*[108]. His intention was to lead us to a different analogy, so that the question would disappear. For an objectivist, as Patterson writes, external facts make assertions true or false. An objectivist would claim for example that if we call some objects 'fruits', we do so because there are indeed fruits.[109] The idea is that if there were no real standard, i.e. were it not for the fact that there are indeed things like fruits in this world, then following a rule would be the same as thinking that one followed the rule. So the criterion of truth must be outside of our mind, and there must be standards independent of rules. Patterson recognises this as a misunderstanding revealed in the *Investigations,* as the objectivist's picture is that of a rule on rails which cannot determine the application of a rule if we are not able to use this independent standard (§ 218). Moreover, the standard might be interpreted variously, so we need something else, something more again to guide us. Hence objectivism does not work. And what about subjectivism? Is the meaning always produced through interpretation? Patterson argues with § 198 of the *Investigations,* which undermines the subjectivist's position: interpretations themselves cannot determine meaning because of the infinite regression of interpretation that needs interpretation, and so on[110] So in fact even subjectivism fails.

Hence, Patterson identifies the shared fallacy of objectivism and subjectivism: they see rule-following as an operation of mind. Wittgenstein then helps us to arrive at a new analogy by perceiving normativity as action: following a rule means being trained to act, so it consists of practice. Then it follows that '[n]ormativity

---

108 Dennis Patterson, 'Normativity and Objectivity in Law' (2001) 43 William and Mary Law Review 325.

109 Ibid, 330. Patterson here uses italics for the term 'really'.

110 Ibid, 334–339.

is concerned not with how we make judgements of correctness and incorrectness, but in what those judgements consist'.[111] Patterson, interpreting his way through the *Investigations*, comes to the conclusion that 'normativity of rule-following—the ground of correctness and incorrectness—is not to be found in the agreement of others *as such*. Agreement is a necessary feature of the normativity of our practices, but the "agreement" must be regularity in reaction to use'.[112] What does this meant for the law? The law is normative too, and so Patterson engages in the task of making legal practise more perspicuous, employing Wittgenstein's method. He claims that the training of lawyers provides them with a set of argumentative skills which are indeed specific, as there is a need to provide persuasive argument leading to correct assertions about the law. Accordingly, he states that *forms of argument* (textual, historical, doctrinal, prudential and perhaps some others) allow rule-following, and so the law is possible thanks to them. This however is all presented rather "out of the blue" for any reader not familiar with Wittgenstein. Readers familiar with Wittgenstein tend to suspect that Patterson is trying to get close to his form of life (in law). Patterson's explanation is that the forms of argument are (i) ways in which we do things with law; (ii) make it possible for us to engage in activities called "law"; and (iii) allow us to demonstrate the correctness, incorrectness, veracity or falsity of assertions about the law.[113] The forms of argument allow for a certain kind of objectivity. They are culturally endorsed and their existence rests upon their use by lawyers. Patterson claims that they could have been different but they are not, although they still might change.[114] Here we can assume that Patterson also accepts the causal "objectivity" of the forms of argument, while at the same time they are "logically" arbitrary; they could have been quite different but they are not. It also follows then that objectivity is '*relative to a domain*'.[115]

Patterson's view might perhaps be rewritten in the form of a reminder like this (compare the reminder in the *Investigations*, § 241):

> "So you are saying that human agreement decides what are true and what are false utterances about the law?"—It is what human beings claim about the law that is true and false; and they agree in the *forms of argument* they use. That is not agreement in opinions but in form of life.

111 Ibid, 342.
112 Ibid, 348 (footnotes omitted).
113 Ibid, 355.
114 Ibid, 363.
115 Ibid.

In my view, the notion of form of life is connected with the level of justification where the "*spade is turned*" (§ 217 *Investigations*), and I just do what I do. Similarly, it is connected with what Wittgenstein wrote in reaction to G. E. Moore's common-sense proof of an external world. In order to have doubts about something, we need to have a system within which such doubts might exist. 'I have arrived at the rock bottom of my convictions. And one might almost say that these foundation-walls are carried by the whole house.'[116] Form of life in fact has such foundations. As no opinions are present at that level, no meaningful discussion is possible. If no meaningful discussion is possible, no justification and no reasoning are needed. Patterson was looking for something in law being part of the form of life, so it would allow solid objective grounds for law. Would it not then be the case that the law's empire would be the lawyer's empire? Laypeople are certainly not acquainted with the forms of argument, but that does not mean that they are not to follow legal rules or in general do things within the law.

The forms of argument are not to be underestimated in any way, but they fix the practice for those who are trained in them. Patterson is on the correct track, I believe, as he is looking for a standard or a matrix that might set some criteria in practice. He is looking for something in the activities called "law" that might be *beyond* correct and incorrect, as this would settle the criteria for correct and incorrect. This something should allow objectivity in law (as this would constrain our actions within this activity), even though this standard could be different, so it is "logically" arbitrary. However, looking in the practice of law we can see more activities than just the things that lawyers do. Even the "list of expressions of legal rules"[117] can play some role in connection with *repeated* practice in applying those rules if we want to refute scepticism about rules and rule-following. On the ontological level, legal norms are surely mind-independent at the existential level,[118] and we are surely trained to follow some laws in some way, so most of the time we do not have doubts as to whether we have obeyed the law or violated it. This is the case also because language is mostly determinate, so there are no huge epistemic constraints for us to find out what the law actually requires us to do.

116 Ludwig Wittgenstein, *On Certainty* (Basil Blackwell 1969) 33, note 248.

117 Cf. *Investigations* §198. Wittgenstein wrote about a list of rules, and in fact refuted the possibility of any list itself connecting rules with action. Nevertheless we have a good deal of practice in following those rules.

118 See the thesis of weak mind-independence of law in Matthew Kramer, *Objectivity and the Rule of Law* (CUP 2007) 6.

And in cases where we have doubts as to the proper way of following or applying a rule, or how, as a judge, the case should be decided, we have methods of legal reasoning that set criteria for a competent quest for the right answer. Perhaps this is as much objectivity as we can get. Is there any other "deeper" bedrock where our spade could ultimately turn?

Pietro Denaro,

University of Palermo, Italy

3. The causality of omissions and the objectivity of human agency

1. Introduction

The paradoxical view that omissions are both non-actions and ways of acting has often been expressed.[1] It is also been argued, often influentially, that omissions do not really cause anything because they are nothing (*ex nihilo nihil fit*). Another popular argument is that causes are necessarily bodily movements (of which more explanation later) and so, under this definition, omissions do not qualify[2]. Other authors have argued that omissions do cause things to happen but do so in a different way than actions. They claim that, unlike actions, which can be observed, omissions can only be referenced according to some norm (the so-called 'normativity of omissions')[3]. This paper is a defence of the causal role of omissions against the first two positions, but also offers some arguments for discounting the normative view.

The terms attributed to the causal properties of omissions have very helpfully been debated and clearly set by John Harris in his seminal works on this topic. He defends the thesis that omissions do have a causal role and dismisses any thoughts that omissions can only be referred to by norms (and are considered

1 Carlos Santiago Nino, *Introducción a la filosofía de la acción humana* (Editorial de la Universidad de Buenos Aires 1987) 5; Georg Henrik von Wright, 'On the Logic of Norms and Action' in Risto Hilpinen (ed), *New Studies in Deontic Logic. Norms, Actions, and the Foundations of Ethics* (Springer 1981).

2 These are the two arguments dealing with the difficulties about omissions analysed by Hart and Honoré in their fundamental work *Causation and the Law*. See H.L.A. Hart and Tony Honoré, *Causation in the Law* (2nd edn, OUP 1985) 447.

3 In the context of the present work, I do not deal specifically with the related issue of the so-called normativity of omissions. This subject is strictly linked to the one I will analyse here though, because the (mistaken) idea that the identification of an omission depends exclusively on the violation of a positive norm of conduct is often elaborated on the basis of the (mistaken) assumption that exactly on this bases the causation of omissions is based, and this is the peculiarity of omissions as compared to positive actions.

causes because they are forbidden).[4] As Harris puts it: 'when someone pointedly turns their back on an event, or washes their hands of it, or puts a telescope to their blind eye, it does not require much imagination to see the connection between these actions and what then occurs'.[5] However, Harris also points out that, we are not entitled to see the failure to prevent something as a cause of harm in every instance where we realize harm could have been avoided.[6] Indeed, if we attribute a causal role to an omission, we also normally think of it as producing only part of the effect.[7] So, where exactly should we draw the distinction between causal and non-causal omissions? A recurrent answer given by legal doctrine is that an omission is the failure to do something that should have been done, not simply avoiding to do something. However, a more satisfactory explanation requires digging deeper.

In what follows, I will defend the idea that we can produce a change both by acting and by omitting to act. Moreover, I aim to show that the differences between actions and events lay in their causal properties, thus undermining the so-called normative thesis of omissions. To appreciate the causal role of omissions, we must first analyse the metaphysical presuppositions that influence our understanding of what actions are. This point is key as I am convinced that these theoretical presuppositions are, most frequently, either underestimated or grounded on wrong premises. Only after having assumed a reasoned position about what actions are, can we start to understand how to differentiate between actions and omissions.

---

4 John Harris, 'The Marxist Conception of Violence', [1974] *Philosophy and Public Affairs* 200.

5 John Harris, 'Bad Samaritans Cause Harm', [1982] *The Philosophical Quarterly* 65. A longer list of examples of causal omission is offered by Jonathan Schaffer in a recent critique of Moore's argument against the causal role of omissions (Jonathan Schaffer, 'Disconnection and Responsibility', [2012] *Legal Theory* 419–20. Such a list, and the variety of examples offered, are not irrelevant. Indeed, as we will see, an argument against Moore's view can be structured starting from the acknowledgement of the causal role of omissions in all the mentioned cases. The premises of Moore's argument ('omissions are nothing') can be questioned on the basis of their resulting in negation of the causal role of conducts to which we attach a causal role. For a more detailed account of Schaffer's argument, see *infra* the following part of this paragraph.

6 Harris, 'The Marxist Conception of Violence' (n 4) 205.

7 There are some peculiar features of causation through allowing, which makes it possible to say that not everything that has not been prevented can be considered as caused, in the same way in which everything which has been positively done has to be considered as caused. However, it is not a reference to a norm which reveals this to us; it is, rather, a reference to each person's causal capacities.

I will first present the terms in which the debate around the causal role of omissions has been phrased, while in the final section I will highlight how such a debate should be restated in the light of more appropriate metaphysical assumptions. My overall aim is to provide an improved account of what omissions are in terms of human agency.

2. The causal role of omissions

Tony Honoré, who devoted a great deal of effort to the analysis and clarification of the debate on omissions, famously observes that:

> 'the idea that an omission could be a cause has been called 'complete nonsense'. Writers who do not go as far as this have, nevertheless, felt that an omission could not really be a cause of harm but merely a condition, or something which might legally be treated as a cause without really being one, or merely a quasi-cause'

He adds, that 'although the view has been advocated that there is no difference of principle between the causality of positive acts and omissions, it is clear from the variety of attempts to circumvent the difficulty that it is felt to be serious'.[8]

The sections that follow present two different influential attempts at arguing against the causality of omissions. The first elaborates on the idea that omissions are simply nothing to reach the conclusion that nothing cannot be the cause of anything. The second focuses on the theory stating that a cause has to be identified with bodily movements.[9]

---

8 Tony Honoré, 'Causation and the Remoteness of Damage', *International Encyclopaedia of Comparative Law* (1983) vol. IX, 13. The art. 40 (2) of the Italian penal code states that 'not preventing an event which it is the legal duty of the *propositus* to prevent is equivalent to causing it. The distinction arises from the fact that there are negative as well as positive conditions of events' (ibid 12). 'The negative conditions are generally numerous; thus, each person's failure to rescue a drowning man may be regarded as a condition of his drowning. But the negative conditions of an event lack explanatory force unless their positive counterparts would be usually present or are morally or legally required', (ibid 13); see also Hart and Honoré, *Causation in the Law* (n 2) 65–6: 'From a common sense point of view, the failure to act is in such cases is a cause or the equivalent of a cause, though no legal liability results. But there may be a legal doctrine, such as the Italian code implies, that in this case the omission is not to be treated as a cause of the harm', Honoré, 'Causation and the Remoteness of Damage' (n 8) 13. Indeed, Honoré stresses that 'it is equivalent to causing' does not mean that 'it *is* causing', and that the norm suggests that only when a duty is there, causation is there too. See also, on this last point, Hart and Honoré, *Causation in the Law* (n 2) 447 (fn 3).

9 These two arguments were pointed out by Hart and Honoré, *Causation in the Law* (n 2) 447.

2.1 Omissions as nothing

The first argument is grounded on the idea that negative descriptions (i.e. someone did not do something) are simply nothing, or have a different value than positive descriptions. This thesis, influentially endorsed by Michael Moore amongst others, presents a theory of causation where omissions have no causal role.[10] Moore claims that the difference between actions and omissions is grounded in a certain metaphysical account of actions and causation. He affirms that 'omissions are simply absent actions. An omission to save a life is not some kind of ghostly act of not saving a life, and certainly not some ghostly kind of killing. It is literally nothing at all'.[11] His metaphysical view is that 'actions are willed bodily movements' and that only actions can be causes.[12] So, according to Moore, actions are events while omissions are absent events or, more simply, nothing at all.

---

10 Micheal S. Moore, 'Causation and Responsibility', [1999] *Social Philosophy & Policy* 2; Micheal S. Moore, *Act and Crime. The Philosophy of Action and its Implication for Criminal Law* (Clarendon Press 1993). More recently, Micheal S. Moore, *Causation and Responsibility. An Essay in Law, Morals and Metaphysics* (OUP 2009). But this is a widely shared view. See, eg, John Kleinig, 'Criminal Liability for Failures to Act' [1986] *Law and Contemporary Problems* 174: 'whereas it is plausible to see positive acts as causally potent, as bringing about certain consequences, it is easy to think that omissions, whatever their status, do not play a causal role in any harmful outcome with which they are associated. For what S fails to do or refrains from doing is to intervene in some harm-causing or harm-threatening chain of events'. For further references see also Honoré, 'Causation and the Remoteness of Damage' (n 8) 13ff.

11 Moore, *Act and Crime* (n 10) 28. More recently, Moore, *Causation and Responsibility. An Essay in Law, Morals and Metaphysics* (n 10) 52–5, 444–51.

12 Moore, *Act and Crime* (n 10) 28. However, it is arguable that Moore endorses the point of view of the jurist, and the reasons he presents for accepting his metaphysics of action are mostly legal reasons. I can imagine that he might have a different view if he were interested in the morally relevant concept of action and its metaphysical presuppositions. At the same time, it should be acknowledged that Moore's 'conceptualization of the act/omission distinction is capable of carrying the moral freight... (of) marking the difference between supererogatory virtues and positive duties, on the one hand, and negative duties, on the other. If... omissions do not *cause* anything, then when I omit to prevent some harm I do not make the world worse; I only fail to make it better. Only when I cause that harm to occur – through my actions – do I worsen the world', Moore, *Act and Crime* (n 10) 28–9. It has to be acknowledged that his view has the advantage of not leading to the conclusion of restricting very much the domain of the supererogatory.

This notion that absences 'cannot serve as causes or effects'[13] forms the basis for Moore's 'No Absences Thesis'.

First, he observes that:

> 'those who oppose the idea that omissions can be causes (on the necessary condition conception of causation), often voice the objection that omissions are never necessary to the production of some result because other conditions are already sufficient to produce that event'.[14]

However, Moore also acknowledges that:

> 'on a necessity conception of causation, those who omit to interfere (say, to rescue the plaintiff) have caused his worsened position. For the other conditions that also caused the plaintiff's harm were not sufficient to produce it; also necessary was that the defendant omitted to prevent the harm from occurring (which, by hypothesis, he could have done)'.[15]

His second objection is based on a kind of *reductio ad absurdum* argument: 'if the absence of an action can be a necessary condition to the happening of some harm, and thus a cause of it, then there are an indefinitely large number of causes for anything'.[16] However, as Moore himself noticed, this argument creates problems for necessary condition causal theory and is not specific to omissions. The same absurd outcome also derives from considering positive actions as causes.[17]

Conclusively, Moore defends his view by affirming that the biggest error made by those who equate omissions to causes is the idea of omissions as existing things or states. He writes:

> 'if I am correct that much of the temptation to treat omissions as causes comes from this identification of nonexistent actions (omissions) with plainly existent things (states), then showing this identification to be false may be reason enough to reject the temptation to which it gives rise'.[18]

---

13 Schaffer, 'Disconnection and Responsibility' (n 5) 401. Moore, *Causation and Responsibility. An Essay in Law, Morals and Metaphysics* (n 10) 436–9.

14 Moore, *Act and Crime* (n 10) 268.

15 ibid.

16 ibid. See also Eric Mack, 'Bad Samaritanism and the Causation of Harm' [1980] *Philosophy and Public Affairs* 244.

17 Moore, *Act and Crime* (n 10) 269. The necessary-condition causal theory is itself untenable: ibid 269–76.

18 ibid 277.

Moore's conception has also been connected to the energy flow conception of causation, assuming that 'absences are nothing' and 'nothing cannot provide either sources or sinks of energy'.[19]

What is most striking in Moore's proposal is his clear-cut equation between actions and things, based on a very suspect view of the metaphysically certainty of what actions really are.[20] Moreover, it can be argued that Moore's idea, that actions are something, while non-actions (and thus omissions) are nothing, is based on a fundamental confusion. Following Tony Honoré, we could argue that what we are involved with here are *descriptions* of actions and omissions. A negative description is different from a non-description and is not a nullity.[21] A negative description can describe the world just as a positive one can. Moreover, if omis-

---

19 Schaffer, 'Disconnection and Responsibility' (n 5) 401. This author refers to the theoretical account of causation elaborated by David Fair, 'Causation and the Flow of Energy' [1979] *Erkenntnis* 219–50.

20 I think, for instance, that from a philosophical perspective it is wrong to compare actions and elephants, as Moore does. See Moore, *Act and Crime* (n 10) 276–7. Moore, *Causation and Responsibility. An Essay in Law, Morals and Metaphysics* (n 10) 53.

21 Honoré makes this point. He observes this criticizing those who try to demonstrate that negative descriptions can be *considered as* positive descriptions: 'none of the attempts to show that omissions are really positive are successful. But there is no need to show this. …The absence of food in the body (starvation) is as real as the presence of arsenic (poisoning). It is real because life has both positive conditions and negative conditions, and so death can be brought about either through the absence of a positive condition of life or the presence of a negative condition', Honoré, 'Causation and the Remoteness of Damage' (n 8) 14. Honoré only seems to accept that, from the point of view of explanatory force, there can be a difference between positive acts and omissions. He indeed writes that 'When the conduct omitted is legally or socially required and is a condition of the harm, there is no difference from the point of view of explanatory force between it and a positive act which is also a condition. The world of social relations is as real a world as the world of physics. When the omission is legally wrongful, there is no difference from the point of view of responsibility between it and a similar wrongful positive act, which is a condition of the harm. From either point of view, it is justifiable to treat at least these omissions as causally related to the ensuing harm', ibid 15. I should add that I also find it difficult to understand the difference, found by Hart and Honoré, between negative and affirmative causal statements, which I believe have the same attitude for describing the world. They write indeed that the difficulty in admitting that an omission can be considered the cause of an occurrence can be overcome: 'the corrective here is to realize that negative statements… are ways of describing the world, just as affirmative statements are, but they describe it by *contrast*, not by *comparison* as affirmative statements do', Hart and Honoré, *Causation in the Law* (n 2) 38.

sions were really nothing, there would be 'no reason why they should figure even theoretically among the conditions of an event'.[22] (A fuller account of the relevance of Hart and Honoré's arguments on the causal role of omissions is provided later.)

Recently Moore's theory of omission has been criticised by Jonathan Schaffer. As he observes, Moore's endorsement of a 'No absence' thesis also leads him to endorse a disjunctivist thesis and to acknowledge, together with a prominent role for causation, mere counterfactual reliance as a source of (forms of reduced) responsibility.[23] Schaffer wants to demonstrate that absence causation is indeed part of the core notion of causation involved in law, scientific explanation and common sense thought. He works out a sophisticated argument showing that every voluntary human movement, insofar as it is based on muscle contraction, is fundamentally based on a process, which involves what this author calls disconnection,[24] that is, in short, an absence. The main argument for the causal relevance of absences is based on the crucial relevance of absences for beheadings, drownings, stranglings and shootings: if they are killings (as they undoubtedly are), absences do have a causal role. However, Schaffer also points out more arguments for attacking Moore's theory of omissions. Particularly relevant among them, in my view, is that counterfactual reasoning is central both to the causality of action and of omission and that absences, as well as presences, can be shaped as agential means to obtain a certain result.[25]

---

22 ibid 447.

23 Schaffer, 'Disconnection and Responsibility' (n 5) 402.

24 ibid 407.

25 ibid 410. The 'Beheading Problem' has been the object of a debate between Jonathan Schaffer and Moore, in which Moore insisted that human actions of this kind (i.e. human actions which involve what Schaffer calls absence) are indeed non-causal, ibid 411ff. Schaffer points out more arguments which support his thesis and the relevance of absences for the mentioned cases (beheadings, drownings, stranglings and shootings): i. Counterfactual reasoning is central both to the causality of action and of omission, following David Lewis's theory of causation. The author remarks that one does not need to identify causation with counterfactual considerations to appreciate the relevance of the latter to causation (ibid 408). ii. Statistical relevance, if it is to be distinguished from the line of reasoning involved in counterfactual arguments (which are, in my view, to be seen as involving mainly statistical considerations), has to be considered crucial both for the causal rationale of actions and of omissions (ibid). 3. Both presences and absences can be shaped as agential means to obtain a certain result (ibid 408–9). 4. Both have a role in scientific explanation (ibid 409–10).

2.2 Omissions and bodily movements

This idea corresponds to the common assumption that a bodily movement is the instrument that allows an action to come into being. Reference to bodily movements is also assumed to be crucial for objectively identifying an action from an external standpoint. Indeed, it is often affirmed that bodily movements are the only aspects of action we can see and perceive, the raw material of our interpretation.[26] In contrast, omissions, 'not being movements, [...] do not make anything move. If, therefore, all causation is movement, as some assert, omissions cannot be causes'.[27]

This notion that causes are necessarily movements was one of the critical targets of Hart and Honoré's accounts of the causal role of omissions.[28] Honoré observed:

> 'undoubtedly, the simplest instances of causal connection, which serve as model or paradigm, are those by which one movement brings about another. But it is also quite common to investigate the cause of something which is not a movement, for instance, a strike or death. In these cases there is no reason why the cause should be a movement, even if one believes that, in general, movements can only be caused by other movements'.

---

26 'Esto asegura que las acciones no son entidades puramente conceptuales, sino que tienen un anclaje en el mundo natural'. (This supports the view that actions are not purely conceptual entities, rather are grounded in the natural world) Daniel Gonzalez Lagier, *Las paradojas de la accion* (Publicaciones de la Universidad de Alicante 2001) 122.

27 Honoré, 'Causation and the Remoteness of Damage' (n 8) 15. For such a view, see eg, Douglas Gasking, 'Causation as Recipes' [1955] *Mind, New series* 483: 'the notion of causation is essentially connected with our manipulative techniques for producing results'. He observes that 'in accounts of causation given by philosophers in the past a specially fundamental role was often played by the motion of bodies. Every kind of change and every kind of natural law was often supposed to be 'ultimately reducible' or to be explicable in terms of it. In this account, too, though in a rather different way, the motion of bodies occupies a special position. Central to this account is the notion of a manipulation to produce A and thereby to produce B', ibid 487. I do not find these theses accurate enough. Indeed, I would argue that human beings would have discovered what causation is even if they would not have been able to manipulate anything, just by looking at what happens in the world.

28 'Preoccupation with the basic simple cases, where causes literally are movements, is the undiagnosed source of the difficulties which some theorists have experienced in seeing how a 'static condition' or a 'negative condition' or an omission could be the cause of anything. ...The analogies with a thing which is active or moves have darkened and continue to darken many a discussion of causation', Hart and Honoré, *Causation in the Law* (n 2) 30.

Honoré also states:

> 'it is arbitrary to confine causal inquiries to inquiries into the question of why a sequence of events was initiated or changed and to exclude the question of why such a sequence was not initiated or counteracted'.[29]

3. Making a difference by omission

In order to fully assess Hart and Honoré's proposal, it is useful to first offer a quick overview of their theory of causality and their arguments for acknowledging that we do make a difference in the world both by acting and by omitting. The idea of 'making a difference' itself needs to be clarified. In Hart and Honoré's account, it seems to presuppose a kind of *status quo*, a stasis, or at least a physiological situation that remains unaltered unless someone intervenes. This is what Hart and Honoré observe to further explain this idea:

> 'human action in the simple cases, when we produce some desired effect by the manipulation of an object in our environment, is an interference in the natural course of events which makes a difference in the way these develop. In an almost literal sense, such an interference by human action is an intervention or intrusion of one kind of thing upon another distinct kind of thing. Common experience teaches us that, left to themselves, the things we manipulate, since they have a 'nature' or characteristic way of behaving, would persist in states or exhibit changes different from those which we have learnt to bring about in them by our manipulation. The notion, that a cause is essentially something which interferes with, or intervenes in the course of events which would normally take place, is central to the common-sense concept of cause, and at least as essential as the notions of invariable or constant sequence so much stressed by Mill and Hume'.[30]

When there is no human intervention, 'the cause, though not a literal intervention, is a difference from the normal course, which accounts for the difference in the outcome'.[31] To this account, Hart and Honoré add that a human cause does not necessarily need to be a human intervention: 'men have discovered that nature is not only sometimes harmful if we intervene, but is also sometimes harmful unless we intervene'.[32] So, both interventions and non-interventions can count as causes.

---

29 Honoré, 'Causation and the Remoteness of Damage' (n 8) 15.

30 Hart and Honoré *Causation in the Law* (n 2) 29.

31 ibid 29, 50.

32 ibid 37. For this reason, I cannot agree with Gasking's view. He affirms that 'men discovered that whenever they manipulated certain things in certain ways in certain conditions certain things happened', Gasking, 'Causation as Recipes' (n 27) 482, and that 'we learn by experience that whenever in certain conditions we manipulate objects in a certain way a certain change, A, occurs', ibid 486. This is affirming half of

This thought lays behind the Marxist conception of violence, as expounded by Harris, and is in line with Schaffer's arguments. It also forms a first approximation of the account of the causal role of omissions that I propose to endorse here. In such a context, one should also keep in mind that other human agencies are part of the 'nature', which can be the cause of the considered consequence.[33]

3.1 Hart and Honoré's causal principles

One of the aims of Hart and Honoré's endeavour to clarify the concept of causation in general, and in law in particular, was to affirm the existence of causal principles. They wanted to deny the arbitrariness or irrationality of this selection (on a certain assumption that normative theses about causation would indeed imply arbitrariness or irrationality, while the causation thesis would not be in this sense normative).[34] The causation thesis, as defended by Hart and Honoré, is presented as a reply to modernist theorists who argue that

> 'it should be recognized that there is no question of fact involved in a question of causation beyond the condition of sine qua non... (and) after that we are to say that A caused X if, as a matter of policy, it is expedient, or just, to hold A responsible for X'.[35]

Their account of causation is based on 'the notion, prominent in Hume and Mill, that particular causal statements implicitly appeal to and claim to instantiate

---

the truth, for at the same time, the same individual recognized that whenever they did *not* manipulate certain things in certain ways in certain conditions certain things happened (at least in the organic world), and what we have learnt by experience is also what occurs when we do not manipulate objects.

33 Indeed, the idea of making a difference is often referred to situations where what I can do might also be done by someone else. See John Gardner, 'Complicity and Causality' [2007] *Criminal Law and Philosophy* 57ff.

34 The need to establish properly causal principles is at the roots of the theorization of causation, which can be represented as a progressive theoretical endeavour leading to emancipation from animism. While before nature and society were both explained by reference to the same normative principle of imputation (also natural changes or effects were attributed to the will and responsibility of a certain subject), modern science, via causal principles and explanations, has introduced a different epistemic model for understanding nature, including also, at a later stage, human behaviour. These are Kelsen's arguments: Hans Kelsen, 'Causality and Accounting' in Hans Kelsen, *Essays in Legal and Moral Philosophy* (Springer 1973) 154–64.

35 Philippa Foot, 'Hart and Honoré: Causation in the Law' [1963] *The Philosophical Review* 511. See also Richard Fumerton and Ken Kress, 'Causation and the Law: Preemption, Lawful Sufficiency, and Causal Sufficiency' [2001] *Law and Contemporary Problems* 87–8.

empirical generalizations'.[36] Following this statement, they argue that abnormal conditions and voluntary human actions 'have a prior claim to be selected as causes of an unexplained event'[37] (from a set of conditions that together are sufficient to bring about that event). They suggest that the determining factors are 'the contrasts between what is abnormal and what is normal in relation to any given thing or subject matter, and between a free deliberate human action and all other conditions'.[38]

Voluntary human actions have priority in being selected as the cause[39] over actions deemed as unintentional' (by mistake or accident), 'involuntary' (in the absence of normal muscular control), 'unconscious', or made under coercion, duress, or other kinds of pressure (such as legal or moral obligations).[40] However, Hart and Honoré add that 'sometimes an action done under coercion is spoken of as voluntary', referred to in law as *coactus voluit* (consent under compulsion)[41].

Abnormal conditions are judged by contrasting them with a normal course of events. For this, Hart and Honoré take a functionalist perspective, whereby certain functions can be attached to a process, while others can be considered accidents. Normal factors, or mere conditions, are 'just those which are present alike both in cases where such accidents occur and in the normal cases where they do not'.[42] However, this functionalist perspective raises philosophical problems in some cases: for instance, taking life and death as events, as effects, it is in some cases difficult to establish which should be considered the normal course of events, whether the one which leads to living or the one which leads to dying. The most reliable account sees normality as *regularity*, or what normally happens.[43] Thus,

36 Tony Honoré, 'Introduction' in Tony Honoré, *Responsibility and Fault* (Hart 1999) 2. See in particular on this, Hart and Honoré, *Causation in the Law* (n 2) 44ff.

37 Honoré, 'Introduction' (n 36) 6.

38 Hart and Honoré, *Causation in the Law* (n 2) 33. See also Foot, 'Hart and Honoré: Causation in the Law' (n 35) 506.

39 Hart and Honoré, *Causation in the Law* (n 2) 41ff. Hart and Honoré observe that 'such a voluntary action is often regarded both as a limit and also as still the cause even though other later abnormal occurrences have provisionally been recognized as causes', ibid 42.

40 That a moral obligation can be understood as an instrument of constraint for one's will is, obviously, not so clear. It depends on one's general view on morality.

41 ibid 41.

42 ibid 34. See also Foot, 'Hart and Honoré: Causation in the Law' (n 35) 507.

43 This is the rationale behind our idea that the gardener's omission and nobody else's omission is the cause of the death of the flowers: the first is a deviation from the normal routine, while the second is in conformity with the normal routine. See Hart and Honoré, *Causation in the Law* (n 2) 38.

Hart and Honoré's theory is grounded on the availability of a normal, expected run of things; 'if, on the other hand, there is an inquiry without this, … their thesis about abnormal conditions will not hold at all'.[44] Indeed, as noticed by Harris, 'we are entitled to say that drug companies are causally responsible for some deaths even though no customary practice of vaccination against cancer has become second nature'.[45] A more serious problem, especially in law, is in cases where what is deemed normal is undesirable or morally wrong. Take a concentration camp, for instance, where killing was normal, we would still be right in saying people should not be killed. So, even though we have an account of a normal functioning, what if normal functioning is always a disaster?[46]

To support their thesis, Hart and Honoré insist that what is normal and what is abnormal is 'relative to the context in two different ways, and it is important to see precisely what this relativity is. Otherwise we may surrender prematurely to the temptation to say that the distinction between causes and mere conditions, which depends upon it, is arbitrary or subjective'.[47] This relativity to the context makes possible that 'the distinction between cause and conditions may be drawn in different ways',[48] and different contexts influence our judgement on what is normal and what is abnormal. However, if in this way they are ready to admit that the selection is somehow led by the purpose of the inquiry,[49] they want to reject the idea that every element is equally entitled to be selected as the cause.[50] Certain ordinary causal principles cannot be violated[51] and these enable us to affirm that 'conditions are mere conditions as distinct from causes because they are normal'.[52]

---

44 Foot, 'Hart and Honoré: Causation in the Law' (n 35) 508.

45 See Harris, 'The Marxist Conception of Violence (n 4) 203.

46 ibid 206.

47 Hart and Honoré, *Causation in the Law* (n 2) 35, where they enumerate two senses of this relativity.

48 ibid 35.

49 'What count as the cause of an event depends on the purpose of the inquiry', Honoré, 'Introduction'(n 36) 3.

50 Hart and Honoré, *Causation in the Law* (n 2) 24–5, where they refer to an explanatory and an attributive context. For some criticisms, see M.P. Golding, 'Causation in the Law' [1962] *The Journal of Philosophy* 89–90.

51 See ibid 90.

52 Hart and Honoré, *Causation in the Law* (n 2) 39. Mackie's notion of causal field, inspired by John Anderson's '*The problem of causality*', has also to be taken into account. This author explains that 'causal statements are commonly made in some contexts, against a background which includes the assumption of some causal field. A causal statement will be the answer to a causal question, and the question 'What caused this

3.2 Omissions and the necessary reliance on an ongoing process

Most relevant for my present argument is Hart and Honoré's acknowledgement that actions and omissions have the same causal role. One of the key arguments for reaching this conclusion is that their selection process for causes operates in the same way with regard to positive and negative conditions. At first sight, it seems that their two priority selection classes, abnormal events and voluntary human actions, exclude omissions. However, in relevant contexts, voluntary omissions could easily be included in the second class or be conceivably classed as abnormal events[53]. Hart and Honoré's aim was to identify causal principles without having to appeal to normative considerations. The fact that they did not specifically acknowledge omissions, understood as behaviours violating positive norms of conduct, to be selectable as causes is, for the moment, a minor issue that can be

---

explosion?' can be expanded into 'What made the difference between those times, or those cases, within a certain range, in which no such explosion occurred and this case in which an explosion did occur?' Both cause and effect are seen as differences within a field; anything that is part of the assumed (but commonly unstated) description of the field itself, will then be automatically ruled out as a candidate for the role of cause', John L. Mackie, *The Cement of the Universe: A study of Causation* (Clarendon Press 1980) 34–5. See also John L. Mackie, 'Causes and Conditions' in Edward Sosa and Micheal Tooley (eds), *Causation* (OUP 1993) 39ff. Starting from the notion of causal field, the cause has to be something not included in the description of it. However, he observes, 'it is in general an arbitrary matter whether a particular feature is regarded as a condition (that is as a possible causal factor) or as a part of the field'. Mackie 'Causes and Conditions' 40. This is why 'there will not in general be any one item which has a unique claim to be regarded as *the cause* even of an individual event, and even after the causal field has been determined. Each of the moments in the minimal sufficient condition, or in each minimal sufficient condition, that was present can equally be regarded as the cause. They may be distinguished as predisposing causes, triggering causes, and so on, but it is quite arbitrary to pick out as 'main' and 'secondary', different moments which are equally non-redundant items in a minimal sufficient condition, or which are moments in two minimal sufficient conditions each of which makes the other redundant', ibid 47.

53 Some theories of omissions refer to the regularity of actions as one of the criteria for determining which, among the different unrealized lines of action, has to be qualified as omission. See for instance Eric D'Arcy, *Human Acts* (Clarendon Press 1963) 42–3: 'A's not-having-done-X is said to be an omission only if X was in some way expected of A; and that may be verified in two ways. First, it may be expected because X is something that A usually does, or people usually do, in the situation in question. [...] Second, we also speak of A's not-doing-X as an omission when X is required of him by some rule with which he is expected to comply'.

set aside[54]. No relevant differences can be found in the counterfactual considerations necessary for attributing a causal role to an action or an omission. When a particular action is picked out as the cause, it can be supposed that, without that element, the effect considered, the relevant difference, would not have been realized (and often another effect, another difference, would have been realized). The same applies when an omission is the selected cause. Thus, we do make a difference in the world both by doing and by allowing: as John Harris puts it, 'if we are able to change things, to elect not to do so is also to determine what will happen in the world'.[55]

Once it is recognized that both actions and omissions are causes, it can still be argued that there are causal or moral differences between them. Here, I am only concerned with differences at the causal level. To cause something by omission, a necessary condition has to be satisfied, which is not necessary in the case of commission. From the standpoint of causal processes, omissions have to be distinguished from actions, even though they both have a causal role. In the case of an omission, what is caused is necessarily produced by an already ongoing process. By contrast, an action can either start a new process and/or rely on an already existing process. If there are no relevant ongoing processes, human agency can only make a difference in the world by acting, not by omitting.

A fuller account can be offered by resorting once again to Hart and Honoré's arguments. These authors suggest this kind of specificity when remarking on the peculiar role of voluntary human intervention in the context of causality. What I am arguing is slightly different, but elaborates on the same idea. This specificity cannot be reduced, in my view, to the role of human intervention in causal processes, but should be recognized in animal intervention and animal will more

54 I think this is actually a weakness of Hart and Honoré's defence of the causal role of omission, a weakness which I attribute to their desire to define causal principles totally independently of any reference to norms. On this point, see Harris, 'The Marxist Conception of Violence' (n 4) 203ff.

55 This is how John Harris opens his seminal paper: ibid 192, and he affirms that probably this idea 'is as old as any thinking on responsibility'. He then adds that 'for obvious reasons, the idea is only employed when the things that happen are of some significance', ibid. This is a similar thought to the one expressed by Hart: 'only where an outcome is thought unfortunate or felicitous is its cause commonly spoken of as responsible for it'. H.L.A. Hart, 'Postscript: Responsibility and Retribution' in H.L.A. Hart, *Punishment and Responsibility: Essays in the Philosophy of* Law' (Clarendon Press 1970) 210ff. However, there is no reason to limit the significance of happenings to moral significance, in the context of a causal inquiry.

generally, in the context of causal processes.[56] Indeed, even if many processes can be considered already ongoing, for instance all the processes described by physics or biology, and in these processes one can intervene indifferently either by doing or by allowing, some processes are not ongoing, that is to say those processes which are precisely initiated by animal will and whose input is animal action. These are cases of causation which can only be explained in terms of doing and not in terms of allowing. Can this specificity of causation by action vs. causation by omission be taken to support the common view, exposed by Honoré, that 'it is primarily by positive acts that people do harms and create risks of harm to others, in the sense of changing things for the worse, whether by violence, pollution, speed of movement, destruction of property, or in a score of other ways'?[57] It should be stressed, incidentally, that this view is not incompatible with the Marxist doctrine of violence, as expounded by John Harris, insofar as it purports to attribute priority to violence by positive acts. However, Harris would also acknowledge negative ways of creating violence.

Honoré adds:

> 'Of course this view of the primary threats to our individual and collective well-being depends on our living in a relatively stable (as it were, Newtonian) world, in which people and objects on the whole continue as they are unless something intervenes to change them. People reasonably attach importance to this continuity since their survival and that of the others depends on it'.[58]

Is Honoré right in affirming that people primarily do harm by positive acts (after acknowledging that non-doings can also cause harm)? I do not find this view correct and I think that this (mistaken) view is not supported by my argument on the specificity of causation by omission. I will try to explain why.

First of all, why do I find Honoré's argument mistaken? I think the emphasis should be placed upon Honoré's reference to a Newtonian picture of the world. Indeed, I do not think this can be considered an accurate account of the world we live in and of how we understand it. Such a picture describes the world as a state of affairs that includes people, objects and regularities (ongoing processes, part activated by animal intervention and part independent of such intervention). These

---

56 For related considerations, more specifically about the actions of non-human animals, see Harry G. Frankfurt, 'The Problem of Action' [1978] *American Philosophical Quarterly* 161ff.

57 Tony Honoré, 'Are Omissions Less Culpable?' in Tony Honoré, *Responsibility and Fault* (Hart 1999) 63.

58 ibid.

ongoing processes are continually leading to changes, which may be considered morally harmful, morally good, or morally irrelevant. However, the assumption that it is primarily by positive acts that people do harm is grounded, in my view, on an underestimation of the relevance of the harm caused by letting harmful processes go on, and on an overestimation of the goodness of the current state of affairs.

Let us now go to the second, less relevant question. Why is this (mistaken) view not supported by my previous acknowledgement of the specific feature of causation by omission? There is an easy answer. Honoré's argument, as is now clear, wants to defend a different, and I think more controversial, thesis about the difference between acting and omitting. I have simply stated that some differences in the world can be made only by acting, and not by allowing. To do something by allowing, some processes have to be already ongoing, and this is not always the case. Honoré, by affirming that 'it is primarily by positive acts that people do harms and create risks of harm to others', introduces a normative, moral, standpoint and reaches a conclusion which I don't believe to be grounded. In the context of the present discussion, let it suffice to note that if 'it is primarily by positive acts that people do harms and create risks of harm to others', then the Newtonian world, 'in which people and objects on the whole continue as they are unless something intervene to change them' is assumed to be something which is overall morally good. It has to be acknowledged that Honoré is right in describing such a Newtonian picture of the world as a common and widely established view. However, it is far from clear whether we are correct in considering the current state of affairs as good.

4. The metaphysical presuppositions of a theory of omission

Until now I have argued that, since what we normally consider as omissions do make a difference in the causal chain of events, they are to be considered as causes. The main argument, following Hart and Honoré's suggestions, has been that omissions should not be understood as negative events or non-descriptions, but rather as negative descriptions. However, from this perspective one can see further problems. If omissions are negative descriptions, does this mean that actions are just positive descriptions, or are they also something else?

The main debate about descriptions of actions and their ontology has focused on whether we should view every action description as a separate action, or include many descriptions under one action. Opposing views come from Davidson, who, following Anscombe, advocates a single action with many descriptions[59]),

59 Donald Davidson, 'On Action' in Donald Davidson, *Essays on Action and Events* (Clarendon Press 1980). G.E.M. Anscombe, *Intention* (Harvard University Press 1963).

and Goldman, who offers a 'maximizing' account of actions, whereby each action description refers to distinct acts[60]. It should be noted here that in order to affirm that all actions are *propositional* (as Anscombe did), you do not have to commit (as Anscombe did not) to a maximizing ontology of actions[61]. Issues concerning the identity of actions can be separated from ontological arguments about their existence.

In terms of the current discussion, a better way to frame this debate is in terms of the objectivity of actions and their descriptions. This is the basis upon which Moore argues that omissions are simply nothing, while actions are something.

4.1 Moore's metaphysics of action

Moore's argument and the thesis affirming the causal irrelevance of omissions is based on a distinctive metaphysical account of what actions objectively are. His well articulated metaphysics of action is linked to the Davidsonian scheme of considering actions as events (i.e. particular facts referenced in space and time). This is in line with a common view that actions are a specific kind of event.[62] However, as Schaffer has pointed out, Moore's metaphysical premises lead to totally counter-intuitive results:

> 'since it is obvious that absences can be causal, this fact can shed light on what absences are and how the metaphysics of causation works. In other words, while Moore argues from certain semantic and metaphysical premises to the conclusion that decapitation cannot cause death, I am reversing the argument and arguing from the premise that decapitation can cause death to the denial of some of Moore premises'.[63]

---

60 Alvin I. Goldman, *A Theory of Human Action* (Princeton University Press 1976). Alvin I. Goldman, 'The Individuation of Action, [1971] *The Journal of Philosophy* 761.

61 Onora O'Neill, 'Modern Moral Philosophy and the Problem of Relevant Descriptions' in Anthony O'Hear (ed.), *Modern Moral Philosophy*, 54 *Royal Institute of Philosophy Supplement* (Cambridge University Press 2004) 305. G.E.M. Anscombe, 'Modern Moral Philosophy' [1958] *The Journal of the Royal Institute of Philosophy* 124.

62 It is often affirmed, though, that even if one is ready to accept an ontology which includes events, alongside material and immaterial objects, one should further decide how to better define them, and that is to say whether they should be considered abstract universals (Goldman, Chisholm) or instead particulars, determined by reference to spatial and temporal coordinates (with reference to actions-events, Davidson). (However, it should be noticed that the feasibility of an acceptance of their existence prior to an agreement on their definition is questionable).

63 Schaffer, 'Disconnection and Responsibility' (n 5) 415–6.

In line with Schaffer's examination of Moore's premises, we can further question their reliability. One line of argument could follow questioning the influential view defended by Davidson that identifies actions as events. From this, he elaborates the opposition between actions and omissions (considered as non-events). It could be disputed that omission claims necessarily denote absent events; they could also denote actual events in the world.[64] It could even be disputed that actions are events at all (von Wright).[65] A promising idea based on this last suggestion is that actions and omissions are just different ways to produce an event. From this perspective, events are not actions but the effect of actions and omissions to be judged on grounds of their causal efficiency.

In the final part of this section, I suggest a different but complementary line of argument criticizing Moore's metaphysical premises. In order to discuss the objectivity of actions and omissions, I first need to ground a theory of omissions on a metaphysics of what human agency objectively is (rather than the metaphysical objectivity of actions); human agency being understood as the way in which humans are able to make a difference in this world.

Until now, the idea that we can make a difference in the world by both acting and omitting has been analysed with reference to two main metaphysical presuppositions: what an action is (a necessary reference for contrasting to it omissions) and what the world modified by our action is. I would now like to introduce the relevance of a specific debate within objectivity in law, which focuses on the objectivity of values. Law is about evaluating facts and actions. Issues of objectivity are raised both with regard to how to evaluate facts and actions, and how to know about their existence. We can ask questions about how actions should be shaped as objects of our knowledge, how we should picture the *status quo,* the reference for determining the so-called difference we make, and in what sense such a *status quo* is objectively determined.

---

64 ibid 426.

65 'The notion of a human act is related to the notion of an event, *i.e.* a change in the world. What is the nature of this relationship? It would not be right, I think, to call acts a kind or species of events. An act *is* not a change in the world. But many acts may quite appropriately be described as the bringing about or effecting ("at will") of a change. To act is, in a sense, to interfere with "the course of nature"' Georg Henrik von Wright, *Norm and Action. A Logical Inquiry* (Routledge and Kegan Paul 1963) 35–6. This view has been very influentially opposed by Davidson's alternative, which is now mainstream: see Donald Davidson, 'The Logical Form of Action Sentences' in Donald Davidson, *Essays on Actions and Events* (Clarendon Press 1980) 113–4.

The reason for introducing these questions is that I intend to claim that the debate on the objectivity of actions and omissions is very often framed in the wrong terms: a metaphysics of human agency modelled on the metaphysics of action, from which derives the idea of omissions as a 'bad copies' of actions. For argumentative reasons, I will nonetheless start from the debate on the objectivity of actions to illuminate some of the inherit problems.

4.2 Making a difference and objectivity

We see a difference between what we do and what happens to us, so, on the basis, we differentiate between actions and events. Moreover, the objectivity of actions starts to get quite ambiguous. For instance, if an action has been realized, it becomes a matter of fact and so can be referred to as objective. Indeed, we cannot affirm, without contradiction, that an action has been both realized and not realized. In this sense, actions (along with events) are objective and are part of our objective world. Using the correspondence theory of objective reality, we can build a concept of objective knowledge. If someone's belief is considered correct, then all other beliefs that do not correspond with this must be judged to be wrong. A belief can be considered correct with regard to objective reality (i.e. directly accessible to our experience) and/or objective standards of evidence. In this sense, objective knowledge is where someone's belief is to be considered correct under one of these two standards of correctness.[66]

With regards to objectivity of action, there is a question of whether actions should be described from a subjective or objective point of view; more exactly, whether an explanation of an action requires reference to the set of subjective elements motivating it, or whether it can also be given independently. For instance, von Wright's account of action, and his distinction between its results and its consequences, strongly depends on consideration of the agent's intentions.[67] Closely related is the issue of whether or not we need to refer to reasons for actions in order to describe them, and, if so, whether these reasons have an objective status. This is relevant for the distinction between actions and omissions in the sense that emphasis on the relevance of intentions can reduce the importance of

66 With regard to this kind of objectivity, one might question whether this second area of objectivity (objectivity of knowledge) is supervenient on the first (objectivity of reality).

67 In line with Anscombe. For this reason this theory of action is open to criticisms, which address the appropriateness of attributing an action to an agent even if it is in some way unintentional (for instance, because a certain intentional state had to be expected by the agent).

references to bodily movements, so favouring omissions (commonly considered as absences of movements) as potential category of actions.

A different line of arguments linked to this debate focuses on the relevance of movement and causal processes for describing actions. On the one hand, actions are often identified with neural activity, muscular contractions, and overt hand movements, while on the other they may be described as 'the mere effects of the agent's overt action'.[68] This idea is often associated with the maximizing theories of action, which need to find a basic action, upon which other actions are based.[69] Following Anscombe and Davidson, these basic actions are commonly identified with bodily movements, although, as Wilson and Shpall put it, 'there is plenty of disagreement about where basic agency starts and stops, whether within the agent's body or somewhere on its surface'. They continue: 'what could conceivably rationalize any set of discriminations between action and non-action as one traces along the pertinent complex causal chains from the initial mind or brain activity, through the bodily behaviour, to the occurrences produced in the agent's wider environment?'[70]

A final strand to the debate can be found in Hart and Honoré's account of causation. Their arguments for the relevance of bodily movements to identify actions enables them to avoid any references to actions as a purely mental or conceptual, and so provides an objective anchorage. However, not all movements are actions and, what is most important, I do not see why not moving should not be considered as a way of acting. The opposite view, that actions always presuppose a bodily movement, corresponds to the mainstream theory of action. But why should we limit the area of action to exclude activities like watching (which do not imply bodily movements)? Or riding in a wheelchair? Or flying in an aeroplane piloted by someone else? Or listening to a concert? I side with John Harris's argument, that 'it is far from clear (unless it is simply a matter of stipulation) that I cannot act without moving my body'.[71] Of course, these are activities different from building a house or writing a book. However, this has more to do with differences in the impact of their agency in the world than with the involvement of bodily movements.

---

68 George Wilson and Samuel Shpall, 'Action', *The Stanford Encyclopedia of Philosophy (Fall edn, 2012)* <http://plato.stanford.edu/entries/action/> accessed 20 December 2013.

69 Arthur C. Danto, 'Basic Actions' [1965] *American Philosophical Quarterly* 141.

70 Wilson and Shpall, 'Action' (n 68) 10.

71 Harris, 'Bad Samaritans Cause Harm' (n 5) 65.

Here we get to a key point. I think that an object reference can be perfectly satisfied by referring to bodies able to move, but not to bodily movements *per se.*[72] From this, we can extrapolate to movements that make change in the world the idea of human agency. This, in my view, is the best objective reference for defining both human action and human agency. Indeed, the frequent argument that bodily movements are the best reference to identify actions because we have control over our bodies[73] is a *non sequitur*, in my view, from the generalised fact that we have a high degree of control over our bodies. We can only derive a conclusion about the nature of human agency, not about human actions. If we were able to move our bodies, full human agents, we would be responsible for what we do whether our body is moving or not.[74]

Introducing the following distinction will be useful in order to give an account of human agency that attributes the correct relevance to bodily movements and acknowledges the proper role of omissions as instruments for making a difference. As A.R. White once observed, 'philosophers sometimes use "do", "action", and "act" indifferently'. As suggested by White, 'not everything one does, much less everything one is accountable for, is an action or an act'.[75]

---

72 The relevance of what is in a (specific or standard) agent's control to define what is an action is remarked on by Gonzalez Lagier (Gonzalez Lagier, *Las paradojas de la accion* (n 26) 126) and is also a objective reference for determining what is and what is not an action. This author distinguishes between what is fully within, fully outside, or partially within the agent's control.

73 Federico Jose Arena, 'La identificación de la acción individual' [2008] *Analisi e diritto* 1.

74 On the basis of this argument a difference between what we do and what happen to us is often maintained. Frankfurt notices that 'the most salient differentiating characteristic of action: during the time a person is performing an action he is necessarily in touch with the movements of his body in a certain way, whereas he is necessarily not in touch with them in that way when the movements of his body are occurring without his making them' (Frankfurt, 'The Problem of Action' (n 56) 158). This is true, and it explains the difference between actions and events. However, it should be added that also during the time a person is performing an omission (or omitting an action) he *can* be in touch with the movements of his body in a certain way, whereas he is necessarily not in touch with them in that way when the movements of his body are occurring without his making them'.

75 Alan R. White, 'Introduction' in Alan R. White (ed.), *The Philosophy of Action* (OUP 1968) 1. This author suggests to see them in a particular relation: 'in ordinary language these are words of decreasing scope' (ibid). I am not specifically endorsing this suggestion, however.

'Do', as observed by White, can be substituted for any episodic verb, including: acts, actions and activities (eg 'kill', 'move', 'work'); accomplishments (eg 'discover'); happenings (eg 'fall'); ways of passing the time (eg 'sleep'); attempts and omissions.[76]

On the other hand, 'action is commonly used to point a contrast between a state of movement and a state of quiescence, between action and inaction, activity and inactivity'.[77]

With the help of this clarification, it becomes easier to see in what sense I have been right in asserting that human agency does not only make a difference by acting, and how I was wrong in insisting that omissions have to be considered in the same way as actions. Omissions have to be differentiated from actions on the right grounds in respect of their relevance to a full account of human agency. This view aims at dismantling the necessary conceptual link between human agency and observable bodily movements, and realigning the connection between human agency and action. It can be combined with Hart's and Honoré's account of omissions as interferences that are able to make changes in the world. This thesis separates the idea of making a difference in the world, what human agency is, from its exclusive link with theories of action and from the identification of actions with bodily movements.[78] It offers a much richer account of human agency. However, it also acknowledges that certain changes can only be realized through action, as omissions always rely on relevant ongoing processes.[79] Most importantly, this

---

76 ibid.

77 ibid.

78 Perhaps, substituting doing with acting, I could agree with Honoré on the correctness of the widely held view 'that the distinction between doing and not-doing is ultimately connected with bodily movements, and that doing involves bodily movements in a way in which not-doing does not'. Honoré, 'Are Omissions Less Culpable?' (n 57) 51. Not because we can make changes in the world primarily by bodily movements, but rather because primarily we act by bodily movements. ibid 52: Honoré refers to Hart and Honoré *Causation in the Law* (n 2) 23–32: 'But why should bodily movement mark such a divide in our thought and language? Has the distinction a rationale? A close study of causal language and thought suggested that the reason why movements feature so prominently in our assessment of responsibility is that we have a picture of the world as a matrix into which, by our movements and especially our manipulation of objects, we introduce changes'.

79 I think this specificity, which depends on the causal specificity of making a difference by omission, is one of the main sources of misunderstanding about the presumed relevance of bodily movements for action: the fact that certain changes can only be made by an active intervention, jointly with the fact that active intervention, in most cases, derives from bodily movements. Indeed, this is the only reasonable way to differentiate

account of human agency opens a way to the acknowledgement of omissions as fundamental elements of human agency. It also liberates a theory of omission from the restricted pathways determined by trying to adapt the theoretical framework of actions to account for omissions.

A specific metaphysical account of human agency also requires a specific metaphysical account of reality. If both actions and omissions can make a difference, this difference needs to be found with reference to a reality that would otherwise remain unmodified. This *status quo* cannot be seen as a still life, but more appropriately as a machine in movement, ever changing along regular paths.[80] It has to include objects and people as well as ongoing processes. As remarked by Harris, as well as by Hart and Honoré, we do think that the world is also modified by our lack of intervention. The world, in a certain sense, is constantly modified without any human intervention.[81] However, we also continually contribute to such a modification because of our agency, either by acting or by omitting. Our ability to change the world, which is the core of the notion of human agency, is put into practice both by acting and by omitting. And the world, whether we intervene (by acting or by omitting) or not, will in any case change. What we can register is that it will change in a different way, depending on whether the picture includes the changes made by human agency or only those which are independent of such an intervention.

---

between actions and omissions by referring to intentions: the intention to start a new process can only be furthered by acting.

80 A further issue is the normative character to be assigned to such a change or to such an unmodified scenario. Hart and Honoré focus on the idea that harm can derive from human inaction, but there is no reason to think that ongoing processes are continually harming, benefiting or determining normatively neutral changes in the world. However, in this paper I have not taken into consideration the normative level at all, and I have not distinguished, as I think would be appropriate, between omitting (which refers to the violation of a norm) and allowing. This would imply rephrasing the argument, and extending the value of what we allow to a wider normative area than that of the negative value of omissions, also including the good results of what we allow.

81 A further issue is the normative character to be assigned to such a change or to such an unmodified scenario. Hart and Honoré focus on the idea that harm can derive from human inaction, but there is no reason to think that ongoing processes are continually harming, benefiting or determining normatively neutral changes in the world. However, in this paper I have not taken into consideration the normative level at all, and I have not distinguished, as I think would be appropriate, between omitting (which refers to the violation of a norm) and allowing. This would imply rephrasing the argument, and extending the value of what we allow to a wider normative area than that of the negative value of omissions, also including the good results of what we allow.

5. Concluding remarks

It makes little sense to discuss the differences between actions and omissions if this debate is not grounded on some prior assumptions about the metaphysics of human agency. It is not possible to understand what omissions are using a theory of human agency modelled on the concept of action. Actions should not be considered as events, nor omissions as non-events, but rather both as human instruments used to bring about events. A full account of human agency should only be partially based on a restatement of the model action.[82] The model which stresses the role of intentional states or willed bodily movements can play a satisfactory function in explaining actions in the context of human agency, though perhaps it could also be restated and refined.[83] The crucial point is to acknowledge that the whole scope of human agency cannot be reduced to the action model, but also needs to account for the basic role played by omissions. The latter can only be understood through a theory of omissions, not a theory modelled on action. The model of omissions is one of non-intentional agency; an agency fundamentally responsible because of its role in the causal network of this world. Omissions are not 'bad copies' of actions. Rather the omission model and the action model are just two of the basic modes of human agency, fundamental and irreducible to one another.[84]

---

82 Such a restatement could start, for instance, from one of the classical loci of the identification of actions, and in particular of actions as events: see Donald Davidson, 'Agency' in Donald Davidson, *Essays on Actions and Events* (Clarendon Press 1980) 43–61.

83 Andrew P. Simester, 'Agency' [1996] *Law and Philosophy* 161ff. In any case, it must be remarked that affirming that every action is intentional, under some of its descriptions, is different from affirming that the basic model of action is the intentional one.

84 This different way of shaping human agency could be partially explained referring to Scheffler's account of doing and allowing as primary and secondary manifestations of human agency (and insisting more on the fact that they are both manifestations, and less to the fact that instances of allowing are secondary). See Samuel Scheffler, 'Doing and Allowing' [2004] *Ethics* 215. It can be argued that such an account of human agency would also lead to the restatement of the idea of human identity, often explained in terms of something which is, to a great extent, built having in mind intentional action.

PART II Analytical Perspectives

Maciej Pichlak
University of Wrocław, Poland

4. Objectivity and Institutional Reflexivity in Law

1. Introduction

The aim of the paper is to explain how and what kind of objectivity is possible within law. The explanation is greatly needed as the discrepancy between the presence of the idea of objectivity in practice and the difficulties with its theoretical justification is easily noticeable. Hence, the proceeding considerations try to recommend and slightly reformulate one of the existing methodological approaches to this problem. I will concentrate on the institutional approach, which, in my opinion, addresses this issue most accurately.

The starting point of this essay is the observation of the breakdown of a Cartesian view on objectivity in law. By the Cartesian view I understand the perspective based on a strict distinction between the subject (*cogito*) and the object (*res cogitata*) of cognition. It is fairly clear that after all the skeptical lessons jurisprudence has taken, it is virtually impossible to describe relations between the law and the lawyer using Cartesian language. Thus, legal judgments[1] cannot be objective in the strong sense of this term.

Having chosen the post-Cartesian starting point, I am not going to look back. The majority of reasons for the impossibility of 'strong objectivity' are well-known and there is no need to discuss them here. Nearly twenty years ago, Jules Coleman and Brian Leiter in their inspiring essay[2] persuasively highlighted some of those reasons, the 'problem of access' being one of the most significant among them, as it had also been present in Descartes' genuine philosophical system.

In spite of these theoretical difficulties with the explication of objectivity, the considered idea remains a vital part of our legal practice and of the consciousness of a typical lawyer (at least within the European legal culture). This assumption

---

1 For the meaning of the term 'judgment' in this context see Gerald J Postema, 'Objectivity Fit for Law' in Brian Leiter (ed), *Objectivity in Law and Morals* (Cambridge University Press 2007) 105.

2 Jules L Coleman and Brian Leiter, 'Determinacy, Objectivity, and Authority' in Andrei Marmor (ed), *Law and Interpretation: Essays in Legal Philosophy* (Oxford University Press 1998) 256.

relies not only on a common intuition of lawyers and legal scholars,[3] but also on the results of the comparative research into the language of judicial decisions.[4] The research has proved not only the universal presence of arguments based on a notion of objectivity in practice but also a broad variety of connotations of the very notion. Hence, a predicate 'objective' in the language of judicial decisions may refer, e.g., to something 'provable, measurable,' 'dependent on legal standards,' 'factual, empirical,' 'external to a subject' as well as 'just, fair' or 'sufficiently justified.'

This practical relevance of the argument from objectivity is the point from which the call for its explanation and justification emerges. Of course, it is possible that this call finds no plausible answer: ultimately, the idea of objectivity may reveal its fictitious or oppressive nature. Such a conclusion would be in line with remarkable theories rejecting the legitimacy of the idea: feminist theories, critical legal studies and other. Yet, I assume that we should face the challenge: before we reject the idea of objectivity, we should search for its plausible interpretation. In fact, as Gerald Postema has convincingly shown, the majority of critiques may be read as the attempts of a search for a deeper and better justified interpretation of the idea under scrutiny.[5]

For these reasons, in what follows I will opt for a generally affirmative attitude to the idea of objectivity in law. In fact, in the first part of this paper such an affirmation may seem very strong and somewhat out-of-date in its modernistic rhetoric. In Sections 5 and 6 I shall suggest the need for a small, yet relevant, change and some softening of this generally affirmative viewpoint.

Admittedly, the interpretation of the idea of objectivity we are searching for faces even more challenging task than a mere description of this idea. Such an interpretation should also explicate the aforementioned diversity of its connotations. As one may conclude from the research that has elicited this diversity,[6] the term 'objective' includes at least two main groups of meaning: it may express compliance with some external facts or standards as well as the demand for legitimacy and fairness. I shall call these two basic meanings: 'objectivity as a fact' and 'objectivity as a moral ideal.' Thus, we need to answer the question how it is possible that one term combines such obviously different meanings. Once again, there might be no good answer to such a question. The semantic complexity of the term under examination may be

---

3 See e.g. Kaarlo Tuori, *Critical Legal Positivism* (Ashgate 2002) 7.

4 The research covered judicial discourses in nine European and one non-European country (Brazil), as well as that of The Court of Justice of The European Union. Forthcoming publication 'Critical Comparative studies on Objectivity in Law'.

5 Postema (n 1) 102.

6 Forthcoming publication 'Critical Comparative Studies on Objectivity in Law'.

purely coincidental. Yet, if there exists any theoretical interpretation that is able to explain this complexity, it has to be seen as better than its alternatives.

2. Beyond idealism and conventionalism

The first question we must face is one of the sheer possibility of objectivity in law. As I will try to show, a plausible answer requires putting it into a broader context of the question about foundations, which provide objectivity to any social or political practice. And the way to answer this question is through poetry.

In the 'Elegy of Fortinbras', Zbigniew Herbert, the Polish poet, confronts two different attitudes to the world, which at the same time provide two different answers to the question about founding principles in politics, about foundations of life in the political community. The poem is built on a simple rule of combining the opposites, yet conducted in a masterly way. It is an imaginary speech of Fortinbras, one of the protagonists of Shakespeare's *Hamlet*. Fortinbras, who is an officer of the Norwegian army, has been assigned by Hamlet to the Danish throne shortly before Hamlet's death. In the final scene of the play we see Fortinbras arriving at the royal castle just to find Hamlet and other protagonists of the drama dead. In Herbert's poem, Fortinbras recites the elegy over the dead body of the Danish prince:

> Now that we're alone we can talk prince man to man
> though you lie on the stairs and see more than a dead ant
> nothing but black sun with broken rays
> I could never think of your hands without smiling
> and now that they lie on the stone like fallen nests
> they are as defenceless as before The end is exactly this
> The hands lie apart The sword lies apart The head apart
> and the knight's feet in soft slippers
>
> ...
>
> Anyhow you had to perish Hamlet you were not for life
> you believed in crystal notions not in human clay
> always twitching as if asleep you hunted chimeras
> wolfishly you crunched the air only to vomit
> you knew no human thing you did not know even how to breathe
>
> ...
>
> Adieu prince I have tasks a sewer project
> and a decree on prostitutes and beggars
> I must also elaborate a better system of prisons
> since as you justly said Denmark is a prison

> I go to my affairs This night is born
> a star named Hamlet We shall never meet
> what I shall leave will not be worth a tragedy
> It is not for us to greet each other or bid farewell we live on archipelagos
> and that water these words what can they do what can they do prince[7]

As I have already mentioned, one may perceive Hamlet and Fortinbras in that scene as the representatives of two different perspectives on the foundations of objectivity in political practice. To ascribe a particular perspective to Hamlet is rather an easy task: with his belief 'in crystal notions' he may be seen as a representative of idealism, which I have already rejected above. Hamlet used to search for the foundations in the realm of abstract ideas, which resembles 'chimera-hunting': ideas cannot offer sufficient and objective grounds for any political decisions. In the final scene, we find Hamlet passed away, lying down 'in soft slippers.' As I have declared, I find no special pleasure in tracing his weak points. Instead, we had better take a closer look at the alternative approach represented by Fortinbras.

At first sight, it might be tempting to equate Fortinbras' viewpoint with conventionalism because of his 'down-to-earth' perspective. He is a Norwegian officer, who abandons general ideas and focuses on actual practices. The problems of a sewer system, prostitutes and beggars, all these trivial and tedious issues of everyday life are precisely those on which common social practices are presumed to be grounded. Conventionalism, as Leiter and Coleman have suggested,[8] adopts a view of 'minimal objectivity', which interprets objectivity as a mere effect of a common social practice.

If Fortinbras followed a conception of minimal objectivity, it would be a disappointing outcome, as the conventionalist version of objectivity cannot provide any solid ground for practice. Conventionalism has been criticized by Leiter and Coleman as, generally speaking, depending on turbulent and deceptive convictions. In particular, conventionalism has been said to lead to three difficulties: the impossibility of explaining rational disagreement among participants of the practice, the analogical impossibility of explaining the case of global error, and the lack of any critical means against the dominant ideology, reflected in agents' beliefs and actions.[9] One may crudely say that this kind of 'weak objectivity' is too weak to be objective. Hence, conventionalism fails as a real alternative to idealism.

---

7 Zbigniew Herbert, 'Elegy of Fotinbras' in Zbigniew Herbert, *The Collected Poems 1956–1998* (Alissa Valles ed, Harper Collins 2007) 186–187.

8 Coleman and Leiter (n 2) 260.

9 *ibid* 260–263.

Nevertheless, Fortinbras differs in an important respect from a typical conventionalist. Being a soldier, he is described as firm, determined, forceful and successful both by Shakespeare and Herbert. None of these characteristics fits the standpoint of conventionalism. Thus, if one is looking for the typical representatives of a conventionalist approach, they will rather choose other protagonists of the Shakespeare's play: Rosencrantz and Guildenstern. These two are the former friends of Hamlet, who are now spying on him. They always adapt their conduct to actual situation and, probably unconsciously, serve the unlawful king, Claudius. Rosencrantz and Guildenstern reflect weak points of conventionalism as described by Coleman and Leiter: inconstancy, dependence on dominant ideology, etc., which makes this perspective unable to offer any grounds for practice. Finally, in the last scene of the Shakespeare's play, we find not only the Danish prince but also his deceptive friends dead.

What makes the difference between Fortinbras and the king's spies? What lets him succeed where others fail? To answer these questions, we should concentrate on the most basic description of his persona: Fortinbras is a soldier. What enables him to share the aforementioned characteristics is the fact that in all his actions he relies on a solid institutional structure of the army. This is the institution he participates in, which lets him act in a proper way; this is the institution which provides grounds for political practices. And these are new institutional settings that he attempts to introduce in order to establish grounds for executing power in his new realm. Therefore, Fortinbras may be perceived as a representative of an institutional approach.

3. Objectivity as an institutional fact

The role of social institutions in guaranteeing the objectivity of practice could hardly be overestimated. Institutions offer solid grounds for objectivity: although they are constantly constructed and reconstructed within interactions of social agents, they remain independent from particular actions of these very agents. A distinctive domain of the factual (German *Faktizität*) is brought into life by institutions: the domain settled with a unique kind of symbolic objects, which, in consequence, allows to apply the notion of objectivity. This process of creating institutional objects may be described as the concept of reification, Marxian in its origins. However, in this case it seems more suitable to use the more neutral term of objectification. The term, which has been proposed by Peter L. Berger and Thomas Luckmann,[10] refers to a process in which symbolic constructs created by

10 Peter L Berger and Thomas Luckmann, *The Social Construction of Reality: A Treatise in the Sociology of Knowledge* (Anchor Books 1966).

social agents begin to be perceived as factually existing and being external to these very agents. In that respect, Berger and Luckmann may be seen as the intellectual descendants of Durkheim. It was the French sociologist who suggested treating 'social facts as things,'[11] which is probably the most clear and radical expression of the need for the idea of objectivity within sociological inquiry.

The details of the theoretical proposals of Berger and Luckmann are questionable, even within the institutional perspective. Nevertheless, it is due to such an understanding of the process of objectification that the term 'objective' is employed not only as an equivalent of some kind of neutrality or impartiality of the agent, but also in a stronger sense: to express the fact that an action is grounded on an object of a unique kind. On the other hand, within such perspective there is no need for idealization to explain the possibility of objectivity of practice. In this respect, the institutional approach remains 'conceptually clearer,' as opposed to the majority of significant theories within jurisprudence, like the aforementioned conception of Leiter and Coleman, and also those of Dworkin or Alexy.[12] All these scholars, in spite of numerous dissimilarities between their genuine standpoints, share the same need for introducing some 'ideal factor' to explain how the objectivity of legal practice is possible. For all of them, the *real* objectivity is possible only as a postulate, expressed with recourse to such an 'ideal factor': 'ideal epistemic conditions' for Leiter and Coleman, judge Hercules for Dworkin, principles of rational discourse for Alexy. As we may notice, it is not the case of an institutional approach that provides the concept of objectivity as a purely social phenomenon.

Furthermore, the notion of objectivity expresses one more feature of social institutions, which is relative autonomy of the subject and the object created within an institution. The subject – object relation is based on mutual autonomy due to the fact that the institutionally created object is external to the agent. The autonomy remains relative because to grasp such an object, one must inevitably be a part of the institution. It is virtually impossible to possess any knowledge on institutional reality from a radically detached, external point of view.

For the preceding reasons, it would be highly unsatisfactory to equate social institution with, and only with, the actual beliefs of the institution's participants, as this would be that version of a fallacy of reductivism which is characteristic of

11 Émile Durkheim, *The Rules of Sociological Method* (Steven Lukes ed, The Free Press 1982).

12 See Coleman and Leiter (n 2); Robert Alexy, *A Theory of Legal Argumentation: The Theory of Rational Discourse as Theory of Legal Justification* (Oxford University Press 1989); Ronald Dworkin, *Law's Empire* (Belknap Press 1986).

conventionalism. It is clear enough that the opinions of social agents are important, however, they are not the only factor determining the shape of social institution. Among other significant factors we may also indicate social mechanisms and structures which go beyond what the agents think. Using Marxian vocabulary again, this dimension of institution could be described through the concept of 'false consciousness' as a set of these beliefs of agents that fail to meet the real structural characteristics of social institutions. However, it is again possible to employ a dictionary less directly involved in the critical perspective. Was it not this feature of modern institutions that Vaclav Havel had in mind referring to their 'impersonal power'? This *sui generis* 'objective' because, independent from particulars, this aspect of institutional life is reflected in the common experience of the contemporary citizens that some things just happen 'above and beyond' them, within impersonal institutional mechanisms for which no one wants to take responsibility.[13]

4. Two faces of objectivity

4.1 Objectivity as a moral ideal

I hope that so far good reasons have been provided to accept the possibility of objectivity in law which needs no recourse to any idealizing assumptions. Objectivity in law may be as concrete and as far from idealism as a sewer system or prostitution. Nevertheless, if objectivity was limited solely to this factual level, it would have to be seen as pitifully one-dimensional. Although the perspective offered above explains how objectivity is possible, it says nothing about its worth. Yet it is a common desire, if not a fact, for the law to be objective not only in a deceptive sense of fitting into actual institutional standards but also in a more ambitious sense of being just or sound. Employing the already offered terminology, there is a desire that objectivity existed not only as a mere fact, but also as a moral ideal.

The desire is witnessed not only by the aforementioned research into adjudication but also by the history of the Western legal culture. It is a remarkable fact that the idea of objectivity counts for an important component of both of the most influential intellectual traditions within that culture: natural law and legal positivism. Moreover, this idea is not only a common notion for both traditions but also the grounds for their mutual critiques. Thus, the matter of dispute between them is not whether law should be objective, but which of the traditions provides more

13 I believe that this is the kind of experience which in the days of the 2010–2012 global crisis was able to lead thousands of proponents of The Indignant Movement onto the streets of the European and North American cities.

plausible expression and justification of the examined idea.[14] In that perspective, Hamlet seems to be right: the hunting for the chimera of objectivity does not cease. It is John Finnis,[15] among others, who follows its tracks within the natural law perspective. In the domain of positivist tradition, there is an apparent interest in it not only from the so called Ethical Legal Positivism[16], but also classical analytical theories (e.g. of Herbert Hart or Joseph Raz[17]) discreetly follow the chimera. But the stake is even higher; objectivity seems to reflect not only our habitual pereption of the law, but also our manner of perceiving ourselves: as equal and autonomous moral subjects for whom to become the object of someone's arbitrary power would mean to deny our nature.

4.2 Factual and ideal: the 'modest objectivity' perspective

Objectivity as an institutional fact and objectivity as a moral ideal: the concept under scrutiny 'takes' something from Fortinbras as well as from Hamlet. Still, the question rises whether the former is right when talking about 'living on archipelagos.' Do these two faces of objectivity have anything in common? It is one of the aims of this paper to explore such a possibility; to answer the question whether the factual and ideal dimensions of objectivity may be linked together.[18] The respective theory explicating the nature of such a link should meet at least two prerequisites: firstly, taking the complexity of the concept of objectivity into account, the two distinctive dimensions should not be conflated with each other; secondly, a link between these two should be sufficiently theorized: the theory should provide sufficient grounds for the explication of such a link.

---

14 For more see Maciej Pichlak, 'Między aksjologią a ontologią dyskursu konstytucyjnego: Obiektywizacja wartości w prawie' [2013] Przegląd Prawa i Administracji 39 ('Between Axiology and Ontology of Constitutional Discourse. The Problem of Values Objectification in Law').

15 John Finnis, *Natural Law and Natural Rights* (Oxford University Press 1979), Part Two, Chapters I–III.

16 See e.g. Tom Campbell, *The Legal Theory of Ethical Positivism* (Dartmouth 1996); Jeremy Waldron, 'Normative (or Ethical) Positivism' in Jules L Coleman (ed), *Hart's Postscript: Essays on the Postscript to The Concept of Law* (Oxford University Press 2001).

17 Herbert L Hart, *The Concept of Law* (Clarendon Press 1961); Joseph Raz, *The Authority of Law: Essays on Law and Morality* (Oxford University Press 1979).

18 The problem, limited here to the issue of law's objectivity, refers to one of the main questions about the nature of law in general. In this context, it has been a key matter of concern in, among others, Jürgen Habermas, *Between Facts and Norms: Contributions to a Discourse Theory of Law and Democracy* (MIT Press 1998); and Robert Alexy, 'On the Concept and the Nature of Law' (2008) 21(3) Ratio Juris.

Before I propose a solution to these questions I will try to offer a more in-depth explanation of the two aforementioned requirements, taking the concept of Leiter and Coleman as an example. The linkage between the factual and the ideal is crucial for their idea of 'modest' objectivity, including the defence against an objection of slipping into idealism. According to the authors, modest objectivity differs from its equivalent within idealism in a way that its requirements ('ideal epistemic conditions' in Coleman's and Leiter's terminology) are not *a priori* but are defined only through the reconstruction from the actual beliefs of the participants of the examined practice. The procedure was called 'unpacking concepts.'[19]

The theoretical project of Leiter and Coleman seems to fail in both points I have introduced. Firstly, the concept of 'unpacking concepts' is surprisingly vague. The authors provide no clue as to how such a procedure could be possible, nor how it should be conducted. The notion of unpacking concepts is intuitive rather than anchored in some coherent and plausible theoretical standpoint. Secondly, what is even more important, the whole idea of unpacking concepts seems to be a hopeless mixture of conventionalism combined with idealism: on the one hand, objectivity as a fact can be realised only by a recourse to idealizing assumptions; on the other hand, objectivity as a moral ideal is dependent on accidental empirical conditions. Defining objectivity standards ('ideal epistemic conditions') would be like asking Shakespeare's Guildenstern and Rosencrantz how the two of them understand morality, justice, faithfulness, etc.[20]

4.3 Factual and ideal: institutional perspective

Facing all these methodological difficulties, it is the institutional approach that offers a helpful hand. It is social institutions that unite the factual with the ideal, not only in theoretical reflection but also in real life. An institution is a place where previously abstract ideas are embodied and realized within social mechanisms. Such an embodiment is not necessarily complete or fully accurate. Yet, it has a

19 Coleman and Leiter (n 2) 266–271.

20 Let me notice that due to these facts the conception of Leiter and Coleman is open for the same critiques as these so convincingly formulated by themselves against conventionalism – among them first and foremost a dependence on dominant ideology. See above in Section 1.

power to transform ideas into 'objective claims'[21], which truly impact on practice. As Habermas puts it: 'If not realized, [an idea] is at least consequential.'[22]

Although the ideal and the factual are united at the level of practice, they remain conceptually distinct: ideas which bring life into institutions do not have to be only reconstructed from actual practices; on the other hand, practices can be plausibly described independently of their axiological meaning. Empirical and axiological inquiry may be treated as two different and distinct types of analysis. In fact, this distinction is absolutely necessary if, subsequently, an explication of their mutual relations were to be possible.

On the other hand, these two described dimensions of institutional life resonate with one another (German: *räsonieren*[23]) at the level of practice. Ideas provide institution with a 'sense of relevance', whereas social mechanisms secure a 'sense of reality.' And this is a dialectical relationship: these two aspects not only explain one another but are also the grounds for mutual criticism. Currently accepted ideas may be criticized as too abstract or impracticable; currently shared practices: as unjustifiable or violating relevant ideals. But, to capture this dialectics, one needs to clearly distinguish both aspects, instead of conflating them within one unifying perspective.

5. Institutional reflexivity

So far, I have tried to argue for the thesis that the institutional approach offers a plausible explication of the concept of objectivity. In particular, the conjunction of the ideal and factual components of social institution has been portrayed as the advantage of that approach, as it has captured a two-faced nature of objectivity: as a fact of social practice and as a moral ideal. These two faces, I have claimed, should not be conflated with each other: one may more suitably see them as confronting each other in a dialectical debate.

The above argumentation notwithstanding, one may have fair doubts at this point. The complex nature of social institution might allow for a methodologically correct explanation of objectivity; the problem is that it is the very nature which

---

21 Jürgen Habermas, *The Structural Transformation of the Public Sphere: An Inquiry Into a Category of Bourgeois Society* (Thomas Burger and Frederick Lawrence trs, MIT Press 1989) 36.

22 *ibid.*

23 The German word *räsonieren* is not only a term from the domain of acoustics where it means intensifying of an oscilation (of a sound). It may be also translated as 'to deliberate' or 'to reasonably debate'. Similar is the French term *raisonner*.

is responsible for the practical difficulties in achieving objectivity. How can we find room for objectivity within this never-ending dialogue between the factual and the ideal? I will attempt to outline the answer in the final part of the paper; but, for now, we need to take a closer look at the nature of such a doubt, as well as at the vision of institution implied by hitherto considerations.

If objectivity is an institutionally created phenomenon, then what serves it best is an institution which is stable, immutable and external to the subject. It is an image of institution peculiar to Durkheim and his followers. We go back to the Cartesian perspective, where institution is a prosthesis of the metaphysical, referential world, settled by the Cartesian objects.

Once we have rejected the Cartesian perspective in general terms, there are no good reasons to adopt it for describing an inner institutional reality.[24] Moreover, there are serious doubts whether such a description may be suitable for a contemporary state of affairs. Thus, the description of an institution which has been offered above, brings another view. If institution is a place of dialogue between the ideal and the factual, it cannot but be open to constant inner criticism. Life within the realm of institution is not limited to compliance with a given 'eternal' standard but becomes a process of reflexive mutual adaptations between the agent and institutional standards in permanently turbulent circumstances.

Thus, the need for another variety of institutional approach emerges: a variety which centres its analysis around the observed reflexivity of the institution. Such a 'post-Cartesian' understanding of institution has been proposed by Anthony Giddens. According to the British sociologist, reflexivity remains a crucial structural feature of the society of 'late modernity.' The notion of reflexivity refers to the constant readiness for a change of both theoretical (knowledge) and practical (rules of conduct) foundations of institution. Giddens explains that 'the reflexivity of modern social life consists in the fact that social practices are constantly examined and reformed in the light of incoming information about those very practices, thus constitutively altering their character.'[25] Hence, we are talking about the readiness not only for a change of some component of institutional life in compliance with its immanent logic (such a possibility may be called the 'weak form of reflexivity'), but also for a reform of that very logic, that is basic determinants of

24 Nevertheless, it should be noticed that there are significant authors who choose such a solution of the problem of objectivity, see e.g. Artur Kozak, *Myślenie analityczne w nauce prawa i praktyce prawniczej* (Maciej Pichlak ed, Wydawnictwo Uniwersytetu Wrocławskiego 2010).

25 Anthony Giddens, *The Consequences of Modernity* (Polity Press 1990) 38.

the institution's reflexivity (the 'strong form of reflexivity'). In that way, reflexivity becomes a basic principle of social reproduction.[26]

Reflexivity in that interpretation implies a potential or actual critique of institutional logic. Nevertheless, it seems plausible that, as far as reflexivity is included into that very logic as its crucial component, it can take a form of a total criticism. The reach of its sting cannot but be limited and partial. If that was not the case, reflexivity would not be an internal element of institution but it would drive to the demolishing of the latter. From the practical as well as logical point of view, a total critique constitutes an unattainable *limes* of the institutional reflexivity[27].

The thesis on the reflexivity of contemporary social institutions may be corroborated by the observation of the legal order. Its changes, which have been noticed since the end of the past century, allow to draw a conclusion about the growing significance of reflexivity within law. Let us recall just a few phenomena which foster such a growth: among them are such various examples as the alternative methods of dispute resolving (ADR), the increasing role of judicial review in the continental law systems, complicated relations between public and private law, the 'multi-centrality' of contemporary legal orders, as well as institutions of civil disobedience or transitional justice. As we may notice, this catalogue contains institutions which are rather peripheral to the legal order, as well as the ones located in the very heart of the order. All of them presuppose the possibility of questioning the actual rules of the system's logic and the need for the reflexive monitoring of the adequacy of these rules.

6. Towards the concept of 'reflexive objectivity'

After the above introduction of the notion of reflexivity, it is time to focus on the aforementioned doubt: is there any room for objectivity within such a vision of social institution? Do these two concepts, reflexivity and objectivity, not exclude one another? I am not able to provide a complete answer to such a question here. Still, I will try to give an outline of two points which would form a part of such an answer. I believe that these points demonstrate that reflexivity and objectivity do not necessarily clash and may concur with one another. If we accept them, the consequence is the acceptance of a possibility of a *sui generis* 'reflexive objectivity' of social institutions, law included.

26 For more see Paweł Jabłoński and Maciej Pichlak, 'Miejsce refleksji krytycznej w instytucjonalnej wiedzy o prawie' (2013) LVII–LVIII Principia.

27 In regard to law, Kaarlo Tuori has exposed that inevitably partial nature of an internal critique; see Tuori (n 3) 28–30.

The first point refers to the limited nature of the critique within reflexivity described in the last section. The reflexivity of institution does not imply destroying this already instituted sphere of factuality on which the objectivity of practice is grounded. Paradoxically enough, the very notion of reflexivity presupposes the existence of this, open to criticism, objective domain, since without the latter there would be no chances for reflexive acts to arise: there would be nothing what may have become a matter of reflection. Furthermore, the very act of reflection cannot be taken from an 'empty point' but must be based on some standards immanent to the reflected institution. Hence, each act of critique presupposes the fact of bearing and accepting the standards which form the grounds for criticism. An institutionally constructed object, together with the concept of objectivity, does not disappear, but weakens its ontological status: instead of the Cartesian *res cogitata*, we find a processual construct. It hardly changes anything in the way agents experience institutions in everyday life, as external and determining conduct. This seems to be a perspective taken by Giddens, whose conception of objectivity I employ herein. Let me repeat: reflexivity presupposes the existence of a realm of factuality and, by that, it presupposes the possibility of objectivity as a fact.

The second point goes one step further. It demonstrates that reflexivity not only allows for objectivity, but may, to some extent, support it. This is the case of objectivity as a moral ideal: by exposing deficiencies and weaknesses of the actual state of institutional settings, reflexivity creates a chance for a more complete realization of this kind of objectivity. Postema, who works on a very similar conception of reflexivity as offered here, writes: 'Reflexivity, openness of every aspect of the deliberative practice [...] is essential to the integrity of the process and its claim to objectivity. But reflexivity is an empty promise unless there are places to stand, models to follow, and resources to draw on to mount challenges.'[28] Reflexivity not only presupposes objectivity as a social fact, but it is simultaneously presupposed by objectivity as a moral ideal: the ideal, on which the legitimacy of the modern law is grounded.

28 Postema (n 1) 123.

Lidia Rodak

University of Silesia, Katowice, Poland

5. "Essentialism of a kind" and "objectivity of a kind" as necessary for law

"There is nothing a bit surprising in the thought that objective standards are applicable only through adjudicative subjectivity. It is an objective question as to who crossed the line first, but it has to be judged by the line judge, the photo-finish adjudicator, or the like[1]".

N. MacCormick

Introduction

In part one, I will show the limitations of the essentialist and the anti-essentialist positions[2] using the example of the debate between different schools of Feminist Jurisprudence. As a conclusion from the limitations of this debate, I will introduce the position of "essentialism of a kind" as a proposition for objectivity in law. "Essentialism of a kind" is necessary for legal discourse because it can provide recognition to subjectivity. Legal discourse needs a kind of "strategic essentialism" in order to protect the rights of citizens in general (as essentialism does), but at the same time it needs to be open to recognition of "the others", which is not included in the essentialists' definitions.

(II) In part two, I consider the similar roles played by objectivity and essentialism, especially in their "of a kind" forms. This middle way contains the essentialist core but is at the same time anti-essentialist in the sense of being open to recognition of "the other". I will conclude that law necessarily needs objectivity of a kind,

---

1 Neil MacCormick, 'Reasonableness and Objectivity', Notre Dame Law Review, vol. 74:5, 1517–1603.

2 Essentialism entails objectivity but not the other way around, anti-essentionalism is not identified with subjectivism – as a position that denies the distinction between "what seems right" and "what is right". See more: Jules. L. Coleman, Brian Leiter, 'Determinacy, Objectivity and Authority', in Andrei Marmor (ed), *Law and Interpretation* (Oxford, Clarendon Press, 1995) 252. In this article, taking into account the differences between objectivity and essentialism, I consider their role in the legal discourse as identical, what allows me to apply conclusion from the essentailism-anti\essentailism debate to objectivity in law.

both to provide the categories that form the solid structure of law and to provide mechanisms by which these categories can be open to individual particularities and deal with matters that fall outside existing categories. Starting with the normative formulation of "objectivity of a kind", I will show how objectivity functions in practical discourse by approaching it on the descriptive level.

Part two introduces the internal conditions for "objectivity of a kind", which are formulated from the characteristics of objectivity in practical discourse. Objectivity that functions in practical discourse seems to be based on coherence, which in turn provides narrative contextual sense. The institutional character of law and the specificity of legal argumentation, together with the function of law, are sets of conditions for internally shaping the soft conception of legal objectivity. The conclusion that follows is that legal objectivity is a dynamic not a static concept; and one that blurs the division between essentialism and anti-essentialism. Objectivity in law has a dynamic potential that is determined by the indeterminate character of practical legal discourse. In this way it is able to reshape the firmly established categories that belong to the core.

2.

Feminist criticisms of objectivity are not just social criticisms but also reflect the arguments in the essentialist/anti-essentialist debate. This debate begins with the definition of the essentialism. There are two basic versions of essentialism: one based on the assumptions of realism (i.e. strong objectivity) and so-called internal essentialism[3] (i.e. soft objectivity, also referred to as modest or minimalist in its various shades). The first position assumes the evaluative criteria to be external and remain accessible to our cognition as a permanent, complete, and *a priori*. The second proposal assumes that the evaluation criteria are developed internally and by various philosophical proposals. For example, it could be the effect of power as dictated by the ranking in a social hierarchy. Alternatively, it could be a question of earlier assumptions, such as reliance on the criterion of utility, the free play of social forces, consensus, etc.

The core of anti-esentialism is mainly based on the thesis that there is no metaphysical transcedental grounding for evaluating judgments concerning individuals or anything else. However, this position does not necessarily have to lead to the collapse of objectivity. into subjectivity.

---

3 Martha C. Nussbaum, 'Human Functioning and Social Justice: In Defense of Aristotelian Essentialism' in Ngaire Naffine (ed), *Gender and Justice* (Ashgate Dartmouth, 2002) 223–68.

Feminism, essentialism and anti-essentialism

The Feminist Jurisprudence debate can be presented as an ongoing discourse between essentialism and anti-essentialism, or, to put it another way, the defenders of universal categories and their critics. On a very general level, essentialism is treated as a position which threatens the status of women and minorities. The central defining characteristics do not take into account the diversity of all women and minority groups but focus on abstract categories, which are themselves very often discriminatory. Feminism started as a full-bodied anti-essentialist movement with the anti-fundamental theses of eclecticism, taking into account the many various sources of acquiring knowledge. The consequence of this openness is a willingness to change beliefs and the ways in which they are verified in light of new experiences; these experiences often being richer than our current terms and concepts. Thus, feminism undermines the rigid social structures, showing that generalization and universalisation, and therefore the essentialist approach, ignores the roles members of minority groups play in the larger social system.

However, during the feminist debate, it became clear that many of the proposals challenging the essentialism (such as the various definitions of women as defined by men as subordinate) resulted in another essentialist thesis, or at least some form of it. Generally speaking, we can say that the first wave of feminism began with the anti-essentionalist slogans acting against the established structures and definitions. The essence was to question the accepted definitions of being a woman. In the second wave, feminists focused on building their own concepts. These were different from those deconstructed by the first wave and became essentialist in themselves. A classic example is MacKinnon's definition of a woman who is white and heterosexual[4]. As a result, the third wave became fully anti-essentialist, questioning all definitions, and put forward a level of subjectivity and non-categorized individualism in which everything is permitted and nothing is definitively established as a foregone conclusion. (Julia Kristeva[5], Judith Butler[6]).

---

4 Catharine MacKinnon, 'Feminism, Marxism, Method and the State: An Agenda for Theory', Signs, Vol. 7, No 3, (1982), 514–54.

5 Julia Kristeva, 'Woman can never be define' in Eleine Marks and Isabelle de Courtivron (eds), *New French feminism*, (New York, Schocken Books, 1984) 196; Julia Kristeva, 'Women's Time', Signs, Vol. 7, No. 1, (Autumn, 1981) 13–35; Julia Kristeva, 'The meaning of equality' in Kelly Olivier and Lisa Walsh (eds) *Contemporary French Feminism*, (Oxford University Press, 2004) 91.

6 Judith Butler, *Uwikłani w płeć. Feminizm i polityka tożsamości*, trans. Karolina Krasuska, (Warszawa, Wydawnictwo Krytyki Politycznej, 2008) 270.

The postulates of anti-essentionalist feminists challenge the traditional model of law and have only been implemented to limited extent, mostly in family law and criminal law. At a fundamental level, the law (defined as a system of abstract and general norms) identifies its addressees as a class of legal subjects determined by general names. Categories of general names refer to the generic characteristics of legal subjects that are indicative of their behavior being repeatable. This is clearly an abstraction. At an individual level, or even at the level of subjectivity, it results in the lack of recognition of these subjects by law, and therefore fails to both realize and protect their interests. The current shape of law does not take into account the demands of the second wave feminists, who stressed that women should be treated differently from men. The law still places women and men in the same group as subjects of law. It currently only considers the request of the first wave of feminism, which despite initial intentions became an essentialist one, and, because of equality reasons, treats both sexes as if they were identical.

In the face of anti-essentionalist assumptions upon which feminism has grown, you could ask whether feminists really need anti-essentionalism This question is particularly important because the main objective of their struggle is recognition. To be recognized, there must be a group with some defining features for their recognition. One solution to meet constraints facing full-blooded versions of essentialism is a type of essentialism proposed by M.C. Nussbaum.

The rejection of essentialism causes the destruction of the "privileged group" boundaries. Because there is no group, there is a free admission to the discourse by minorities, groups or individuals who were previously excluded, and so oppression and exclusion are seemingly removed. However, the negative consequence appears to be a private system almost unable to function beyond the individual level. A subject not covered by any category remains outside the functioning of the legal system. Therefore, it seems that maintaining at least some form of essentialism is necessary to recognize the individuality and diversity of membership, acceptance and inclusion. This brings doubts as to the nature of anti-essentialist feminist jurisprudence and any actual advantage in defying definition.

On the map of different conceptions of objectivity in law, both full-blooded essentialism (strong objectivity) and anti-essenstialism (subjectivism) remain at the extremes, still too controversial to apply in practice, as confirmed by the example of Feminist Jurisprudence. While the soft conception of objectivity in law (modest and minimal) combines the advantages of both strong objectivity and subjectivity and avoids the criticisms directed towards them. "The thin vague theory of the good" represents soft objectivity in law and proposes a middle way that combines moral sentiments with essentialism and represents a new approach to objectivity. One that is worth including on our map.

This approach is presented in "Essentialism of certain type" by Martha C. Nussbaum. Her *"Thin vague theory of the good"* proposes a kind of essentialism that is the internal version of Aristotle's essentialism[7]. Considering the two moral sentiments, respect and compassion, provides the opportunity to hear and also recognize those who are excluded from the group, those who would never be accepted by the realists due to their full-blooded essentialist approach. The theory combines the features of Aristotle's essentialism, according to which human life has some specific features and shape, together with the recognition of what is not firmly defined or "vague". The main task of Nussbaum's essentialism is to take into account the various local, individual conceptions of human life. The "Thin vague theory of the good" is not a metaphysical concept, but is based on two premises: recognition of another as human being, regardless of the differences we encounter in his or her definition; and the idea of consensus regarding the characteristics that mark the boundaries of human life.

2.

The practical use of objectivity in the application of law is commonly the subject of criticism and strong attacks. In this part, I focus on objectivity in practical legal discourse in order to demonstrate that its role is much more complex than has previously been discussed in the literature[8]. The main attack on objectivity has mostly been based on anti-essentialist arguments formulated by the Feminist Movement (as described in Part 1). The main objection to objectivity was *expressiss verbis* in that it 'masks inequality" by hiding the power relations that exist in societies. The

7 Martha C. Nussbaum, 'Human Functioning and Social Justice: In Defense of Aristotelian Essentialism' (n 3) 223–68.

8 See more detailed literature: Jules Coleman and Brian Leiter, who helpfully discuss this literature in detail. Jules Coleman and Brian Leiter, *Objectivity in Law and Morals*, (Cambridge Univeristy Press, 2001) 331–49.
A short review of arguments introduced in the jurisprudential literature: the use of objectivity in practical legal discourse is an object of criticism, mainly made by feminist movement: Martha Minow, 'Justice Engendered', 101 Harvard Law Review 10 (1986); Ann C. Scales, 'The Emergence of Feminist Jurisprudence: An Essay', 95 Yale Law Journal 1373 (19860); Critical Legal Studies – Joseph Singer, 'The Player and the Cards: Nihilism and Legal Theory', 94 Yale Law Journal 1 (1984); Duncan Kennedy, 'Form and Substance in Private Law Adjudication', 89 Harvard Law Review 1685 (1976); Critical Race Theory – Kimberley Crenshaw, 'Race, Reform, and Retrenchment: Transformation and Legitimation in Anti-discrimination Law', 101 Harvard Law Review 1331 (1988); Richard Delgado, 'The Inward Turn in Outsider Jurisprudence', 34 Wm. & Mary Law Review 741 (1993).

Feminist Movement postulated a complete rejection of objectivity, describing it as a "hypocritical notion[9]". Critical Legal Studies also attacked objectivity as nothing more than a successive tool of rhetoric, which makes the process of decision taking deductive and non-personal, leaving judiciary discretion as a masquerade under the rule of law.[10]

It's important to stress here that the above criticisms were made against the so-called strong conception of objectivity, which has its origins in philosophical realism. However, if we deconstruct the way in which objectivity is used in legal discourse, it reveals that it is also widely used in the soft sense. By describing the different usages of objectivity in legal practice, it's possible to show how objectivity functions as an argument in practical usage. By deconstruction and description of all the elements that constituted an argumentative situation, both objective and subjective, it's possible to identify what is behind the shell of what is called objective (i.e. examples of objective judicial discretion, which combine a mixture of subjective judgements and objective standards). Approaching the problem of objectivity in legal discourse from a descriptive level makes it possible to reformulate its role in legal discourse. This methodology and conclusion are taken from conclusions from "Objectivity in legal discourse: the comparative perspective", an extensive research project on objectivity in practical legal discourse covering 12 different legal systems[11]. From this research,

9 See more: Sandra Harding, 'Rethinking Standpoint Epistemology: What is Strong Objectivity?' in Ann E. Cudd, Robin O. Andreasen (eds) *The Feminist Standpoint Theory Reader. Intellectual and Political Controversies*, (Routledge, New York London); Amartya Sen, 'Positional Objectivity', Philosophy and Public Affairs, Vol. 22, (1993); Martha C. Nussbaum, 'Human Functioning and Social Justice: In Defense of Aristotelian Essentialism', (n 3); Carol Gilligan, *In a different Voice: Psychological Theory and Women's Development, Library of Congress Cataloging in Publication*, (USA 1993); Catharine MacKinnon, *Difference and Dominance: on Sex Discrimination*, 211–21, quoted in Hillaire Burnett, *Introduction to Feminist Jurisprudence*, (Cavendish Publishing Limited, London Sydney 1998); Martha Minow, 'Justice Engendered', (n 8) 211–21, quoted in Hillaire Burnett, *Introduction to Feminist Jurisprudence*, (Cavendish Publishing Limited, London Sydney 1998); Ann C. Scales, "The Emergence of Feminist Jurisprudence: An Essay," 95 Yale Law Journal 1373 (1986).

10 Duncan Kennedy, 'Form and Substance in Private Law Adjudication', 89 Harvard Law Review 1685 (1976), accessed from http://duncankennedy.net/documents/Form and Substance in Private Law Adjudication.pdf As Duncan Kennedy said: it is the pseudo-objectivity of the rule-as applied." As Richard Delgado speaks of critical race theory's "distrust of law's neutral and objective facade."

11 Full data is included in the final Report of the Project "Objectivity in Legal Discourse: the Comparative Perspective". Research was carried out 2010–2012.

I would like to introduce a different role of objectivity in legal discourse, which is not only a tool of argumentation used to exclude subjects, close the discourse, or to oppress legal subjects, but one that provides narrative sense to legal narration.

The internal conditions for "objectivity of a kind" are formulated by the characteristics of practical legal discourse, which is the way objectivity is applied by the courts. At the practical level, this enables the possibility for general categories to be adjusted in different situations according to their narrative contextual sense. In this way, "'objectivity of a kind'" can act as a flexible concept, preventing unjust exclusion of subjects.

1. A major function of objectivity in practical discourse is to provide coherence to arguments, which in turn creates narrative contextual sense[12]. The concept of objectivity is specified by the following:
   1.1 The character of legal discourse, its institutional character, ("the nature of the thing", its concept).
   1.2 The specificity of legal argumentation and legal reasoning, with the special role attributed to coherence.

1.1 The institutional character of legal discourse

Objectivity as "the nature of the thing"

The concept of "the nature of the thing" has been used in very broad range of contexts[13], from the doctrine of legal voluntarism to anti-formalistic and anti-legalistic doctrines[14]. This illustrates the flexible nature of the concept and gives interpretive guidance.

There are two levels whereby objectivity could be explained by "the nature of the thing". The first is in practical legal discourse, where objectivity plays an

---

12 See a more detailed description in: Lidia Rodak, *Objectivity as Coherence in Practical Discourse*, (Post-conference Proceeding, Peter Lang) 1–15.

13 For example, the nature of the thing, according to A. Asquini, is a social construct that represents common consciousness, and has social and economic functions. Individual reasoning can be achieved with reference to the common consciousness. This position cannot be identified with objectivism or naturalism. According to Norberto Bobbio, this interpretation of the nature of the thing is mixed up with equality. See more, Norberto Bobbio, La natura delle cose. See webside: http://www.lex.unict.it/didattica/materiale09/storiamedavanzato/vocabolario/Bobbio_La_natura_delle_cose.pdf.
See also, Tomasz Gizbert-Studnicki, Konepcje "natury rzeczy" w zachodnioniemieckiej filozofii prawa, (Conceptions of "the 'Nature of Thing" in the West German Philosophy of Law), Etyka, 19, (1981) 133–155.

14 Norberto Bobbio, *La Natura delle cose*, (n 13) 199.

active role in exercising judicial discretion in a broad sense. The other is where objectivity provides a solid structure to the legal system while at same time giving it flexibility and a dynamic nature. G. Radbruch explains "die Nature der Sache[15]" ("the nature of the thing") as follows: "*This approach means translating the reality of phenomena, which have some immanent values, into the world of legal institutions. The nature of the legal order as expressed in varying number and interrelation of legal institutions, has certain immanent qualities that legal science must recognize*[16]" (…) "*moving force in the transformation of legal institutions in response to social change*[17]" The nature of the thing can also be identified with judicial discretion: "*This phenomena can be observed as a dynamic concept by which law, as an instrument of social change, responds to the manifoldness of life and changing social relations.*[18]" Meihoffer suggests the nature of the thing is like "*good faith*" or "*reasonableness*", something that is part of positive law and everyday legal life[19]. Bobbio, stressing the multiple contexts of usages, suggests a more rigorous way of defining its meaning and even adopting a different vocabulary in order to reach precise communication. As first, he refers to it as "teleological reasoning"[20] in defining the sociological moment in legal rules. He then proposes calling it "a socio-economic function" within legal rules.

Objectivity as "the nature of the thing" in judicial discretion

The analyses of objectivity in the context of judicial discretion[21] shows that objectivity in practical legal discourse is used most often in cases where "*extra legem* standards" need to be applied. A clear example of this are cases where discretion is exercised. Exercising discretion is directly linked with the subjective character of the evaluation process, yet the final evaluation is still called objective. How then do you resolve this apparent conflict and make clear the "mystery of judicial discretion"?

Examples from the court rulings show that the application of judicial discretion is based on "objective standards", "commonly shared objective standards", "external criteria", or other examples (using Bobbio's words) of "teleological reasoning".

---

15 Gustaw Radbruch, *The Nature of Things as a Juridical Form of Thinking* [Die Natur der Sache als juristische Denkform], 1948.
16 Wolfgang Gaston Friedmann, *Legal theory,* (London, 1967) 203.
17 Gustaw Radbruch, *The Nature of Things as a Juridical Form of Thinking* (n 15).
18 Wolfgang Gaston Friedmann, *Legal theory,* (n 16) 203.
19 ibid.
20 Norberto Bobbio, *La Natura delle cose*, (n 13) 212.
21 Report of the Project "Objectivity in Legal Discourse: the Comparative Perspective".

"Reasonable person" is a common example applied in many different legal systems as an objective measure for the objective interpretation of contracts. Objectivity in the process of legal discretion is defined according to the interpretative style: it may be linked with the text[22], the intention of the parties[23], or the interpretation from a third-person perspective[24] – all of them are called objective.

The objective character of exercising discretion can be explained by reformulating the conception of legal objectivity. The lesson from these examples is that it is necessary to accept subjective elements as part of the process of taking legal decisions. Objectivity provides framework that allows law to deal with all the elements that compose arguments when taking final decisions: those elements that are evaluative, justified, reasonable, and finally objectivised are the ones that are counted. Exercising discretion is the "process of objectivisation" that allows elements which have a different status to be incorporated into a common legal framework. The character of objectivity in practical legal discourse is very different than the one derived from the Cartesian scheme; it is soft, adjusted to the character of legal discourse, and is necessarily composed from subjective elements.

---

22 Judgment of The Supreme Court of Poland, 2001.11.09. [wyrok SNIII RN 145/00 OSNP 2002/19/450] *"(...) the objective interpretation of contracts shows the real sense, the meaning of the contract, which it is necessary to grasp when doubts of interpretation have appeared"*. The aim of objective interpretation is clearly indicated but it gives no real information of what constitutes objective interpretation. The next quote says, *"that objective interpretation is going to reconstruct the content of the contract on the basis of a linguistic examination"* (2001.11.09. SN III RN 145/00 OSNP 2002/19450).

23 Principles of International Commercial Contracts UNIDROIT, art. 4.1. "A contract shall be interpreted according to the common intention of the parties. 2. If such an intention cannot be established, the contract should be interpreted according to the meaning that reasonable persons of the same kinds as the parties would give it t it in the same circumstances".
Art. 4.2. The statements and other conduct of a party should be interpreted according to that party's intention if the other party knew or could have not been unaware of that intention. 2. If the preceding paragraph is not applicable, such statements and other conduct should be interpreted according to the meaning that a reasonable person of the same kind as the other party would give to it in the same circumstances."

24 Annick De Boeck and Mark Van Hoecke, 'The Interpretation of Standards clauses in European Contract Law in Standard Contract Terms' in Hugh Collins (ed) *Europe: A Basis for and a Challenge to European Contract Law*, (Wolters Kluwer 2008) 211. German contract law incorporates an "objectified subjective approach" and according to this "*the meaning is what a reasonable outsider would assume it to have been meant.*"

1.2 The specificity of legal argumentation and legal reasoning

2.2. With regards to the nature of law itself[25], to what extent interpretation and coherence have a special role to play in legal reasoning? Interpretation addresses the problem of linguistic indeterminacy in law (inherited from indeterminacy of language generally – vague predicates and family resemblance concepts). Coherence addresses the inconsistency of the sources of law[26], making it necessary for judges to resort to non-legal sources in order to resolve disputes – in the cases where there are legal gaps for instance.

In a certain sense, coherence is a way to deal with the consequences of indeterminacy. Coherence is more than logical consistency amongst propositions, but it is not clear from the many accounts of coherence exactly what this something more amounts to.[27]

N. MacCormick distinguishes two types of coherence: normative and narrative. In his view,[28] normative coherence is a unity of principles in a legal system, contending that the coherence of a set of legal norms consists in their being related, either by virtue of being the realization of some common value or values, or by virtue of fulfilling some common principle or principles.[29,30] Because "*(…) any system of practical reason necessarily requires the framing of hierarchically related rules and*

25 There are thus three things (at least, there may be others) which legal theorists could mean by legal reasoning: (a) reasoning to establish the existing content of the law on a given issue, (b) reasoning from the existing content of the law to the decision which a court should reach in a case involving that issue, and (c) reasoning about the decision which a court should reach in a case, all things considered.

26 Jules L. Colman, Brian Leiter, 'Determinacy, Objectivity and Authority', (n 2) 217–19.

27 Kenneth Kress, 'Legal Reasoning and Coherence Theories: Dworkin's Rights Thesis, Retroactivity, and the Linear Order of Decisions', California Law Review (1984), 72, 369–402.

28 Neil MacCormick, 'Coherence In Legal Justification' in Aleksander Peczenik, Lars Lindahl, Bert van Roermund (eds) *Theory of Legal Science, Theory of legal science: proceedings of the Conference on Legal Theory and Philosophy of Science*, (Lund, Sweden, December 11–14, 1983 Dordrecht, Boston, Hingham, MA, U.S.A.: Sold and distributed in the U.S.A. and Canada by Kluwer Academic Publishers, 1984) 235–51.

29 Raz also characterizes coherence in law in terms of unity of principle. On his view, the more unified the set of principles underlying those court decisions and legislative acts which make up the law, the more coherent law is.

30 Neil MacCormick, 'Coherence In Legal Justification', (n 28) 238. "*The coherence of a set of norms is a function of its justifiability under higher order principles and values(…) provided that the higher or highest order principles and values seem acceptable as delineating a satisfactory form of life, when taken together* (…)"

principles of conduct exhibiting consistency over time and universality over cases, this being essential to the achievement of a rational order superimposed on what would otherwise be a chaos of particular purposes.[31]"

The function of coherence can be characterized as "making sense" or "hanging together[32]" Narrative coherence can be characterized as the general common sense principle. It has justificatory force in making decisions about matters of fact (the idea of rationality plays a special role here). We make the world intelligible for ourselves and one of the conditions of intelligibility is the supposition that what we perceive is real[33]. Summing up, normative coherence justifies normative conclusions and narrative coherence justifies factual conclusions. This perspective is not only a semantic narrative but also a semantic-pragmatic narrative. Rational agents can transform brute facts into coherent legal narratives within a framework of common pragmatic rules. This process of transformation ends up with creating objective legal facts by adapting them to the legal narration. The aim of this qualification is to single out this type of legal fact from those previously described, and to show that their process of construction is different in the vast majority of cases, while at the same time still being able to call them objective. The semantic-pragmatic approach is based on the conception of institutional legal facts in a narrative and normative context developed by N. MacCormick. Going step by step, the process of applying the theory of coherence to the legal facts means that brute facts first have to be grasped and then transformed into institutional facts. The narrative-normative context then forms the basis for the justification of this transformation. The minimal condition for the transformation is that the fact is coherent with its normative context and accepted by the community of legal professionals. All legal facts are contextualized entities and fit together in the same way as with narrative coherence.

1.3 The Argument from Objectivity in Legal Discourse

The general characteristic of the "legal usage of objectivity" has a special meaning and a particular role in legal discourse that is related to the assumption of objectivity of law itself. This assumption is taken by legal practice almost literally and what follows from this is that everything that is "legal" is treated as "objective" in a practical legal discourse. This is expressed by the importance and strength given to certain types of arguments qualified as objective during the process of balancing

31 ibid 237–38.
32 ibid 235–51.
33 ibid 235–51.

arguments. This qualification as objective is delivered by law by its own power of authority. These arguments must also be introduced within legal (i.e. objectified) narration and so can be characterized as syllogistic.

By analyzing case law it is possible to identify the following groups of usage of objectivity[34]:

1. The first group of examples are from cases where the strongest and the most valuable arguments are considered to be those based on legal authority. The argument from objectivity can be seen to come from various sources:
   a. legal rules
   b. legal order
   c. precedent cases
   d. legal dogmatics delivered by facts themselves
   e. descriptive argument, grounded in facts
   f. logical or scientific explanation
   g. arguments delivered by an impartial observer.
2. The second group of examples are cases in which objectivity is applied as a style of argumentation expressed as non-personal narration. Arguments introduced as impersonal rather than subjective are deemed more important. The standards of legal narration say that arguments must be intersubjective and this is provided by accepted justification. Here, objectivity also provides argumentative power in a rhetorical sense[35].

Objectivity as a mixture of objectivity and subjectivity

From all the court rulings under examination[36], only a minority used objectivity in its pure sense. Virtually all contained a mixture of objective and subjective elements. It could be implied from this that there is always the problem of subjectivity when dealing with objectivity in practical use. Claims that objectivity plays a negative role in legal discourse and statements that subjectivity is the ordinary part of legal application both have their own firm places in the jurisprudential debate. Taken together, these two positions characterize legal discourse: there are formal, abstract, objective rules, but these rules need to be applied by real people to particular cases. Despite strong criticisms, objectivity is still a very commonly used argument in a legal discourse. It follows from this that subjectivity is a necessary part of legal

---

34 Lidia Rodak, *Objectivity as Coherence in Practical Discourse*, (n 12) 1–15.

35 ibid 1–15.

36 Report of the Project "Objectivity in Legal Discourse: the Comparative Perspective".

discourse. Objectivity is implicit in the nature of law, and the way it is applied in practical legal discourse is strongly linked with its normative[37], public, abstract, and formal character, together with the necessity of justifying the final decision, and the assumption of authority of law – all these features of law demand objectivity.

Law incorporates subjectivity, but through the process of reaching the final decision the character of this decision has changed into a legal one. Legal judgments or legal facts are constructed through the practice of legal professionals, who deal with the realm of values, goals and beliefs, and they are not purely descriptive. Legal judgments do not aspire to correspond to a human independent word and the correspondence theory of objectivity doesn't fit legal reality[38]. As N. MacCormick express it: *"There is nothing a bit surprising in the thought that objective standards are applicable only through adjudicative subjectivity. It is an objective question as to who crossed the line first, but it has to be judged by the line judge, the photo-finish adjudicator, or the like[39]".*

The legal meaning of objectivity goes beyond the dichotomy of objectivity and subjectivity. What should be considered is the quality of arguments that support "objective decisions" and the degree of subjectivity in objectivity. The spectrum of the usages of objectivity is represented by a wide range of elements, from descriptive to evaluative, and includes special legal usages[40]. In this account, the criticisms made by Legal Realists, Critical Race Theorists, and the Feminist Movement are still valid – objectivity can be abused to mask inequality, close the discourse prematurely, or used simply to add argumentative power. However, it also plays also a vital role in a legal discourse. It allows terms of objective reality in law to be applied to individual cases in an objectified and legal way. It forms a junction, between the formal and material substantive elements of legal systems, enabling the law to be applied at a practical level. Objectivity is a necessary element in the process of adjudication and provides the "extra legal" substance to the process of justification and judicial decision-making. Objectivity provides a common measure and allows the translation of languages from different discourses into a legal one.

---

37 Ernest Sosa, 'Normative Objectivity', in Ernest Garzón Valdés, Werner Krawietz, Georg Henrik von Wright, Ruth Zimmerling (eds), *Normative systems in Legal and Moral Theory*, (Duncker&Humbolt, Berlin 1997) 141–53.

38 Heidi Li Feldman, 'Objectivity In Legal Judgment', *Michigan Law Review* Vol. 92, No. 5 (1994), 1187–1255.

39 Neil MacCormick, 'Reasonableness and Objectivity', (n 1).

40 One of the arguments that are considered by the courts as objective are based on the authority of law. See more, Lidia Rodak, *Objectivity as Coherence in Practical Discourse*, (n 12).

Conclusions

1. The lesson from the anti-essentionalist feminist discourse introduced in part 1 indicates the importance of fulfilling the function of law within an objective legal framework. Without "objectivity of a kind" law doesn't fulfill its regulatory function. The core of legal system is the normative coherence which simply cannot exist without a certain form of objectivity that both preserves the identity of a legal system and enables it to adjust to social reality. It provides stability, predictability and flexibility of legal rules and facilitates just decisions, so fulfilling the regulatory function of a legal system.

The overarching aim of law is to regulate human behavior in a broad sense. Without some objectivity such a function could not exist. Law should provide recognition of legal subjects and this is only possible by adapting the concept of legal objectivity in a soft sense (anti-realist approach).

Without soft objectivity, as objectivity of a kind, law doesn't fulfill its regulative function. As a result, normative coherence, the core of the legal system, would collapse. Objectivity is necessary to fulfill the main aims of law, namely its certainty, transparency, common acceptance, universality, equity before law, and, in a certain sense, democracy. At the very basic level of legal assumption, objectivity provides the values that constitute law, like legitimacy, justification, and its power of authority. It is also necessary for the normative character of law to be thought as objective[41]. Even legal semantics have to be transparent on the level of assessment and is in this sense objective, otherwise there would be no intersubjectivity, understanding or dialogues.

2. Objectivity is the key concept for law since it provides a shared structure for legal systems and guidelines for fulfilling the functions of law. However, it is also dynamic not a static concept.

From the analyses of the jurisprudence of the court, there are large number of examples where objectivity was recalled. Law seems to like objectivity, mainly because it is based on routine. In the vast majority of cases predictable procedures are applied. However, there is always a shadow of uncertainty because they are not fully determined. From time to time, hard cases appear that can be said to create or shape law. What should be stressed here is that objectivity is used in both type of cases, easy and hard ones. Easy cases find their justification in predictability and

41 Robert Alexy, *Law, Normativity and Autonomy*, paper presented during the workshop "The Normative Dimension Of Law", organized by University Centre Saint-Ignatius Antwerp, Centre for Law & Cosmopolitan Values, 2009.

certainty represented by objectivity[42], while hard cases recall objectivity as justice[43]. Tragic cases provide a litmus test[44]. Even these cases may appear to be decided arbitrarily on the basis of subjective judgments, justification for the final decision has to follow objectivised legal standards. These are cases that shape the legal system, indicating its 'new" direction. They create a pattern for future application, which is again based on objective standards, routine and predictability.

There is an internal dynamic of bottom-up legal discourse that doesn't follow the imposed rules of legal system. The impact of the unpredictability of social life that law has to deal with has changed the concept of legal objectivity. "Objectivity of a kind", is open for new input and has the ability to convert it into the legal terms and adjust it to a legal framework. Objectivity of the legal system is based on subjectivity in relation to the extent that hard or tragic cases reshape the legal system. It's like we can observe a planetary system that is stable but, from time to time, comets fall down riot, but as they do so they become part of already new established planetary order.

---

42 C-109/88 ECJ October 1989, Danfos, Handels-og Kontorfunktionoernes Forbund I Danmark v. Dansk, Arbejdsgiverforening, acting on behalf on Danfos. To illustrate the flexibility and argumentative capacity in equity law, the judge's final decision in certain cases can be based on the objective legal rule. Such a decision is motivated not only by equity but also by the values of predicability and certainity (see C-449/08). However, there are also cases, for example indirect discrimination cases (see C-109/88) where judges deliberately refrain from applying to the letter of the law because it would lead to an unjust result. Such a decision is in itself based on an objective argument in order to reach the "one right answer". In both types of case objectivity is a useful tool to provide coherent justification to the decision. This shows objectivity can perform as a good justificatory tool both in the positivistic sense, when taking objective decisions in a legalistic way, and also in the non-positivistic sense, when taking decisions in accordance with a sense of justice.

43 C-109/88; Judgment of the Court (Fifth Chamber) of 22 October 2009, Case C-449/08 (Common agricultural policy – Integrated administration and control system for certain aid schemes – Regulation (EC) No 1782/2003.

44 Manuel Atienza, *Los límites de la interpretación constitucional. De nuevo sobre los casos trágicos.* (Alicante: Biblioteca Virtual Miguel de Cervantes, 2005).

Marcin Pieniążek

Andrzej Frycz Modrzewski Krakow University, Poland

6. The objectivity of the legal text in view of the concept of semantic autonomy. Comments on Paul Ricoeur's theory

Introduction

The issue of the objective meaning of the legal text is of deep interest for the jurisprudence, inter alia, in the context of the issues of interpretation and application of law.[1] The purpose of this article is to look at the analysed topic from the perspective of semantic autonomy of the text, introduced by Paul Ricoeur. The interconnection of the concepts of objectivity and autonomy is justified, among others, due to their definitional relationship, since the former stands for "the existence independent of the entity aiming at cognition",[2] while the latter – for "self-reliance and independence".[3] In turn, among the many definitions of the legal text, one should emphasise the one which proclaims that it is "a finite sequence of linguistic expressions, produced in the form provided by

---

1 Cf. Jerzy Wróblewski, *Legal Language and Legal Interpretation* (Law and Philosophy, Vol. 4, No. 2, Legal Reasoning & Legal Interpretation (Aug., 1985)) 239–255; Maciej Zieliński, *Interpretacja jako proces dekodowania tekstu prawnego* [Interpretation as the Process of Decoding Legal Text] (Adam Mickiewicz University, Prace Wydziału Prawa [Law Faculty Essays] No. 54, Poznań 1972) 85; Wojciech Cyrul, 'Legal Drafting: From Text to Hypertext' in *Law and Legal Cultures in the 21st Century: Diversity and Unity* (ed. M. Pieniążek, Oficyna Wydawnicza AFM, Kraków 2009) 14ff. The issue of the interpretation and application of law will be analysed in points 2 and 4.

2 After: *Uniwersalny słownik polskiego PWN* [*Universal Polish Dictionary of the National Scientific Publishers*], Vol. K-Ó (ed. S. Dubisz., Wydawnictwo Naukowe PWN [National Scientific Publishers], Warszawa 2008) 1054. The etymology of the adjective "objective" can be sought in the Late Latin phrase *obiectio* – "restraint". After: Władysław Kopaliński, *Słownik wyrazów obcych i zwrotów obcojęzycznych z almanachem* [*Dictionary of Foreign Words and Phrases in Foreign Languages with Almanac*] (Oficyna wydawnicza RYTM, Warszawa 2006) 403.

3 After: *Uniwersalny słownik polskiego PWN* (n 2), Vol. A-J, 156. The etymology of the adjective "autonomous" can be traced in Greek *autonómos* – "self-governing; independent". After: Kopaliński, *Słownik wyrazów obcych* (n 2) 54.

the author, legally empowered to law-making process, relatively complete and internally coherent, published in a legally regulated manner, whose primary illocutionary force[4] is prescribing."[5]

Ricoeur's views, outlined below and developed on the border between hermeneutics and analytical philosophy of language,[6] allow to overcome the impasse in the form of associating the objectivity of the legal text with its unambiguity, as practised in the "scientific jurisprudence". It should be recalled that the methods of interpretation, postulated by legal positivism and based on the thesis of the constant sense of a normative act, led to a loss of flexibility in applying law. In turn, counter arguments against the positivist paradigm resulted in utterly subjectivist and intuitive methods of interpretation, postulated by some hermeneutical trends, thus creating a danger of a loss of intersubjective communicability of the meaning of the legal text and the certainty of law application.[7]

Therefore, this article treats Ricoeur's views as the foundation of formulating the concept of "the third way" of thinking about the notion of the objectivity of the legal text. First of all, it refers to the hermeneutics of literary texts by inscribing the issue at hand into the paradigm of the humanities.[8] At the same time, however, the proposed concept of the semantic autonomy of the legal text draws from the linguistic structural analysis, defining the horizon of the subjective

---

4 Illocutionary force as perceived by John L. Austin. Cf. John L. Austin, *How to Do Things with Words* (Harvard University Press, Harvard 1975) 98–132.

5 After: Ryszard Sarkowicz, Jerzy Stelmach, *Teoria prawa* [*Theory of Law*] (Wydawnictwo UJ, Kraków 1996), 72 (the author quotes the definition of legal text proposed by E. Stabrawa). The text is lexically defined as "a sequence of written words and sentences that make up a certain whole, expressing the specified content". After: *Wielki słownik wyrazów obcych* [*Great Dictionary of Foreign Words*], ed. M. Bańko (PWN, Warszawa 2003) 1240. The etymology of the noun "text" is a Medieval Latin concept of *textus* – "text, paragraph, verse", derived from the Latin word *textilis* – "weaved". After: Władysław Kopaliński (n 2) 569. Cf. Teresa Dobrzyńska, *Tekst. Próba syntezy* [*Text. The Approach to Synthesis*] (ed. Instytut Badań Literackich, Warszawa 1993). Cf. Jeff Conklin, *A Survey to Hypertext* ('MCC Technical Report', Nomber STP) 356–86.

6 On the reasoning of the undertaken exploration of the borderland between hermeneutics and analytically oriented ordinary language philosophy, see Paul Ricoeur, "From Existentialism to the Philosophy of Language" [Spring, 1971] 10, Criterion 18.

7 On the advantages and disadvantages of the reception of hermeneutics in the philosophy of law, see Jerzy Stelmach, Bartosz Brożek, *Methods of legal reasoning*, Springer Science & Business Media, Berlin 2006, pp. 173–175.

8 Broadly about the specifics of the legal text in the context of the theory of literature, see Marcus Galdia, *Legal Linguistics* (Peter Lang, Frankfurt am Main 2009) 247–270.

interpretation. The basis of the undertaken reasoning is provided by Ricoeur's views, outlined, inter alia, in the work *Speaking and Writing, The Model of the Text: Meaningful Action Considered as a Text, The Hermeneutical Function of Distanciation* and *Reflections on the Just*.[9]

The article is divided into four sections. The first one discusses the concept of the text, from the perspective of Ricoeur's ideas, with particular attention paid to the differences existing between the written text and live discourse. The second section brings us closer to the concept of the semantic autonomy of the text, discussed by Ricoeur in the context of the author, the primary addressee and the sociopsychological conditions of the creation of the text. The third section outlines the views of the philosopher in respect of the structure of the text which constitutes the precondition of its objectivity, as well as the role played by literary genres in the objectivization of the meaning of the text. The fourth section introduces the concept of reference and iconic augmentation that model the autonomy of the world, opened up by the text. In each of these sections, Ricoeur's views are related to specific characteristics of the legal text, which – on the basis of the proposed paradigm – makes it possible to determine the nature and delimitation of its objectivity.

1. The concepts of text and discourse in the context of the specifics of the legal text

The jurisprudence indicates the specific characteristics of the legal text in respect to other types of texts. R. Sarkowicz and J. Stelmach point out at the following features: 1) the specific language, referred to as the legal language;[10] 2) poor literary form, which is forced by the attention to precision; 3) formalized and complex structure (divided into articles, paragraphs, etc.); 4) the particular conception of the author of the legal text – a rational legislator; 5) proceduralized techniques of

---

9 See below.

10 Tomasz Gizbert – Studnicki argues that the legal language is a unique "register of ethnic language". Cf. Tomasz Gizbert – Studnicki, 'Język prawny a język prawniczy [Legal Language and Juridical Language]' [1972] Vol. 55, Zeszyty Naukowe Uniwersytetu Jagiellońskiego, Prace Prawnicze; Tomasz Gizbert – Studnicki, 'Język prawny z perspektywy socjolingwistycznej [Legal Language from Sociolinguistic Perspective]' [1986] Vol. 26, Zeszyty Naukowe Uniwersytetu Jagiellońskiego, Prace z nauk politycznych; Zygmunt Ziembiński, 'Le langauge du droit et le language juridique. Les criteres de leur discretement' [1974] Vol. 19, Archives de philosophie du droit.

interpretation. These features are in close correlation with the "topic" of the legal text, namely prescribing socially relevant human behaviour.[11]

Paul Ricoeur's research opens up the possibility of a new insight of jurisprudence into the specific nature of the legal text. The issue of the text is in fact widely discussed by Ricoeur who considers it a key problem of hermeneutics.[12] Ricoeur enumerates five features which "constitute the criteria of textuality": 1) the realization of language as a discourse; 2) the realization of a discourse as a structured work; 3) the relation of speaking to writing in a discourse and in the works of discourse; 4) the work of discourse as the projection to the world; 5) discourse and the work of discourse as the mediation of self – understanding.[13]

The specific properties of the "work",[14] i.e. the text, are analysed by Ricoeur in correlation with the issue of discourse and the hermeneutical dialectic of event and meaning.[15] The philosopher argues that the fundamental difference between the discourse and the text is based on diversity of live speech and fixed writing".[16] Writing indeed results in a loss of mutual "here and now" of the participants in the dialogue and it entails a greater distance of the meaning of written words and a specific event of a discourse. Therefore, in Ricoeur's views, the hermeneutical dialectic of the event and the meaning explains the transition from speech to writing.[17]

The peculiar transience of the event of discourse raises the question of the method of consolidating its meanings. Therefore, by referring to the theory of the Russian linguist, R. Jacobson (outlined in the article *Linguistics and Poetics*),[18]

---

11 Ryszrad Sarkowicz, Jerzy Stelmach (n 5) 70–9.

12 Paul Ricoeur, 'Task of Hermeneutics' in John B. Thompson (ed), *Hermeneutics and the Human Sciences* (Cambridge University Press, Cambridge 1981) 44.

13 Paul Ricoeur, *The Hermeneutical Function of Distanciation in From Text to Action. Essays in Hermeneutics* (Northwestern University Press, Evanston, 2007) 76.

14 On the concept of "work", see Paul Ricoeur (n 13) 80.

15 ibid 77.

16 The inherent interrelations between hermeneutics, text and writing, are presented in the following manner by Ricoeur: To the extent that hermeneutics is text-orientated interpretation, and inasmuch as texts are, among other things, instances of written language, no interpretation theory is possible that does not come to grips with the problem of writing. After: Paul Ricoeur, Speaking and Writing in Interpretation Theory: Discourse and the Surplus of Meaning (TCU Press, Fort Worth, 1976) 25.

17 ibid.

18 Roman Jacobson assigned the highlighted six "factors" involved in communicating the discourse – namely the addresser, the addressee, the code, the message, the context, the contact, respectively to six functions: emotive, conative, metalingual, poetic, referential,

Ricoeur suggests that the difference between speech and writing concerns the relationship of the specific message to its medium (channel).[19] At the same time, Ricoeur states that the form of "the alphabet, dictionary or grammar" is subordinate in relation to the proper object of consolidation, i.e. the discourse. Language in fact constitutes a timeless system, namely – in contrast to discourse – it is not considered as an event.[20]

Ricoeur extensively analyses the role of writing as a medium of consolidating living speech, thus signalling the implications for law itself. According to Ricoeur, the scale of social and political changes associated with the invention of writing highlights that the latter is more than just a "substantive consolidation" of discourse. Ricoeur notes that "the possibility of transferring information over considerable distances without serious distortions" is correlated with the birth of political power, just as "the record of accounting rules" is associated with the onset of the economy, while "the rise of archives" is associated with the beginning of history". More importantly, Ricoeur states that "recording laws as adjudication patterns, independent of the opinion of the individual judges" conditioned "the birth of justice and legal codes". The scale of the said social impact leads Ricoeur to the conclusion that writing, by consolidating discourse, not only protects it from destruction, but also radically modifies its communication functions.[21] Therefore, Ricoeur emphasizes that discourse and text are believed to be phenomena of substantially different specificity, inter alia, due to the fact that the relation between writing and reading differs from the relationship between speaking and listening.[22] While the spoken discourse refers to the entities specified by the situation of the dialogue, the written text is addressed to an unknown reader, namely potentially to "anyone who can read". Although, according to Ricoeur, there are limitations of a potentially universal circle of the recipients of the text, resulting from the social nature of readers' reception, yet, at the same time, the claim that the text is addressed to everyone "remains valid as a limit of any sociology of reading".[23]

---

phatic. Cf. Roman Jacobson, 'Linguistics and Poetics' in *Style in Language* (Massachusetts Institute of Technology Press, Cambridge 1960) 350–377.

19 Paul Ricoeur (n 16) 26.

20 ibid 27.

21 ibid 28.

22 ibid 29.

23 Paul Ricoeur writes: (...)This universality is only potential. In fact, a book is addressed to only a section of the public and reaches its appropriate readers through media that are themselves submitted to social rules of exclusion and admission. In other words, reading is a social phenomenon, which obeys certain patterns and therefore suffers from specific limitations. After: ibid 31.

In Ricoeur's opinion, the universalization of the reception constitutes one of the most striking and, at the same time, paradoxical effects of writing. Written discourse – precisely because it gains a material carrier – becomes in Ricoeur's opinion – "more spiritual", being free from the constraints of the direct contact between the partners in the communication process.[24] The specificity of the text depends on the fact that when detached from the constraints of the situation of the dialogue, it creates new circles of its recipients. In this way, as Ricoeur writes, the work may broaden the scope of communication or create its new varieties; therefore the scope of the reception of the text is difficult to predict and remains open.[25] This observation provides the basis for the thesis of the autonomous existence of texts (works) in social reality.

It should be noted that these abovementioned ideas created by Ricoeur shed new light on the key features of positive law, reflected in particular in the context of legal discourse. Ricoeur rightly points out that the act of writing down law is closely correlated with its universalist validity, as expressed in Middle Ages maxim "*Lex non obligat nisi promulgata*".[26] Referring to the hermeneutical dialectic of event and meaning it can be stated that the normative meaning becomes independent from law making event through the communication channel in the form of statutory law. In other words, the codified law is detached from any particular discourses, which constitute a prerequisite for adopting new law and it opens up to an unlimited number of future interpretations and applications.

The philosopher's comment on a "more spiritual" nature of the text, liberated from the constraints of a particular situation of a dialogue is reflected in the abstract and general characteristics of the legal norm, interpreted from the legal text. The "liberation" indicated by Ricoeur refers in this case to the act of departing from a direct contact between the legislator and the addressee of the legal text. As a result, the norms like "whoever at his fault caused injury to another person, is obliged to remedy it" are open to an infinite number of applications and they include more and more extensive circles of recipients. At the same time, the abundance of circumstances causes that the range of the references of norms in respect to reality is unlimited.[27]

---

24 ibid 31.

25 ibid 31.

26 This principle was expressly presented by St. Thomas Aquinas in *Summa Theologiae*. After: *Łacińska terminologia prawnicza* [*Latin Legal Terminology*] (ed. Jerzy Zajadło, Oficyna a Wolters Kluwer business, Warszawa 2009) 43.

27 This issue will be further developed in section 4.1. in the context of descriptive aspect of normative reference.

The striking fact is that the modern legislator, when providing a relatively wide subjective and objective scope of the act of law, does not make any claims to predict all possible references of the normative message. On the contrary, universal, general and abstract determination of the scope of regulation introduced by the legal text aims at opening it up to the widest circle of states of facts. Therefore, writing down laws results in the autonomisation of the legal text in respect to the legislator, presupposed recipient, as well as psychosocial determinants of law making process in a certain place and at a specified time.

2. The concept of semantic autonomy of the legal text

As mentioned above, in Ricoeur's opinion, writing down the discourse causes that the original intention of the author and the meaning of the text begin to diverge. Ricoeur emphasizes that due to it being recorded, the text gains a specific feature, namely semantic autonomy, which is a consequence of interfering into the relation between "mental intention of the author and the verbal meaning of the text". Semantic autonomy is therefore expressed in the fact that the meaning of the text transcends the author's intention, while the fate of the text "eludes the finite horizon, in which the author lived".[28] Therefore, according to the philosopher, "one needs to discover and explain the text not in relation to its author, but rather in terms of its immanent meaning and reality presented and revealed by it".[29]

The said specificity of the legal text, and in particular the abstract and general nature of the legal norms, results in transcending "the finite horizon" of the legislator, conditioned by the circumstances of time and place of lawmaking. This transcendence, seen as the expression of the semantic autonomy of the legal text, allows unfolding to more and more new circles of its addressees the normative options offered by the world of legal duties.[30] The question about the "proposal of the world" revealed by the text is directly related to the issue of the interpretation and it places in the foreground the question of the meaning of the text which is no longer rooted in the historical event of the author's record. In the theory of law this issue is of particular interest due to the concepts of authentic and historical interpretation that connect the legal norm with the act of will of historically understood sovereign and emphasize the meaning of the text determined by the legislator. I believe that in the jurisprudence the perspective of authentic and historical interpretation cannot be utterly rejected, at least in view of the role played

28 Paul Ricoeur (n 16) 30.

29 Paul Ricoeur (n 12) 53.

30 The issue of the world of the text is analysed by Ricoeur (n 13) 84–86.

by *ratio legis* in the interpretation of a particular legal regulation (see below). As Ricoeur believes, the fact of detaching readership interpretation from the original intentions of the author may not lead to the conclusion that the author's meaning is completely meaningless. Ricoeur raises this issue by referring again to the hermeneutic dialectic of event and meaning. According to the philosopher, the absence of a dialectic between intentional event of the record and the meaning of the text would result in either transferring the emphasis of the author's intention as the intentional fallacy[31] or in "the text absolutization", namely "hypostatizing it as an authorless entity".[32] In other words, the fallacy would consist in a failure to perceive the autonomy of the text or in forgetting that it constitutes "a discourse uttered by someone to someone else about something".[33] For this reason, in Ricoeur's opinion, the problem of author – message relation cannot be in any case ignored and removed outside the inner dialectic of semantic autonomy.

In the case of semantic autonomy of the legal text the abovementioned dialectic takes into account certain specific assumptions, concerning both the author – legislator as well as the author's meaning of the legal text. I believe that it is, primarily, an idealizing assumption of a rationality of the legislator,[34] being the interpretative premise of the legal text which does not prejudge the content of the interpreted legal norm but which ultimately allows for adopting a coherent vision of the world of legal duties.

The second assumption is an illocutionary force of legal texts, determined by the author – legislator, aimed at developing human action.[35] It should be added that in his works devoted to the theory of narrative, Ricoeur developed the dialectic of description, prescription and action. In this context the specificity of the legal texts is

---

31 At this point Paul Ricoeur uses the concept applied by William K. Wimsatt. Cf. William K. Wimsatt., M.C. Beardsley, *Intentional Fallacy* in *The Verbal Icon: Studies in the Meaning of Poetry* (University of Kentucky Press, 1954) 3–19.

32 Paul Ricoeur (n 16) 30.

33 ibid 30.

34 Cf. Sławomira Wronkowska, *The rational legislator as the model for the real lawmaker in Polish contributions to the theory and philosophy of law* (ed. Zygmunt. Ziembiński, Editions Rodopi B. V., Amsterdam 1987) 147–164; Mark Van Hoecke, *Law as communication* (Hart Publishing, Oxford – Portland Oregon 2002) 156–7; Jan Zimmerman, *Administrative law [Prawo administracyjne]* (Oficyna a Wolters Kluwer Business, Warszawa 2014) 123.

35 Cf. footnote 4.

expressed in moving strongly to the fore of the normative aspect associated with prescribing, as the element that modifies the self-narrative of the interpreting entity.[36]

Thirdly, ignoring any cases of utterly discretionary and "detached" interpretation, a relevant assumption is provided by *ratio legis* underlying the legal text, which serves a moderating role in the dialectic of the author and the message. *Ratio legis* does not prejudge the outcome of the interpretation, but it suggests a normative horizon of the dialectics of the event, namely law making and meaning, i.e. the interpreter entering the world of legal duties. A similar role is played by the preamble of normative acts, revealing the intentions of the author of the legal text that belong to the sphere of legal policy.

Thus, thanks to the presumption of the rationality of the legislator, determination of the illocutionary mode of communication, and indicating its *ratio legis*, the legal text, though it lives its own life, remains a discourse uttered "by someone, for a certain purpose, about something". These observations indicate that the semantic autonomy of the legal text can be considered a special case of the general theory of semantic autonomy as understood by Ricoeur. This topic will be developed below in the context of the deliberations undertaken by G. H. Taylor. It may be the case that due to its peculiarities the legal text may also deserve to be regarded as an "objectively different" literary genre (this issue will be raised in section 3.2.).

According to Ricoeur, the semantic autonomy of the text has two other important dimensions. It stands for making the meaning of the text independent not only from the author's intention (intentional horizon), but also from the text's original audience as well as from the cultural and sociological conditions of the text's creation.[37] The semantic autonomy of the text in the context of the presupposed circle of the addressees manifests itself in the subsequent instances of "unfolding the world of the text", whose originality stems from the perception of new interpreters.[38] As Ricoeur writes, the inherent feature of the text is the fact that it is open to an infinite number of readers and thus to the multiple interpretations.[39] Therefore,

---

36 In light of Ricoeur's views, legal interpretation would start with prescribing and would go through describing the states of facts to "the operation of the addressee of the legal norm, thus creating a structure of the hermeneutical legal syllogism". See, section 4.

37 The article of G. H. Taylor can be considered as a unique example of referring Ricoeur's views to the issue of judicial application of law, in particular to the interpretation of the Constitution by the Supreme Court of the United States. Cf. George H. Taylor, *Ricoeur and Law: the Distinctiveness of Legal Hermeneutics* (ed. S. Davidson, The Continuum International Publishing Group, Inc., London 2010) 86.

38 Cf. Paul Ricoeur (n 13) 84–6.

39 Paul Ricoeur (n 16) 31–2.

the philosopher claims that the problem of assimilating the meaning of the text is as paradoxical as the problem of its authorship. The said paradox takes the form of "a hermeneutical conflict"[40] because "the powers of the reader and the powers of the text itself clash in a momentous struggle that controls the entire dynamics of interpretation".[41] Therefore, as Ricoeur writes, the essence of the autonomy of the text is "the dialectics of the address that is both universal and accidental". The philosopher believes that though – on the one hand – autonomous text creates ever new circles of the addressees, it is – on the other hand – only their reaction that provides the text with "the importance and meaning", since it opens up the world of the text (reference).[42]

It would be hard to find a better example of "a universal and accidental" addressee of the text than the abstract addressee of the legal norm, typically designated by means of the pronoun "whoever".[43] Even if the legal act creates a circle of addressees by using generic bases, such as "natural person", "a national", "political party", or "court", the subjective scope of its regulation is subject to constant changes. The dynamism of the said change is multiplied by generally described subjective scopes, i.e. the circumstances of regulation. Thus, the dialectic nature of the addressee and the circumstances of regulation are considered in the modern legislation to be a predetermined feature of the legal text which meets – to the greatest extent – the discussed dimension of semantic autonomy. At the same time, Ricoeur's comment on attaching "validity" to the legal text by means of addressees' reaction, is aptly reflected in the law application process. Compliance with the legal norms by an individualized addressee and their application in specific circumstances is a measure of the "meaning" of the legal text and the evidence of the effectiveness of its illocutionary aspirations. It should be added that when Ricoeur writes about "the hermeneutical conflict between the powers of the reader and the powers of the text", the dialectics of a universalizing norm and a specific case touch upon the issue of

40 Cf. The collection of Ricoeur's articles – *The Conflict of Interpretations* (ed. Don Ihde, Continuum, Northwestern University Press, 2004).

41 Paul Ricoeur (n 16) 32.

42 ibid 31.

43 Cf. Article 148 of the Criminal Code; article 415 of the Civil Code, etc. In the Polish legislation, the pronoun "whoever" is consideredthe broadest manner of determining the scope of subjective regulation, indicated in the "Principles of legislative technique". Cf. The Regulation of the President of the Council of Ministers of 20 June 2002 on "The Principles of Legislative Technique" (Journal of Laws No. 100, item 908), § 144.1. If the legal norm is to be addressed to any natural person, the addressee of this norm is indicated by means of the word "whoever".

legal syllogism. This problem has been discussed by Ricoeur, among others, in his book *Reflections on the Just*, where, in a direct commentary on R. Dworkin's practical syllogism, the philosopher raised the issue of the harmonization of universalizing the narrative of the legal text and the narrative of the specific case in the interpretative and argumentative process.[44]

Semantic autonomy is also manifested in the fact that the text transcends socio – psychological conditions of its creation and opens up to unlimited sequences of readings, placed in the new, constantly changing contexts. Ricoeur writes that the text decontextualises itself from a psychological and sociological point of view and then it recontextualises itself in the act of reading.[45] In the case of the legal text, recontextualization involves, inter alia, the act of transcending in the interpretation the primordial, ideological base of the statute which allows an autonomous duration of codification, irrespective of the changing contexts of political power. It should be clarified that, according to Ricoeur, the assumed ideological perspective limits the perspective of the world that can be opened up before the reader by means of the text (as I indicated, this view requires some verification due to the issue of *ratio legis* of the legal text). Nevertheless, the conception of decontextualisation and recontextualization of the legal text is confirmed in the long term in law application practice. A specific example here can be provided by the conception – implemented in Poland in the transition period – of the continuity of the legal system with the changing political and economic system,[46] which constitutes the ideological context of the emergence of numerous legal acts that are currently in force in Poland.[47]

The "emancipation of the text" is ultimately expressed in transcending the above three restrictions (authorial meaning, the original addressee and socio – psychological context of creation) and thus it constitutes "the most fundamental condition for the recognition of a critical instance at heart of interpretation".[48]

44 Pail Ricoeur, *Reflections on the Just* (Chicago University Press, Chicago 2007) 69–70. Cf. section 4.

45 Paul Ricoeur, 'Hermeneutics and Critique of Ideology' in John B. Thompson (ed), *Hermeneutics and the Human Sciences* (Cambridge University Press, Cambridge 1981) 91.

46 What I mean here is a long process of transition from socialism to capitalism, and from controlled economy to a free market economy.

47 There are a number of normative acts that were adopted in the socialist period, which are – after relevant amendments – still in force to this day: Act on the Attorneys Profession (1982), Act on Legal Advisers (1982), Act on Prosecution (1985), Act on the Constitutional Court (1987), etc. Some Polish legal texts in practice proved their autonomy, remaining unchanged while experiencing different political systems, such as the Law on bills of exchange and promissory notes (1936).

48 ibid.

A unique example of applying the concept of semantic autonomy in the American jurisprudence is presented in G. H. Taylor's article *Ricoeur and Law: the Distinctiveness of Legal Hermeneutics.*[49] Taylor *reviews Ricoeur's emphasis on the semantic autonomy of the text and provides examples drawn from the American legal context that "generally support and extend" the significance of Ricoeur's insight.* These examples are drawn from the case law of the Supreme Court of the United States and they concern the interpretation of the U.S. Constitution. Taylor stresses that *despite the great contest in the United States between liberal and conservative jurisprudential approaches (…) there is (…) general consensus that legal interpretation should attend to a text's meaning rather than to the authorial intention lying behind the text.*[50] The first of the examples cited by Taylor, being an inherent part of the perspective of the semantic autonomy of the text, is associated with the famous court decision in Brown v. Board of Education of 1954, issued on the basis of Fourteenth Amendment to the U.S. Constitution.[51] Taylor points out that *in Brown the Supreme Court had to decide whether it was constitutional under the equal protection requirement of the abovementioned Amendment for states that permit segregated public schools.*[52] When adjudicating in the said case, the Supreme Court did not apply the authentic interpretation[53] of the concept of 'equal protection' from the times when this amendment was adopted, arguing that the determination whether *the framers of the Amendment* believed racial segregation in public schools to be constitutional is inconclusive. Instead, *the Court went on to rule on the basis of contemporary understandings of equality that segregation was indeed unconstitutional.*[54] Taylor notes that the above interpretative decision in practice constituted the realization of Ricoeur's views, since it made the actual meaning of the text independent of the intentions of the authors of the Amendment, who most probably did not perceive the problem of segregation.[55] The second example cited by Taylor is associated with

49 See below.

50 George H. Taylor (n 37) 85. A diverse view is presented, inter alia, by Stanley Fish. Cf. Stanley Fish, 'Intention is All There is: a Critical Analysis of Aharon Barak's Purposive Interpretation in Law' [2008] Vol. 28 Cardozo Law Review 1109–1146.

51 347 U.S. 483 (1954).

52 George H. Taylor (n 37) 86.

53 This conception stands for the interpretation undertaken by the same body which established a given norm. After: Lech Morawski, *Wstęp do prawoznawstwa* [*Introduction to Jurisprudence*] (Wyd. Dom Organizatora, Toruń 2006) 163–164.

54 George H. Taylor (n 37) 87.

55 Taylor refers, inter alia, to the views presented by Antonin Scalia and Ronald Dworkin. Cf. Antonin Scalia 'Response' in *A Matter of Interpretation: Federal Courts and the Law* (Princeton University Press, Princeton, NJ 1997) 144; Ronald Dworkin (n 55) 118.

the interpretation of the concept of "cruel and unusual punishments", found in the Eighth Amendment, adopted in 1791. Widely discussed Supreme Court rulings that refer to the latter, i.e. *Atkins v. Virginia*[56] (2002), *Roper v. Simmons*[57] (2005) and *Kennedy v. Louisiana*[58] (2008) related, respectively, to the possibility of ruling the death penalty against *someone with extensive mental disabilities, someone under age of eighteen and someone who raped a child (but did not kill it).*[59] In these court decisions, the Supreme Court ruled that it could not apply the original meaning of the phrase "cruel and unusual" because the Eighth Amendment *"draw[s] its meaning from evolving standards of decency that marks the progress of maturing high society"* and decided to apply the *"evolving standards of decency"*.[60] It should be noted that in all the three abovementioned decisions the Supreme Court held that the death penalty under the Eighth Amendment would be "cruel and unusual".

It should be emphasized that Taylor does not follow blindly the path traced by Ricoeur but he perceives the specificity of the interpretation of the legal text in the context of the special status of the author of this text, what distinguishes him from the authors of "literary texts". Taylor concludes that *the author of the legal text does retain a significance in legal interpretation that is not required in other fields. Because a legal author – a legislator or the court – requires obedience to the terms of a text, its expression is limited to the range of its legitimate authority.*[61] According to the author, the specificity of the semantic autonomy of the legal text also applies to the addressee of the legal text, whose intention in the interpreting process is not to aim at "enriching one's world" but at implementing practical purposes, related to the interests of the client or of the legal system.[62] This aspect stands for the verification of the conception proposed by Ricoeur.

3.1 The structure of the legal text as an objectivizing factor

Ricoeur strongly associates the question of the autonomy of the text with the issue of its structure. It should be clarified that the philosopher, though he does not hide his admiration for the achievements of C. Lévi – Strauss, indicates the restrictions characteristic for structuralist philosophy.[63] As a result, Ricoeur stresses the

56 536 U.S. 304.
57 543 U.S. 551.
58 128 S.Ct. 2641 (554 U.S. 407).
59 George H. Taylor (n 37) 89.
60 ibid.
61 George H. Taylor (n 37) 85.
62 ibid 92.
63 Cf. Paul Ricoeur, 'Structure and Hermeneutics' in (n 40) 27–60.

difference between structuralist philosophy and "the structural examination of specific texts", as postulated by him.[64] It refers to the semiotics of A. J. Greimas[65] which, according to Ricoeur, "perfectly illustrates the objectivising, analytical and explanatory proximity of the text in accordance with the structural conception".[66] As noted by the philosopher, this conception consists in "taking into account the relevant rules of text composition". Composition rules are of a procedural nature, while their application has the characteristics of objective analysis. An additional catalyst of the analysis is writing itself, since it "attaches to the work composition" and provides "the support of eternal signs" to objectivizing procedures. The philosopher emphasizes the practical importance of this approach that allows "to find what is best in the text", namely to capture its "internal articulations, independent of the authorial intentions, i.e. of its subjectivity". That aspect of the studies on the text is crucial for Ricoeur in the context of the abovementioned view, according to which "the text defines its author and has a meaning for itself". The semantic autonomy of the text, understood in such a way as noted by the philosopher, "opens it up to the approaches which take into account only its objectivity, as the uttered, written, and thus objectified text". In other words, Ricoeur perceives a close correlation between the objectively existing structure of the text and removing its meaning from the author's original intention in future interpretative efforts.[67]

Ricoeur's views meet the pursuit of jurisprudence to objectivise the meaning of the legal text by means of the canon of rules that moderate its structure. First of all, they shed new light on the role of the principles of legislative technique,[68] which constitute a set of procedural, structural and linguistic rules defining the construction of normative acts.[69] These rules formalize the composition of legal texts,

---

64 Paul Ricoeur, *Critique and Conviction: Conversations with François Azouvi and Marc de Launay* (Columbia University Press, New York 1998) 73.

65 More broadly on the possible reception of A. J. Greimas' views in the legal theory; Bernard Jackson, *Semiotics and Legal Theory* (Deborah Charles Publications, Liverpool 1997).

66 Paul Ricoeur, *Refleksja dokonana* [*Reflection Achieved*] (Wydawnictwo Antyk, Kęty 2005) 33.

67 Paul Ricoeur (n 64) 73.

68 In Polish law, these principles are set out in the Annex to the Regulation of the Prime Minister on the 'Principles of Legislative Technique' and the 'Law on the promulgation of normative acts and other legislative acts' as of 20 July 2000 (Journal of Laws No. 197, item 1172, as amended).

69 On the issue of theoretical and legal aspects of the rules of legislative technique, see: Maciej Kłodawski, 'Hipertekst a technika legislacyjna – o możliwości zmiany paradygmatu polskiego prawodawstwa' '[Hypertext and Legislative Technique – on the Possibility of

imposing constraints on every conceivable *ratio legis* of the normative act. From the perspective of Ricoeur's views, a formalized composition of the legal text is thus an instrument of autonomizing its meaning vis-à-vis the subjective intention of the legislator. The assumptions about the division of the normative act into the general, detailed and final part, correlated with the adopted diversification of provisions into legal definitions, derogating provisions, rules of conflict, interim provisions, etc., allow to "find" that which is essential in the legal text and "to capture its inner articulations", namely to bring its autonomous normative meaning. Due to this technique, a written normative act, to paraphrase Ricoeur, defines the will of the legislator and has a meaning for itself. When taking a broader perspective, it can be perceived that the compliance with the objective principles of legislative technique makes it possible to overcome the ideological determinants of law making, thus providing a guarantee of its stability in the face of political and social changes.[70]

As mentioned above, according to Ricoeur, the tool of objectivization is also a record in itself, which "joins the composition of the work". It should be emphasized that the principles of legislative technique, compliant with the abovementioned standpoint, uniformly regulate the issue of the structure of the text and the phrases contained in the legal text. In other words, the "analytical approach", due to the close relationship between the text and the composition of the provisions, includes both the macro scale of the normative act as well as the micro-scale of specific expression of the legal language. An objective analysis of the structure of the legal text and the legal language autonomizes therefore the meaning of the normative act with respect to the intentions of the historical author, thus playing an important role in future interpretations. An additional premise of autonomization is an unclear ontological status of the legislator, who is to be a rational and transparent entity, correlated at the same time with concepts such as "the will of the people" or "the representation of the sovereign", etc. For these reasons, the conception which is justified in the context of Ricoeur's views is the systemic interpretation, referring, inter alia, to the construction of the normative act; whereas the justification for the historical and authentic interpretation, referring to the legislator's original intention is disputable (cf. the comments on *ratio legis* contained in section 2). Finally, the structure of the legal text constitutes a permanent element of semantically autonomous legal text, open to future, dynamic interpretations.

Changing the Paradigm of Polish Legislation]' in Aleksandra Samonek (ed) *Teoria prawa. Między nowoczesnością a ponowoczesnością* [*The Theory of Law. Between Modernity and Postmodernity*] (Wydawnictwo Uniwersytetu Jagiellońskiego, Kraków, 2012) 99ff.

70 Cf. section 2.

It should be added that Ricoeur, by relating the analysed issue with the hermeneutical theory of interpretation, considers objectivization as "the obligatory transition through explanatory action, which precedes the return to "the party expressing itself". The philosopher has here in mind some aspects of the hermeneutic circle, associated with the dialectic distanciation and appropriation[71], as well as explanation and understanding.[72] From the perspective of jurisprudence, the said "transition through explanation" can be considered a hermeneutic vision of law application process in which subsumption is expressed in dialectics of the objective structure of the legal text and the subjectivity of the interpreter.[73]

Ricoeur summarizes the role of a structural approach to interpretation in the following way: "To understand the text is to follow its movement from sense to reference,[74] from what one says to what one talks about. In this process the mediating role of structural analysis objectively justifies this approach and purifies the subjective approach. It protects us definitively before identifying understanding with an intuitive act of capturing any intention underlying the substrate of the text".[75]

3.2 Legal text as an autonomous literary genre

The question of the structure of the text leads Ricoeur to analyse the considerations devoted to the specifics of different literary genres. Ricoeur raises the question of their role in both the writing of the text itself, as well as in the creation of its variants, such as "poems, narratives or essays". The philosopher believes that literary genres "in their origins" remained "in the same relation to the text as generative grammar is related to the grammaticality of particular sentences". Therefore, Ricoeur notes that literary genres have a function similar to "phonological, lexical and syntactic codes" that "govern" the units of the text, namely sentences.[76] Referring to the problem of the text structure, Ricoeur states that the function of literary genres is to generate "new units longer than sentences" and to organize them as the units which are not reducible "to a simple sum of consecutive sentences".[77] The philosopher stresses that

71 Cf. Paul Ricoeur, 'Appropriation' in John B. Thompson (ed), Hermeneutics and the Human Sciences (Cambridge University Press, Cambridge 1981) 182–7.
72 Cf. Paul Ricoeur, *Explanation and Understanding* in *From Text to Action. Essays in Hermeneutics*, (Northwestern University Press, Evanston, 2007) 125–7.
73 In respect of the hermeneutic law application model, see section 4.1. and 4.2.
74 On the concept of reference see section 4.1.
75 Paul Ricoeur, 'The Model of Text: Meaningful Action Considered as Text' in (n 72) 165.
76 Paul Ricoeur (n 16) 32.
77 ibid.

some of the written wholes are directly produced by the strategy typical of various literary genres, such as poetry.[78] Given the written record as a substantive carrier of the text, conditioned by the literary genre, semantic autonomy of the text as well as "the features of manifestation" (as indicated in point 1 above), characteristic of writing, Ricoeur concludes that the language can be considered as a craft material. Thus, if we consider literature to be such craft, what becomes crucial is the interrelation between writing and creation of a given text. In other words, the record remains in a close correlation with the structure, typical for the texts of particular genres, usually generated by the rules of producing literary compositions.[79]

Having in mind Ricoeur's views, it can be argued that the normative message, correlated with the formal requirements of the legislative technique, determines the specificity of the autonomous literary genre, namely the legal text. This genre is based on "phonological, lexical or syntactic codes", codified in the principles of legislative technique and forming a unique structure and record of laws and regulations. To paraphrase Ricoeur, these principles "generate units longer than legal provisions" that cannot be mistaken for another type of literary text. Moreover, the legal text as a genre is equipped with specific strategies of creating its own subgenres (for example, under the Polish law, the principles of legislative technique regulate separately the formal requirements applied to statutes and regulations). This model brings to mind firmly formalized poetic genres, such as a sonnet or dramatic genres, such as ancient tragedy (the principles of which were expounded by Aristotle in "Poetics"[80]). Next, the requirements of legislative technique cause that lawmaking, more than any literary work, is considered as a craft whose material is provided by the legal language. Finally, in accordance with Ricoeur's views, in the text of statutes or regulations there is manifested the strictest correlation between the record (legal provisions) and the structure (the structure of a normative act), moderated by precise rules of composition.[81] This interrelation between the record and form, undertaken on the basis of the principles of legislative technique, justifies the fact of deeming the legal text "objectively separate" literary genre.

78 Paul Ricoeur (n 16) 34.

79 ibid.

80 Stephen Halliwell, *Aristotle's Poetics* (ed. Stephen Halliwell, Chicago University Press, Chicago 1986) 369.

81 Cf. Andrzej Malinowski, *Redagowanie tekstu prawnego. Wybrane wskazania logiczno – językowe [Editing Legal Texts. Selected Logical-Linguistic Aspects]* (Wyd. LexisNexis, Warszawa 2006); Tomasz Zalasiński, *Zasada prawidłowej legislacji w poglądach Trybunału Konstytucyjnego [The Principle of Proper Legislation in the Views of the Constitutional Tribunal]* (Wydawnictwo Sejmowe, Warszawa 2008).

4.1 The concept of normative reference and its role in autonomizing the meaning of the legal text

Semantic autonomy, within Ricoeur's meaning, is correlated with the issue of text references. In fact, the autonomy is a consequence of the difference occurring between the intended authorial sense and reference, which the text opens before the interpreter.[82] According to Ricoeur, hermeneutic dialectic of the authorial sense and reference is characterized by "a greater complexity", compared with the correlated dialectic of the event and the meaning. The philosopher maintains that it constitutes a model of manifesting in writing such meanings that transcend the original intention of the author. According to Ricoeur, "reference transcends the intended meaning in a peculiar way, namely, the very meaning is considered as the catalyst through which the reference manifests itself, being thus guided by "[the interpreter's] thought (…) through the meaning towards different types of extra-linguistic entities, such as objects, states of affairs, facts, etc."[83]

Therefore, Ricoeur argues that the semantic autonomy of the text (which opens it up "for an infinite number of potential readers at unspecified time") is reflected in the changes of the scope of reference. Their most important consequence is that – according to the philosopher – the interpreter "embraces the world" opened by the text rather than the meaning correlated with particular circumstances of its creation. As Ricoeur notes, "what we aim to understand is not something hidden behind the text, but something open before it".[84] Simultaneously, Ricoeur defines "the world" as "a collection of references opened by texts, including (…) descriptive texts". The philosopher believes that in this sense we can speak, for example, of "the world" of the ancient Greeks, "which does not consist in imagining every time the reality of their lives, but on the realization of non-situational references designated by the descriptive statements of facts".[85]

Ricoeur expresses a personal view that the world is "a collection of references exposed by all kinds of texts, both descriptive and poetic, which he read, understood and loved". Consequently, hermeneutic understanding of the text consists in "placing among the predicates relating to our situation all the senses which form *Welt* (the

---

82 Ricoeur applies the differentiation between sense and reference after G. Frege, *Űber Sinn und Bedeutung* (French translation. [in:] Ecrits logiques et philosophiques, transl. C. Imbert, Paris 1971) 102ff.

83 Paul Ricoeur (n 16) 34. In another text Ricoeur adds that "reference stands for the claim of a proposition to reach reality". See Paul Ricoeur (n 13) 85.

84 Paul Ricoeur (n 75) 165.

85 Paul Ricoeur (n 16) 36.

world) from *Umwelt* (environment)".[86] In other words, according to Ricoeur, "all that points towards a possible world" is subject to understanding. At the same time, understanding has nothing to do with a direct perception of the author's mental life or with the emotional identification with his intention of thought. In the philosopher's opinion, the correlate of "personal assimilation" of the text is not "something that could be felt, but rather a dynamic meaning liberated by explication", identified with the power of opening a certain world by the text.[87] For this reason, the interpretation, "having less than ever to do with the author and his situation",[88] aims to capture the proposal of the world opened up by the text reference. The references uncovered by texts include visions of the world that enable "the extension of the horizon of the interpreter's existence." This latter observation was developed by Ricoeur in the article *The Hermeneutical Function of Distanciation*.[89] The philosopher consistently holds that "only writing", due to its semantic autonomy, "reveals (...) the purpose of the discourse, namely the act of projecting the world".[90] The analysed issue has been commented by Ricoeur as follows:

> "What we have said (...) invites us rather to think of the sense of the text as an injunction starting from the text, as a new way of looking at things, as an injunction to think in a certain manner (...) The text speaks of a possible world and possible means of orienting ourselves in it. The dimensions of this world are adequately open, exposed by the text".[91]

Ricoeur's views, as quoted above, constitute one of the most interesting points of reference to the concept of semantic autonomy in the context of the issue of the legal text. This reference relates to two correlated issues, i.e. a normative reference of the legal text and the hermeneutical law application model.

The issue of the meaning and the reference of the legal text places in the foreground the normative question. As already indicated, according to Ricoeur, the manifestation of the reference involves orienting "interpreter's thoughts" through

---

86 ibid 37.

87 Paul Ricoeur (n 75) 167. This view expresses Ricoeur's critical stance towards utterly intuitive trends in hermeneutics and phenomenology.

88 Paul Ricoeur (n 75) 165.

89 Paul Ricoeur (n 13) 87–8.

90 Paul Ricoeur (n 16) 37.

91 Paul Ricoeur (n 75) 165. Translation on the basis of the Polish edition; the translation of the second sentence is taken from the paragraph left aside in English translation. Cf. Paul Ricoeur, 'Model tekstu. Znaczące działanie rozważane jako tekst [The Model of Text: Meaningful Action Considered as Text]' in Aleksandra Jasińska – Kania (ed) *Współczesne teorie socjologiczne* [*Modern Sociological Theories*] (Wydawnictwo Naukowe SCHOLAR 2006 Vol. 2) 1017.

the meaning "towards different types of extra-linguistic entities, such as objects, states of affairs, facts, etc." The philosopher does not claim, however, that the reference must be of a strictly descriptive character. In other words, Ricoeur does not imply that the world opened by the text cannot be the world of duties. Anticipating the discussion on the correlation between acting, describing and prescribing (developed on the basis of the narrative theory[92]) the philosopher describes the meaning as "the prescription originating from the text" or "the prescription to think in a certain way". Therefore, due to the basic illocutionary mode of the legal text, namely regulation, one can talk about catalysing "normative reference" by its very meaning. Its scope in practice is subject to dynamic changes that result in "new openings" of the world of legal duties in the process of legal interpretation. The extent to which normative reference transcends the meaning intended by the legislator can be considered as a measure of the autonomy of the legal text. The semantic autonomy of the legal text is ultimately expressed in the changes of the scope of the normative reference in respect to the original intention of the legislator.

The normative reference of the legal text is of a complex nature. Referring to a popular conception of the structure of the legal norm, I suggest differentiating its two aspects, i.e. one related to description and the other to duty. The former is correlated with the hypothesis of the legal norm (indicating the addressee of the norm and the circumstances of its application), while the latter – with its disposition (indicating a certain pattern of a proper behaviour specified by the legislator). Therefore, the changes in the scope of the normative reference include dynamic transformations of the scopes of hypotheses and dispositions, thus determining the scope of the interpretation of the legal text. It can be accordingly stated that the autonomization of the normative reference in view of the text's meaning has a twofold manifestation: towards the reinterpretation of the patterns of behaviour and towards the reinterpretation of reality. It is only the dialectic of the aspect of description and obligation within the normative reference that allows the interpreter to adequately embrace the "world of legal duties", which at the same time constitutes the world of reality. It is worth noting that in the hypothesis of a legal norm a general determination of the addressee ("who") and an abstract determination of the circumstances ("kills") is an expression of the intended autonomization of the text in respect of the "here and now" of the historical legislator.[93] The lawmaker

92 Cf. Paul Ricoeur, *Soi-même comme un autre* (L'Ordre Philosophique. Editions du Seuil, Paris, 1990) 167ff.

93 Cf. section 2.

presupposes that a descriptive aspect of the normative act is adequately open "for an infinite number of potential readers at an unspecified time". Therefore, due to the legislator's will, abstract and general hypotheses of norms define a broad horizon of "a possible world" of legal duties. However, the autonomization of the text refers also to the scope of the disposition of norms. This process, though spontaneous and unintentional, expresses a departure from the supremacy of the lawmaker's particular meaning towards the semantic autonomy of the legal text. This process results in "extending the horizon of the interpreter's normative existence" to the world of duties placed out of reach for the author of the text.[94]

The meaning of the dialectics of the aspect of duty and description of the normative reference is reflected in the hermeneutical model of law application. In this model, it is expressed in the dialectic of the legal norm and reality. Ricoeur argues that the application of law is the process of agreeing the meaning of the major and minor premises of the syllogism, namely of mutual approximation and adaptation of the interpretations covering both the legal norms as well as the reality. By this very standpoint the philosopher refers to R. Dworkin's concept of a practical syllogism.[95] In the context of Ricoeur's observations there appear further conclusions about the process of law application. First of all, the meaning of the major premise in "the hermeneutical legal syllogism" is not based on the sense of the legal text but rather on the normative reference opened by the latter. This meaning can be understood as the result of the dialectic of the aspect of duty and description of the reference, thus it is the effect of determining dynamic meanings of the hypothesis and disposition of the legal norm. At the same time, the descriptive aspect of a normative reference ("who and under what circumstances") is determined in the process of interpretation with the description of a fragment of reality, covered by the minor premise of the syllogism. Having in mind the outlined perspective, this process should be identified with subsumption, i.e. subsuming the description of the state of facts under an abstract and general legal norm. In summary, the semantic autonomy of the text essentially affects the process of law application, both through the internal dialectic of a major premise and through subsumption involving the determination of the meaning of the minor and major premise in the "hermeneutical legal syllogism". Applying

---

94 Similar views were presented by Mark van Hoecke: a legal rule and a legal text are not one and the same. The text provides information about the rule, but is not itself the rule. This is precisely the reason why the interpretation of a statutory text may produce a result which may deviate from, or even be opposed to, the prima facie meaning of the text. After: Mark Van Hoecke (n 34) 167.

95 Paul Ricoeur (n 44) 69–70.

law, to paraphrase Ricoeur, consists in implementing the normative references, designated by the descriptive interpretations of reality.

4.2 The concept of the iconicity of the legal text

The problem of the reference raises the question of how, i.e. by what linguistic means, the text opens up "the proposal of the world" before the interpreter. Therefore, Ricoeur introduces the concept of iconicity of the text, whose meaning is explained by the analogy to the techniques used in painting. He begins discussing the concept of iconicity by saying that the work of art in the form of a painting, regardless of the use of technique, "is not something less than its prototype in reality". On the contrary, according to Ricoeur, even a minimalistic work highlights certain features of reality. The strategy of the painter is thus based on a particular multiplication which consists in "reconstructing reality by using limited visual alphabet". The philosopher believes that this "strategy of condensation and miniaturization, by presenting less, gives more". As a result, the most important effect of painting is "giving a greater sense to the world by presenting it as a network of simplified characters". Ricoeur concludes that "this effect of saturation and culmination, within a tiny space of the frame and the surface of a two-dimensional canvas, in opposition to the optical erosion proper to ordinary vision, is what is meant by the iconic augmentation.[96]"

In the case of the legal text "the strategy of saturation and culmination", as referred to by the philosopher, is fully realized through the principles of legislative technique. The proposal of the world of legal duties is opened in such a way that the abstract and general legal norm by "presenting less" in its content, "delivers more" possibilities of its applications. In other words, the legal text emphasizes the normative aspects of reality, thus reconstructing them through minimal means of expression. "The network of simplified characters" of the legal language, generated by the principles of legislative technique, constitutes the tool of autonomizing "the proposals of the normative world" with respect to reality. Thus, the premise of the autonomy of the legal text is "iconic augmentation" of the normative aspects of specific cases, expressed in the abstract and the general content of legal norms.

Ricoeur adds that the abstract art bears some resemblance to science, which "challenges the forms of perception by referring them to non-perceptive structures". In both cases (science and abstract art) the act of "radically challenging directness", which results in "an apparent denial of reality" is considered as "the way of glorifying non-figurative nature of things". For these reasons, according to

96 Paul Ricoeur (n 16) 41.

the philosopher, iconicity in a work of art "is regarded as the manifestation of reality more real than a colloquial reality".[97] Referring the above observations to the issues connected with the text, Ricoeur notes that iconicity is equal to "re- writing reality" [also a normative one – the author's note]. In Ricoeur's opinion, the text, namely "the record of discourse", ultimately constitutes a certain transcription of the world, yet not its representation, but rather its metamorphosis.[98] It should be noted that the deliberations on the iconic augmentation constitute the foundation for Ricoeur's later work, devoted to metaphor.[99]

The philosopher's views meet the trend towards making law more scientific, as expressed in transcending the casuistic thinking, i.e. in "challenging the directness". Such act of challenging can be encountered in common law culture in the form of removing the *ratio decidendi* of a case from *obiter dicta* of a particular situation. In turn, in the culture of statutory law, it is expressed in the systems of concepts – developed by legal dogmatics – which, as "non-perceptive structures" serve the purpose of normative redefinition of human action. One can therefore say that the legal texts capture the normative dimension", namely "a more real" dimension than "the everyday reality". This process, autonomous in respect to reality, consists in multiplying its normative dimension to the level of the patterns of a proper behaviour, i.e. to the level of abstract and general legal norms. To paraphrase Ricoeur, it can be said with confidence that the legal text contains a certain transcription of the world, other than its representation, being rather an autonomous, normative metamorphosis.

The last comment will refer to the hermeneutical model of law application. It should be noted that the subsumption, understood as agreeing premises in syllogism, is possible due to the "iconic augmentation" of the normative dimension of reality in the content of a major premise. "Re-writing reality", i.e. capturing its normative aspects, is a precondition for a reverse application of the normative reference to a real human action. From the perspective of Ricoeur's views, law application is therefore considered as a special case of the dialectic distanciation and appropriation,[100] i.e. the movement leading to an autonomous "normative icon" towards a new re-reading of reality.

97 ibid 42.

98 Iconic augmentation is thus considered as the tool of "spiritualising a written discourse", as indicated in section 1. Cf. ibid.

99 Cf. Paul Ricoeur, *The Rule of Metaphor: Multidisciplinary Studies of the Creation of Meaning in Language* (University of Toronto Press, Toronto 2012).

100 See Paul Ricoeur (n 71) 182–6. Cf. section 2.

Conclusion

The aim of the above analysis was to outline the concept of the semantic autonomy as a certain form of understanding the objectivity of the legal text, alternative in respect of the extreme positivist and hermeneutical views. The position presented in the essay refers to the multi-faceted studies of the text, developed by Paul Ricoeur. The proposed concept refers primarily to a flexible methodology of humanities related to the hermeneutics of literary texts, but it also contains some elements of the structural analysis, inspired by the semiotics of A. Greimas. The presented argumentation focused firstly on the concept of the legal text, characterised in opposition to the "living discourse", including the role of writing as a medium of normative communication. A crucial element of the deliberations was the characteristic of the semantic autonomy of the legal text as a view on its independence from the perspective of the legislator's intention, presupposed addressee and the circumstances of its creation. Additional light on the concept of objectivity was shed by the analyses devoted to the structure of the text, supplemented by the observations about the legal text as an autonomous literary genre, shaped by the principles of legislative technique. The final part of the analysis presented the concept of normative reference and iconicity of the legal text, complementary to the picture of the autonomy in the context of the hermeneutical model of law application. The deliberations were supplemented by Ricoeur's comments relating directly to the theoretical and legal issues (including the codification of law and legal syllogism). When making the final remarks on the concept of the semantic autonomy of the text, one can express the belief that it will enrich the jurisprudential discourse dedicated to the objectivity of law.

Jaqueline Sena

University of Sao Paulo, Brazil

7. The imperative of objectivity and neutrality in legal science and its repercussion on judicial activity: an analysis of the ideas of the Latin-American jurist Luis Alberto Warat

1. Introduction

The issue of objectivity and neutrality in legal science is one of the most relevant themes in the theory of law, especially considering its impact on the question about how judges should perform their activity. This discussion has appeared with legal modernity, but it still does not seem satisfactorily resolved. It is possible for magistrates to keep distance from the facts examined as the judicial function supposedly requires? This article will discuss this issue from the ideas of Luis Alberto Warat, an important Argentine jurist, naturalized Brazilian, who has a relevant scientific production in this regard. In particular, the concept of theoretical common sense of the jurists, that he developed, from authors as Louis Althusser, Michel Foucault and Roland Barthes, to describe the imagery that permeates the science of law: a *corpus* of representations, images, beliefs, fictions and pseudo-certainties that underlies the everyday practice of law and that seems to be scientific, but in reality are nothing beyond a *doxa*[1] disguised *episteme*[2]. The theoretical common sense of the jurists is a series of statements that, while seeking true about various aspects of the legal phenomenon, in particular on the meaning of the rules of law, are merely opinions consolidated, common sense, crystallized. A discourse that proclaims itself as strict speaks, supposedly as results of scientific observations, but that shows its vulnerabilities when subjected to a closer examination. Warat supports that even the requirement of objectivity in the production of legal science, as it was formulated in the modernity, integrates the theoretical common sense.

---

1 Greek word which means popular oppinion or common beliefs, used by the author Luis Alberto Warat.

2 Greek word which means knowlegde or scientific knowledge, also used by the author Luis Alberto Warat, in opposition to the concept of *doxa*.

This paper presents the following structure: first, it provides a brief analysis of the appearance of objectivity requirement in scientific practice, a process that starts with the configuration of the knowledge production process undertaken in modernity. Afterwords, it discusses the shortcomings of this model, its impact on the science of law and on the judicial office. Is it possible to achieve neutrality in the science of law and judicial activity? Trying to answer this question is the challenge of this work.

2. Brief observations on the emergence of the need for objectivity in science in modernity

In the context of the development of sciences, modernity brought claims of objectivity, neutrality and purity. Scientific knowledge was constituted on such standards, which were offered as a safe harbor, conditions to ensure consistency and correctness of reasoning. The complexity of the world was reduced in the name of an obsession with order, calculating and manipulating. According to Warat[3], neutrality and objectivity were illusions widespread as condition for progress, because they camouflaged the impossibility of controlling the phenomenal world and ignored the position of men as inevitable participant in the construction of what is called reality.

Waratargues that, in modernity, there was constituted an imaginary of scientific language, a speech that set certain goals for sciences, that, in despite of being impossible to reach, were presented as conditions of scientific, such as neutrality and objectivity.[4] This imaginary would be a specific manifestation of ideology, somewhat hidden in the sciences, disguised as neutrality.

According to Warat,[5] the impossible goals assigned to the scientific statements were:

> eliminating the pluralities of reality through the illusion of creating unambiguous discourses (here, the ideological thinking is manifested by denying the plural character of praxis and knowledge); proposing the artifice of giving an ultimate meaning to scientific statements; establishing the false possibilities of a grammar of production of knowledge free from mythic components; isolating the language of its historical time; representing

3 Luis Alberto Warat, 'Introdução Geral ao Direito vol. II – a epistemologia jurídica da modernidade' (1st edn, Sergio Antonio Fabris, 1995).

4 ibid.

5 All the translations from Portuguese are mine.

> History; considering the error as polyphony and the truth as univocal; imposing the mirage of the system of language as a safe system to understand the world.[6]

Due to this mythologized imaginary of science, full of subliminal significant, the historical sense of the action of building knowledge was ignored. According to Warat, this distance allows the science to consolidate itself as a power device. This understanding of the product of science as something divorced from the historical conditions of its production is only possible from what this author has called "the myth of double rationality"[7]. He said that in modernity, there was an artificial division of rationality in two different levels, "a daily one [rationality], unable to cleanly grasps reality, and a scientific one, which aims to amount to the immaculate knowledge of realty through self-correcting procedures."[8] This distinction, which leads us to believe in scientific rationality as the only sure way of understanding the world – explains Warat – ends up denying the fact that all knowledge is a social product and therefore subject to historical and political constraints. As reported by Warat:

> Therefore, in modernity, the discussion about the possibility conditions of producing knowledge begins. Those conditions would be brought from the subject's consciousness (and, thus, based on a method), which supposedly would have the power to comprehend the essence of reality, society, and also to understand its own nature. And, in the end, as a great paradox, the nature of knowledge, itself, would have no relation with social aspects and with History.[9]

Warat says that the place of truth in science is also idealized and became part of that imaginary previously mentioned. Since Plato, language was understood as a tool that would express the essence of the world observed, by capturing things in their pure form. Looking at the objects the subject would be able to formulate a mental representation about them, which, after, would be translated linguistically. The truth would be found since this speech represents, precisely, the objects examined.

Science has always had the intention of reaching the truth and this feeling is intensified in modernity, as the man's desperate attempt to order the world around them. And, as Warat concludes, "the position of truth is, than, glorified, authoritatively mythologized".[10]

---

6 Luis Alberto Warat, 'Introdução Geral ao Direito vol. II – a epistemologia jurídica da modernidade' (1st edn, Sergio Antonio Fabris, 1995) 470–471.

7 ibid 471–472.

8 ibid 472.

9 ibid.

10 ibid.

3. The theoretical common sense in sciences and its influence on the scientific production of Law

According to Warat, traditional epistemology distinguished two forms of rationality: the scientific and the common sense (or daily). The first established as its issue to define the parameters of what should or should not be considered as science. The second, despite that it is a form of rationality, should be excluded from the supposedly scientific knowledge, because formed by opinions, metaphysical concepts and ideology. In this sense, scientific rationality assumed itself the task of distinguishing truth from error through the distinction between *episteme* and *doxa*, as if that were possible. However, considering the social and political processes of knowledge production, it is perceived that only political decisions can separate the *doxa* from *episteme*. Therefore, Warat concludes that in social sciences there is a "mythological reasoning that legitimizes a political *doxa* disguised as *episteme*."[11]

This would result in an "imaginary reference from which to establish the inhibitions, the silence and censorship of all the speeches of so-called human sciences".[12] With this, the author means that there is a cluster of pre-understandings, of significant instances of pre-discursive meanings that permeate and give shape to the discourse of truth in the sciences. And also regulate the activity of producers and performers of this discourse, avoiding the questioning of the social roots of the truths produced.

Transporting these findings to the science of Law, Warat develops the notion of theoretical common sense of the jurists. According to him, there are clusters of systematic knowledge that claim themselves as theory and several speeches that seems to be scientific, but that bring in their midst, even in a veiled way, series of ideological assertions and justifications. These sets of knowledge that carries with it a cluster of beliefs, even with a kind of pretended abstraction, favor thc reproduction of ideological contents unnoticed. As stated by Warat:

> Ideology, in its historical materiality, provides a system of questions that give answers that favor its own reproduction. There is no doubt that all the ideological responds constitute a body of knowledge. And in order to clarify this last statement, we would say that the abstract character of ideology appears in the form of a theory. Also, we could say that

---

11 Luis Alberto Warat, 'Territórios Desconhecidos – A procura surrealista pelos lugares do abandono do sentido e da reconstrução da subjetividade', (1st edn, Fundação Boiteux, 2004), 75.

12 ibid.

the complex discourses that produces the ideological thinking, which is an abstraction, is what we call 'common sense theory'.[13]

From this observation, Warat distinguishes scientific theories of ideological ones. He said that while the former are dedicated to understanding the reality, the second reconstructs this reality, rearranging it according to ideological constraints, to ensure the reproduction of dominant conceptions and practices. While making reference to reality, ideological theories are controlled by certain interests – generally the ones of those whom somehow collaborated on their production – in such a way that the answers sought are already pre-determinates. These theories would be moral, because they are based on ethical judgments and, as a consequence, they reproduce the dominant social values. It is, therefore, a knowledge deeply marked by the theoretical common sense.

In turn, the scientific theories seek to build a system of concepts able to explain the reality examined, but with the intention of uncovering the hidden ideological content. To Warat therefore, a theory is scientific if it assumes the existence of hidden ideological constraints on accumulated knowledge, in order to understand the data of reality in its historical significance. A research can only be regarded as scientific, according to the author, when it seeks the transformation of the ideological knowledge – which forms the theoretical common sense – into a knowledge that makes clear the role played by ideology in the process of knowledge production. A scientific theory, therefore, is not the one that simply understands the ideology, but the one that extends the dimensions of reality to reveal the axiological factors that influences the knowledge produced.

Thus, the first concern of those who want to make science should be to build a knowledge object according to a methodology that allow to see clearly when the so-called scientific enunciates are produced as part of a moral knowledge. It is necessary that the scientist does not take the knowledge produced before his theory as a landmark, an automatic reference, and problematize it in order to understand in what sense and for what purposes it was produced. The scientist must ask: what interests this accumulated knowledge serves to? In which historic moment it was conceived? What values dos it alludes to? Scientists must take the knowledge produced to build his object of study only after answering such questions. A theory that is expected to be scientific cannot ignore the prior task of clearing the *theoretical common sense* of ideological knowledge; it needs to be identified before becoming a tool of analysis.

---

13 ibid 75.

Also, Warat notes that the function traditionally set to science – including the science of Law -, that is, to describe the data from reality as if they had their own meanings, it completely ignores the historicity of these data. The objects of study are comprehended as if they were not given a concrete meaning, a foreign meaning that is attributed to it and that affects the way this object is perceived. And so, Warat comes to two important conclusions: first, that legal theories should be characterized as *theoretical common sense* and the second is that any work that pretends to be scientific about Law, should begin by reading symptomatic the *theoretical common sense.*

Warat states that this theoretical common sense refers to "conditions of production, circulation and consumption of the truths in the various practices of enunciation and writing of the Law. This is, a neologism proposed so that we can count on an operational concept that serves to indicate the ideological dimension of legal truths"[14]. From these observations, he developed this concept:

> During their daily theoretical, practical and academic activities, the lawyers are strongly influenced by a constellation of representations (…), by habits of censoring what will be stated; by metaphors, stereotypes and ethical standards that anonymously govern and regulate their acts of decision and enunciation. Therefore, it seems possible to say that we have a protocol of enunciation without interstices. A series of linguistic conventions that we found ready, inside ourselves, when we need to speak spontaneously (…). Visions, fetishes, memories, scattered ideas, abstractions that border the boundaries of our words before they become audible and visible, and that, in despite of this, regulate our speech, are some of the key components for approaching the idea of 'common sense theory'.[15]

According to the Warat, the hermeneutic effort undertaken by lawyers in an attempt to understand and reveal the meaning of the rules of law creates, gradually, a kind of standardized legal culture which is composed by a sort of values, prejudices and views of reality that echoes among the bureaucratic practice of Law without the jurists reflect more deeply about their meaning. To Warat, this kind of knowledge – that is often replicated without distinction – has the implicit political function of reassuring the power inscribed in social relations in order to ensure the maintenance of the *status quo*. As reported by Warat:

> Accepting that Law is a technique of social control, we must recognize that its power can only be maintained by the action of establishing certain habits of significance. There is therefore an accumulated knowledge – diffusely present in the networks of institutional state systems – which is a necessary condition for the exercise of the legal control of the

14 Luis Alberto Warat, 'O Direito e sua Linguagem' (1st edn, Cooperadora de Direito e Ciências Sociais, 1976) 14.

15 ibid.

> society. (...). This knowledge develops a invisible language – the 'common sense theory of lawyers' – inside the grammar of the positive law, which, in its turn, serves political ends.[16]

Warat shows that accepting the notion of the theoretical common sense requires a sort of "semiological complicity" that makes possible to agree with the premise that whatever the philosophers or scientists traditionally called truth is just a complex network of meanings constructed by various discourses on the real. This is a clear evidence of the influence of the Philosophy of Language in the author's thought, because the concept of theoretical common sense only could be understood through a pragmatic perspective, that focus on the communicative context in which scientific theories are created – remembering they are nothing but series of logically statements ordered to form a coherent and convincing discourse on specific objects. Consequently, before conceding the existence of a theoretical common sense of sciences, you must accept the premise that the data do not really have its own significance, but the meanings given to them by the various statements built on it. As believed by Warat:

> From this point of view, the reality is the name commonly used in Western thought to the design polyphonic interpretative versions. The world has no distance from its versions. For this reason, we would be forced to admit that the meanings of a text is not extracted from the subject's consciousness or reality, but from the discursive circulation of ideas. Thus, we must admit the existence of a principle of intertextuality of those discourses from which we can conclude that the meaning of a text depends on its own history, and this history depends on the deaf dialogue with other texts of culture.[17]

Thus, Warat develops the category of theoretical common sense of jurists to characterize the set of idealized representations, images, metaphors, prejudices, values and beliefs that form the axiological institutionalized knowledge that legitimizes the science of Law. It is possible to say that it is through this code, subliminally registered under the statements of the legal discourse, which consolidates "the social functions of law, the political dimensions of law and its role in the design of the state."[18]

Those representations about Law, gradually crystallized in the everyday practice of lawyers and other professionals, give rise to the standards on which the legal rationality holds. And once consolidated, those illusory ideas move by inertia and become the support of new false representations. Inside this vicious circle takes place the processes of production of meanings, which feeds the theoretical

16 Luis Alberto Warat, Introdução Geral ao Direito vol. II – a epistemologia jurídica da modernidade (1st edn, Sergio Antonio Fabris, 1995), 15.

17 ibid 15.

18 Luis Alberto Warat, 'A Pureza do Poder' (1st edn, UFSC, 1982) 55.

common sense; at the same time this process is nourished by it. For instance, it seems possible to conclude that in theoretical common sense "we find out the validity of the traditional belief in forced neutrality of scientific knowledge. Thus, it reproduces the old opposition between science and ideology, which undoubtedly strengthens the dreams of lawyers around a pure science."[19]

By pointing out the existence of a common sense in the practice of lawyers, Warat makes a profound critique of traditional hermeneutics, whose goal was to find the correct meaning of the rules of Law and their real effects, as if they have an unambiguous meaning that could be unveiled by the application of technical interpretation. The existence of a common sense in the practice of jurists, that is, illusory conceptions that give the outlines of legal rationality, shows that lots of statements usually considered hermeneutic truths are merely conventions that serve particular interests. With his critical, Warat calls attention to the need of investigating the true reasons that conditioned the birth of some certainties of legal science, especially those that concern its structure or that concern to the meanings attributed to the rules of Law by hermeneutic practice.

4. The relationship between the *theoretical common sense of jurists* and the question of neutrality in the judicial activity

Considering everything that was said, it seems possible to claim that the requirement of neutrality in judicial activity is a part of the theoretical common sense of jurists. The concept of the neutral judge was created to guarantee the proper functioning of the modern liberal state. Magistrates should be simple machineries and act in a way that would not compromise this rational system. It was understood, at that time, that the trials would only be fair if they represent straightly the commands of the rules of laws, which were considered as inherently fair, because they expressed the popular will. As a consequence, based upon the rules of positive law, the judge did not decide according to his personal will, but according to the people will. Any comprehension about the rules of law based on the judge's personal convictions – instead of based on the community's expectations on the legal system – needed to be avoided, because only the literal interpretation of the law was able to assure justice. Magistrates, therefore, was not given to reflect on the consequences of their judgments, because the evaluation of the standard of justice had been done in the course of the legislative process.

19 ibid 56.

It is clear, therefore, that the standard of objectivity in judicial activity was created as an attempt to minimize the influence of subjectivity in judicial decisions.

The figure of neutral judge was reinforced by the rationalism that characterized the positivist legal science in modernity. The "Pure Theory of Law" developed by Hans Kelsen[20] was conceived within this positivist ideal, which treated scientifically and objectively, and resulted in an effort to rid the Jurisprudence of any trace of subjectivism. However, the amputation of the ideology and the sensitivity of the field of legal science is the serious mistake of the modern theory of law, that now we are forced to repair.

Whether the democratic system worked as intended, especially in countries of late modernity[21] as Brazil – that is, if the laws actually represent the will of the people and were not the result of meticulous political discourse that often makes that certain private interests prevail – then there would be nothing wrong with the neutral judge, that limits its own function to a simply operation of applying the rule of law. However, if the magistrate accepts automatically the standards that represent the interests of few groups or persons, then, this neutrality creates injustice and inequality – instead of equality and justice, as it was supposed to.

It turns out that, despite this disparity between the expectations of the democratic system and its actual configuration, the requirement of objectivity in the performance of the judiciary continues to be defended by many people – consciously or not.

It appears that as a consequence of the dogma of objectivity in judicial activity, the magistrate has become a political agent worried about the commands of the rules of law, but away from reality and not prepared to deal with the intersubjective conflicts. At the same time, it appears that judicial action modeled on strict rationality is no longer sufficient to handle today's complex social relations and the crisis of the democratic system. There is no need to undertake such efforts in maintaining a legal system that is inherently unfair, that ensures better conditions of political representation to a few, and that, therefore, reflects the concerns of privileged minorities. It is not possible to accept anymore the figure of the neutral magistrate, who insists on not recognizing the harmful consequences of an aseptic posture facing so many social ills.

Despite its importance, not many scholars study the issue of neutrality in judicial activity. José Renato Nalini, an important Brazilian magistrate and professor of

20 Hans Kelsen, *Pure Theory of Law* (Translation from the Second German Edition by Max Knight, University of California Press, 1967).

21 Reference to the expression used by Anthony Giddens in *Modernity and Self-Identity: Self and Society in the Late Modern Age* (Stanford University Press, 1991).

Law, is one of the few authors, in Brazil, who deals with this question. According to him, judges are public agents responsible by taking decisions compromised with the fulfillment of the promises of the Federal Constitution – which states equality as one of the supreme values of the Federal Republic of Brazil and reducing social inequalities as one of its fundamental goals. Therefore, the combat of the profound inequalities that characterizes Brazilian society requires magistrates that comprehend the importance of the question of neutrality and its repercussions on their activity.

For Nalini, the judges, in this contemporary context, should have the courage to give decisions that compensate the imbalance that often exists between the parts of a process, giving them specific protection when it is required, especially for those who are in a materially lower position.

In this regard, Nalini supports that:

> If the rule of law does not operates as a way of improving the equality through the elimination of factual inequalities, the judge is not prevented from doing so in the concrete case, in the exercising of jurisdiction. As the other branches of the state, the magistrates have the duty of enforcing the promises of the constitution. The judicial power is not a supra-estate or an extra-estate body. It integrates the state and it is also obliged to observe the constitutional rules that provide, in the future, a country with justice, brotherhood and solidarity.[22]

Hence, it becomes clear that breaking with the standard of objectivity in judicial activity entails profound changes in the relationship between the judge and the parts. According to Nalini, this debate necessarily leads to the theme of otherness. The judge that is not neutral is the one who has the courage to leave out the artificial covering that protects him from the contact with the social harms, is the one that recognizes the "put yourself in another's place" as a prerequisite for being a judge. For these reasons, Nalini states that the image of the judge equidistant from the parties, immortalized in the famous "chiovendiano triangle" must be changed by the figure of a magistrate who tries to deeply comprehend the case, trying to feel like each of the parties, and incorporate their personal dramas.

About this issue, Warat makes an important consideration, when he supports that the normative-positivist rationalism set as the basis of legal science tried to "establish the conditions for producing a kind of 'emotional intelligence' about the Law, that is, forms of reason to avoid emotional decisions and arbitrary decisions".[23]

---

22 José Renato Nalini, 'Ética da Magistratura – Comentários ao Código de Ética da Magistratura Nacional – CNJ' (1st edn, Revista dos Tribunais, 2009) 71.

23 Luis Alberto Warat, 'A Rua Grita Dionísio!' (Lúmen Júris Editora, 2010), 57.

According to him, modernity tried to create institutional mechanisms to control the subjectivity of decisions that should be eliminated at any cost, in order to guarantee that the objectivity of the judicial-legal system would not be compromised. However, this idea, as well as impossible, was grounded on the straight view that confounded the lands of sensitivity and arbitrariness, as if they were both the same emotional dimension. For these reasons, the legal practice – which includes judicial activity – is often surrounded by the abstractions of strict logical-dogmatic thinking, which prevent judges, lawyers and prosecutors to reflect on the conflicts from its sensitive aspects. According to Warat:

> On behalf of the need to control the arbitrariness of the judges, the rationalism aborted the possibility of the interpretation of sensitive decisions and excised from the operators of Law their sensitivity. And, thus, the magistrates decide what the parts of the conflict need in such an insensitive way. And, an insensitive decision is nothing but a result of an arbitrary way of deciding. It is a decision far away from justice.[24]

Therefore, it is possible to say that the theme of otherness has been expunged from the legal reason from its birthplace, what produced a serious impact on the process that the judges use to take decisions. In this context, magistrates were encouraged to act in an aseptic, neutral way, according to the canons of the formal legal methods of reasoning. Also, they had anesthetized their human side, which could not be reflected in the decisions taken. However, considering the new contemporary social challenges, it is becoming more and more evident the inadequacy of the paradigm of the stone guest judge.

Recognizing the inadequacy of the paradigm of neutrality in the performance of the judiciary and the urgency on recovering the value of diversity as a prerequisite for fair judicial decisions leads to the conclusion of the necessary judiciary protagonism. Nalini defends it from the ideas of the French magistrate Antoine Garapon[25], who identified three types of justice today. The first would be the "ritual justice", the one that takes place inside the courtrooms and that focuses on the individual matters, a kind of personification of the economic liberalism of the nineteenth century. The second would be the "bureaucracy justice", which, in turn, would be closer to the administration and therefore would be more inclined to the criteria of performance and productivity rather than the legality. This method focuses its concerns in the search for a formula that allows mass dispute resolution and is based in the automation of processes and not on the quality of

---

24 ibid 56.

25 Antoine Garapon, 'Le gardien des promesses. Justice et démocratie' (Odile Jacob, 1996), reffered by the Portuguese translation from Maria Luiza de Carvalho, 'O juiz e a democracia – O guardião das promessas', (Revan, 2001).

the judicial response given. Finally, the so-called "decentralized justice" or "justice of approaching", which emphasizes the participation of the judge with the society and proposes interventions in addition to offices, that is, a direct contact with the conflict even before they become disputes. This is an enlargement of the field of action of magistrates, which usually act only after required, and start to take part of the territory of the conflict, participating in the Security Council, working for the social reintegration of former inmate of the prison system, having regard to situation of homeless people, and other excluded minorities.[26] This justice of approaching is a new form of judicial action, in which the judge seeks to carry out its role as a public agent compromised with social changes and that helps the promises of the Constitution to become true. And it is not possible to understand this new paradigm but from the recognition of inadequacy, disruption and need to overcome the figure of a neutral judge.

Luis Roberto Barroso, a well-known Brazilian professor and lawyer, also treats the theme of the (im)possibility of neutrality in judicial activity. He supports that the judge's impartiality is one of the aspects of the requirement of neutrality in the performance of the judiciary. As stated by Barroso:

> Neutrality is diluted in many different aspects. Some of them are not difficult to implement, such as impartiality – as the absence of immediate interest in the issue – and impersonality – as the acting that aims the common good, not favoring anyone. Only a serious job and the desire to do well done are required to achieve such necessities. But neutrality presupposes something impossible: that the interpreter is indifferent to the results of his or her work. Of course there is an endless number of cases decided by the judicial power that do not raise inside the judges any other feeling than the one of bureaucratically fulfill their duty. Many other cases, however, involve the choice of values and alternatives.[27]

And Barroso continues, seeming to reach the essence of the matter:

> The idea of neutrality of the state, the law and its interpreters, disclosed by the normative-liberal doctrine, builds on the status quo. Neutral is the decision or action that affects neither subverts the distribution of power and wealth in society in relation to property, income, access to information, education, opportunities, etc. Well: such distributions – that is, the status quo – not the result of chance or the natural order. They are the product of the right post. And often have nothing to fair. The social order is the result of fatalities, dysfunction and even perverse history. Use it as a reference of what is neutral is clearly undesirable, because it means the perpetuation of injustice.[28]

---

26 José Renato Nalini, 'Ética da Magistratura – Comentários ao Código de Ética da Magistratura Nacional – CNJ' (Revista dos Tribunais, 2009), 83.

27 Luis Roberto Barroso, 'Interpretação e Aplicação da Constituição. Fundamentos de uma dogmática constitucional transformadora' (Saraiva, 2009), 292.

28 ibid 293.

The reference made by Barroso about maintaining the *status quo* that becomes possible by the neutral judiciary action means nothing more than perpetuate the theoretical common sense of jurists in the science and practice of Law. The reproduction of the *status quo* through a judicial activity that is not worried about the consequences of the trials is a serious obstacle to the dynamism of the Law. It destroys the emancipator potential of judicial action. The judge that does not perceive the existence of theoretical common sense of jurists works as a mere component of the legal system, which is like a machine intended to maintain a state of inertia; a system that not uncommonly regulates social relations in an unfair manner. Thus, magistrates should make every possible effort to deconstruct the theoretical common sense of jurists, in order to avoid the injustice of the maintenance of unfair legal and social structures.

5. Final Considerations

The requirement of neutrality in the performance of the judicial power was born along the consolidation of modern liberal state, especially based on the principle of separation of powers. The intense political, economic and cultural rationalization occurred in Europe in the seventeenth century, allied to the deep appreciation of the individual recommended by the Enlightenment ideal, enabled a series of changes in ways of organizing society then. Added to the rise of capitalism and the increasing power of the bourgeoisie, the cultural changes occurring in the middle of the Enlightenment culminated in questioning the foundations of the ancient regime, in which the sovereign centralized all authority. It was born a new state model, more suited to the commercial and capitalists of the rising bourgeoisie, in which the principles of legality and separation of powers were of great importance as a factor of limiting the power exercised by the sovereign.

The emergence of the rule of Law in the modern state guaranteed equal treatment among citizens, reducing the abuses of the sovereign and representing the popular will. The requirement of neutrality in judicial activity, therefore, was created in order to ensure a legal system guided by the strict legality. Remaining neutral, judges would respect the separation of powers and thus guarantee the functioning of a fair state, this is respecting the people's desire to have their conduct regulated and judged according to their own self-determination represented by Law.

However, this paradigm of objectivity is not more appropriate to deal with contemporary social problems. This is because, in the contemporary days, it seems that the democratic state is becoming less representative and, consequently, the legal system gradually loses its legitimacy. Laws no longer result from the will of the people. They are rather the result of intense political alliances that serve, in large part, the interests of economic elites who wish to see regulated in favor of subjects that concern the community.

Democracy seems to be exercised only by citizens every four years when they are asked to vote. After that, they are not called to discuss and decide the fate of the *polis*: citizens are neutralized to remain in a subordinate position in relation to actions (and inactions) of administrators and elected officials. In times of crisis of the institutions, including the legal system and also the judicial power, it seems necessary to assume the "non-neutrality" in judicial activity and the need to rescue the sensitivity as a new paradigm of work of the magistrates. It is not possible to keep accepting the neutral position of judges in front of a universe that is clamoring for them to stand up.

The present study, based mainly on the ideas of Warat, tried to discuss philosophically the problem of the role of the judge. This author has shown us, through its proposal for identifying the theoretical common sense of jurists that the actual statements of the science of law are not neutral. He also noted that it is not possible to produce neutral legal knowledge, because language itself is not neutral, free from external influences and socio-historical conditions.

From discovering the existence of a theoretical common sense of jurists in the practice of lawyers, it is important to discuss the ideologies disseminated behind this common sense. This is a rebuilding of the epistemology of the science of Law, a knowledge that cannot ignore the fact that power takes precedence over the practical and legal experience.

It is also possible to say that the requirement of neutrality in judicial activity became a petrified belief, which is taken as truth and that had being rooted in culture and legal rationality. This requirement is not understood as an illusion that needs to be criticized and revised. In other words, it has become theoretical common sense. Thus, considering that the paradigm of neutrality does not resists in front a reality that requires the magistrate to take position in the social conflicts, it is possible to conclude that they can not remain inert as the "guest of stone" or simply be the *bouche de la loi*, as referred by Montesquieu. The actual requirement of neutrality in the performance of the judges was integrated into the theoretical common sense of jurists and therefore must be shattered, deconstructed.

Moreover, the exigency of neutrality in the judicial activity also must be rejected because it is not possible to ignore the creative role of the magistrate, who did not simply say the words of the law, since the rules of Law have no meaning in it. The interpreter in the daily hermeneutic practice gives the meaning. Thus, it is impossible for the magistrate to stay away from the rules he deals with, because somehow he constitutes them.

In conclusion, it is possible to say that the magistrate is not and cannot be neutral. First, because there is no objectivity in the act of knowing, since the subject affects the construction of the object – in the case of judges, they influences the construction of the meaning of the rules of law. Second, because, even if they did not realize, judges reproduce the theoretical common sense of jurists, which is not neutral but full of ideological representations and crystallized values that permeates a legal order that is not necessarily fair.

If the theoretical common sense of jurists is composed by different representations, images, beliefs and illusions present in the science and practice of law that proclaim themselves as product of scientific knowledge, but that, in reality, are replete of ideology, then keeping a neutral position implies acting for the maintenance of ideological meanings petrified by the common sense. That is, a judge who insists on exercising the function without questioning the content of the legal structures – and that does not care about the socioeconomic causes of the intersubjective conflicts and is not worried about the consequences of the decisions taken – will have a performance even more ideological than it might be supposed. Magistrates unconcerned with the ideological aspects of science and practice of law and that chooses not to defend any position, in reality, defends the values crystallized in the law, even if they are unfair.

PART III Historical Perspectives

Cosmin Cercel

University of Nottingham School of Law, UK

8. The Purloined Letter: Law, History and the Theory of Totalitarianism

"[*T*]*o conceal his letter, the Minister has resorted to the comprehensive and sagacious expedient of not attempting to conceal it at all*"[1]

Abstract: This chapter aims to further problematize the question of objectivity within legal and historical discourse by exploring the theoretical intricacies raised by the historiography of totalitarianism. It tries to do so by focusing on the ambiguous status of law within authoritarian settings, one marked by a thorough complicity between ideology and 'legal' normativity. Along these lines, this chapter addresses three core questions, namely the structuring role of the theory of totalitarianism in historical and memorial discourses over the law in authoritarian contexts, the historiographical and jurisprudential implications of approaching the past through this framework as well as the construction of meaning through a historical recollection marked by the paradox of evil law. By underlining the pivotal role of the theory of totalitarianism in the politics of representing the past, I attempt through a genealogical reading informed by the work of Giorgio Agamben and Lacanian psychoanalysis to explore the potentialities of a different rendering of totalitarian law as part of legal modernity. In this way I intend to critically examine the limits of representation of law and totalitarianism in both historiographical and jurisprudential setting.

Keywords: law, memory, psychoanalysis, state of exception, totalitarianism

"[*T*]*o conceal his letter, the Minister has resorted to the comprehensive and sagacious expedient of not attempting to conceal it at all*"[1]

1. Introduction: politics, ideology and the communist past

The question I intend to explore in this chapter concerns the representation of communist past in contemporary debates on law, memory and history. I aim to do so by stressing the importance of critical jurisprudence when approaching the communist legacy as well as by underlying the significance of legal concepts

1 Edgar Allan Poe, "The Purloined Letter" in *The Works of Edgar Allan Poe*, Vol. IV (New York: Armstrong and Son, 1884), p. 412 [1844].

infusing historical analyses of communism. Additionally, drawing on a Benjaminian framework, this chapter asserts the need for a non linear theoretical engagement with the past inasmuch as it tries to draw attention on the limits of legal and historical discourse in approaching the traces of communism. As such, I seek to question the pretence to objectivity of the contemporary consensus over the meaning of the totalitarian experience. In doing so, my intention is to set up the basis for a process of clarification with regard the foundational concepts which inform the symbolic mapping of this history as espoused by the theory of totalitarianism. Along this investigation the contemporary historical *cum* political reading of the law within the totalitarian past shall serve me as a basis for addressing the inherent ambiguities of our present understanding of law's place within our polities.

After keeping the headlines of public debate and scholarly investigation during the two decades following the fall of the Berlin Wall and the sudden implosion of the so called communist bloc, the memory of actually existing socialism started to dissipate in the cultural background, leaving instead a (post)ideological consensus regulated by law[2]. This retreat within the field of transitional justice and memory studies is nonetheless problematic inasmuch as the communist past now risks to be closed for hermeneutical intervention and to become conflated with myths and ideological appropriations. To be sure, that is because the privileged site of ideological construction stays within the sphere of unquestioned cultural production, that area of knowledge which is taken for granted and positively determines our understanding of the present. Inasmuch as "ideology presents the existing social relations as both natural and inevitable; particular interests come to be disassociated from their specific location and come to appear as universal and neutral"[3] ideological appropriation operates a closure of critical inquiry by reifying the intellectual spectrum of analysing the past. In this way, the current entry of the past in the sphere of the unquestionable truth prevents us from engaging with the deeper significance of its legacy.

---

2 See *Report from the Commission to the European Parliament and to the Council: The Memory of the Crimes Committed by Totalitarian Regimes in Europe*, COM(2010) 783 (22nd of December 2010) available at http://ec.europa.eu/commission_2010-2014/reding/pdf/com%282010%29_873_1_en_act_part1_v61.pdf (accessed the 14th of July 2014). For the research serving as a basis to this report see *Study on How the Memory of Crimes Committed by Totalitarian regimes in Europe Is Dealt with in the Member States*, European Commission, 2012.

3 Trevor Purvis and Alan Hunt, 'Ideology, Discourse, Ideology, Discourse, Ideology ... ', 1993, Vol. 44, No. 3, British Journal of Sociology, p. 478.

What is often and rather misleadingly referred to as the communist terror[4], the communist dictatorship(s)[5] or the communist illusion[6] seems to have left the space of critical inquiry and settled within the realm of official history, a history written and read according to the ethical, axiological and epistemological presuppositions which are informing our present. Indeed, as the interpretation of the past is not limited by historical situatedeness, rather it is positively influenced by it[7], it is our present which guides our gaze over the debris of communist historical experience[8]. Consequently, the ideological underpinnings of interpretation of the past and the polemical, if not political, power-knowledge relations through which our present regimes of truth are forged partake to the construction of the historical narrative, of the symbolic encryption of the past into the framework of our present.

Historical truth emerges as a result of the interplay of discourses struggling for hegemony inasmuch as the writing of history takes the form of a narrative. As Hayden White notes,

> the very distinction between real and imaginary events that is basic to modern discussions of both history and fiction presupposes a notion of reality in which "the true" is identified with "the real" only insofar as it can be shown to possess the character of narrativity[9].

Narratives on the past are thus not only necessary reactions to a historical traumatic experience[10], but also sites of struggle over the meaning and the overall significance of the trauma. Hence, the formal conceptual framework one uses when reading, unveiling or recalling the traces of communism, is crucial both to the symbolic reconstruction of its nature as it is to the strategies of coming to terms with its legacy. Because "epistemology is a moral undertaking"[11], and historiography is inescapably

4 Robert Conquest, *The Great Terror: Stalin's Purge of the Thirties*, New York: Macmillan, 1968. See also, Robert Conquest, *The Great Terror: A Reassessment*, Oxford: Oxford University Press, 1990.

5 Vladimir Tismăneanu, *Stalinism for All Seasons*, Berkeley: University of California Press, 2003.

6 François Furet, *Le passé d'une illusion*, Paris, Calman Lévy, 1995.

7 Pierre Legrand, "Comparative Legal Studies and the Matter of Authenticity", 2006, Vol. 1, No. 2, Journal of Comparative Law, p. 427.

8 On the positive aspect of prejudice in the theory of interpretation, see Hans Georg Gadamer, *Truth and Method*, 2nd ed., New York: Continuum, 1989, 372–73.

9 Hayden White, "The Value of Narrativity in the Representation of Reality", 1980, Vol. 7, No. 1, Critical Inquiry, p. 9.

10 Hillary Clark, "Introduction: Depression and Narrative", in Id. (ed.), *Telling the Dark* [:] *Depression and Narrative*, New York: State University of New York Press, 2008, p. 2.

11 Paul E. Glenn, "The Politics of Truth: Power in Nietzsche's Epistemology", 2004, Vol. 57, No. 4, Political Research Quarterly, p. 577.

interwoven to politics as "all historical discourse is susceptible of political uses"[12], a close reading of the philosophical and theoretical context informing our present mapping of communism seems important as a first step in devising a conceptual clarification of the basic discursive tenets guiding the historiographical and legal engagement with the communist legacy.

Regardless of the rather long time span the field of totalitarianism, post-totalitarianism and post-communist transitional studies found themselves at the heyday of historical inquiry, political philosophy and political science, little has been achieved in terms of conceptual clarification with regard to the communist experience. It seems that before losing their momentum, the last decades of post-communist studies were not able to bring forward something more than the all too known departing postulates present in public and academic discourse ever since the emergence of the Iron Curtain. Accordingly, communism is still read as an illegitimate regime[13], a dictatorial practice[14], a murderous adventure or an ideology inimical to democracy[15]. What this long debate over the nature of communist regimes and communist ideology has produced is less a thorough and historically informed critical appraisal of the topics at stake than a moral condemnation of an ambiguous historical experience signified by the unclear denominator communism. Of course, no authentic engagement with the past is or can be waged on morally neutral grounds. But the question of the communist past generally and that of Romanian experience in particular have been asked only under the injunction of a moral obligation of condemning communism[16], a reality which stayed for a long period of time yet unexplored, an experience

12 François Hartog and Jacques Revel, „Note de conjoncture historiographique", in *Id.* (eds.), *Les usages politiques du passé*, Paris: Ecole des hautes études en sciences sociales, 2001, p. 14.

13 Reuben H. Markham, *Rumania under the Soviet Yoke*, Boston: Meador, 1949, pp. 191–207.

14 Dorothy Thompson, *The Truth about Communism*, Washington, D.C.: Public Affairs Press, 1948, p. 15.

15 The criminological discourse has been a constant part of the devices mapping communism. It is worth noting how law and history come together in bringing the penal gaze in these area by treating in the days of McCarthyism Marxism Leninism as nothing short than a 'conspirational cult': See, The American Bar Association, *Brief on Communism: Marxism, Leninism, its Aims, Purposes, Objectives and Practices*, St Paul: West Publishing, 1951, p. 6.

16 See e.g., Vladimir Tismăneanu, "Democracy and Memory: Romania Confronts Its Communist Past", 2008, Vol. 617, No. 1, Annals of the American Academy of Political and Social Science, p. 169, where the author states with regard to the activity of the

which has been already naturalised by a moralistic discourse confusing law, ethics and memory. Indeed, communism was not to be explored on the grounds of its emergence, that is historical experience, nor in terms of its deployment, that is under the categories of intellectual history or the history of systems of thought. Rather it was subjected to analysis only under the aegis of a retrospective condemnation.

Under this light, communism is the Other of the Western liberal democratic order which has become the norm to be followed and conceals its ideological call under the pretence of neutrality. Driven by a hermeneutics of silencing, scholars of communism and transitional studies, activists and public intellectuals intervened in the production of a discourse on the past which played a key-role in the symbolic reconstruction of Eastern European polities. This current discourse, or in lacanian terms *disque-ourcourant*[17], pertains to a strategy of repression. Following the traumatic encounter with the dictatorial other, the politico-legal subject redefines itself according to new processes of interpellation[18]. It selectively forgets and selectively remembers the past inasmuch as it builds symbolic limits in order to keep it at distance. Communism is the Other. And after its disappearance, Eastern Europe is already responding to the Western gaze just as it did at the advent of modernity. Note, at this juncture, how the post-1989 descriptions of the communist past on both sides of the continent have enthusiastically re-enacted the vocabulary of the late 18th century clearly delineating between an European East subjected to tyranny and despotism and the enlightened West protected by law and reason[19]. Consequently, Eastern Europe now rejects communism as its inimical alterity, one which it otherwise fostered for five decades and that is to be sacrificed in order for a new order to emerge[20].

Commission that he was chairing, that 'it was meant to pass moral judgment on the defunct dictatorship'.

17 The term coined by Lacan conveys the image of a disc turning ceaselessly around. It emphisizes at once the radical cut between signifiers and signified as well as the inner irrational deployment of any discourse which ultimately is grounded on the irrational assertion of a master signifier: Jacques Lacan, *Le seminaire, vol. XX, Encore, 1972–1973*, ed. by Jacques-Alain Miller, Paris: Le Seuil, 1975, pp. 33–34.

18 According to Althusser we are interpelated into subjects by ideology: Louis Althusser, "Idéologie et appareils idéologiques d'Etat", in *Id.*, *Positions* (1964–1975), Paris: Editions Sociales, 1976, p. 123 [1970].

19 Larry Wolff, *Inventing Eastern Europe* [:] *The Map of Civilization on the Mind of the Enlightenment*, Stanford, Stanford University Press, 1994, pp. 370–74.

20 René Girard, *The Scapegoat*, transl. Yvonne Freccero, Baltimore: Johns Hopkins University Press, 1986, pp. 25–28 [1982].

If post-communist societies' foundational myth rests on the demise of their past politico-juridical regimes, this disappearance of communism takes the form of a representational elimination. As Girard points out, foundational myths require a symbolic rupture which is narratively construed as effacement or as sacrifice insofar as "[s]omething like a 'radical elimination' does really constitute the high point in the mythical drama and it is supposed to play a crucial role in the establishment of the cultural order"[21]. This new order is our present, an intersection of formalized and constituted modes of being together built under the hegemonic imperatives of global capitalism and its politico-legal instantiations.

At the antipodes, the memory of communism keeps the Western critical tradition in a rather embarrassed silence. With some notable exceptions[22], the failure of the communist political project has been avoided either under the label of ideological fabrication or under that of a treason or a deviation of communist praxis from the theoretical core of the guarantor figures of Marxist orthodoxy[23]. From this line of argument a strategy of denial emerged. Not only really existing socialism can hardly be linked to the Marxist tradition, but also, communism never happened[24]. This is the other side of our (post)ideological consensus. The formal structure of this dominant opposition presents itself as radically asymmetrical. On one hand, one notices an outright rejection of the communist experience, albeit one doubled by a disavowed recognition of its existence. According to this stand, the communist remainder needs to be sanitized, excluded and limited through legal and historiographical frameworks informed by a criminological gaze. On the other hand, we are facing a negation of the anti-democratic historical experience of the post-October revolution arch as a part of the emancipatory project of communism. To its view the unsettling experience of real socialism is rejected as outside the sphere of communism. This relation continues to infuse our political imaginaries in Eastern and Western Europe alike under the guise of a continual trial in which one side claims to have found the culprits for the 20th century political crimes tracing their allegiance back to the revolutionary politics and emancipatory struggle – at times going as far

21 René Girard, "Violence and Representation in the Mythical Text", 1977, Vol. 92, No. 5 *Comparative Literature*, p. 924.

22 Alain Badiou, *D'un désastre obscur*, Paris: Editions de l'Aube, 1998; Jean-Luc Nancy, "*La Comparution*/The Compearence: From the Existence of 'Communism' to the Community of 'Existence'", transl. Tracy B. Strong, 1992, Vol. 20, No. 3, *Political Theory*, pp. 371–398; Jean-Luc Nancy, *La communauté désœuvrée*, Paris: Christian Bourgois, 1999.

23 See Hugh Collins, *Marxism and Law*, Oxford: Oxford University Press, 1982, p. 8–10, where the author dismisses the experience of socialist states as pertaining to communism.

24 Gáspár Miklós Tamas, 'A Capitalism Pure and Simple', 2008, No. 32 *Left Curve*, pp. 66–75.

as 19th century or perhaps to the French revolution itself – while the other half-utters almost indistinguishably an *error in personam* defence.

This silent dialogue is, of course, plural: there are voices on the side of the accuser underlining the ruptures and divisions in communist practice from Marx to Lenin and Lenin to Stalin, there are also other who focus on the multitude of political cultures in which Marxism has been deployed, on the economic and social structures of the communist regimes. On the other hand, there are different ways in which the communist praxis is separated from the progressive tradition of 19th century: war-time communism is rather different from the revolutionary line defended by Marx, Stalinism is hardly a form of communism after all, whereas different forms of national communism are indeed just a step away from traditional forms of authoritarianism.

The deployment of these arguments is mainly revelatory for the politics of reading the past and the values informing the historiographical landscape. It is a matter of relating to an experience which is already constructed as being different from our present institutional and cultural framework. For to be sure, from the standpoint of the official history, national memory and institutional practices, the dominant discourse holds for true that the communist experience has been overcome. The communist past has become now only a legal question which has to be addressed in terms of redress and criminal prosecution. History has entered into the apparently calculable, rational and neutral realm of the law and it is rendered through categories such as crime, criminal organisation, restitution, lustration and arguably reconciliation. The past has re-joined the black letter of symbolic structures and it is now part of the flow of knowledge production ceaselessly assuring us that the contours of our present are there to stay. However, whether the law of the present has come to finally overtake communism and inscribe it into its own grammar, what is forgotten is that communism has been from its very beginning imbued with law, that law has been there and it never ceased to punctuate from within communist theory and practice.

At this juncture it seems important to explain the philosophical underpinnings of my intervention. The fact that communist state ideology opened a specific historical dimension for the uses and the understanding of law raises serious questions around our present project of dealing with the past through legal means. To put it in other words, what is forgotten is that the very medium which is at the core of redressing, rewriting and overcoming the past is already marked by it. To put it in other words, what contemporary debates seem to ignore is "the basic and fundamental problem or at least the jurisprudential danger"[25] which lies in the

25 David Fraser, *Law after Auschwitz*, Durham, NC: Carolina Academic Press, 2005, p. 8.

fact that something called communism has happened and it had indeed a lawful existence. Moreover, it would not be unsafe to assert that its mere historical existence for more than forty years has certainly left an imprint over the ways in which law is thought and practiced. In this sense one needs to take into account a historical materialist perspective in order to be able to approach the dialectical link between our present and its intellectual roots.

As a historically constructed and historically situated cultural artefact, legal discourse is an emblematic example for the 'complex interplay in which what is past and what is present are negotiated through material struggles'[26]. As such, every instantiation of the past as a closed experience has to be regarded with suspicion. That is because the past is a flow whose legibility is determined dialectically by its resonance with the movements of a formless present, which constantly recounts its roots and posits itself as a distinct temporality. As Benjamin writes borrowing from the theological discourse, "the past carries with it a temporal index by which it is referred to redemption"[27]. The historical index is the secret link which ties the present to the experiences of the past, which limits the possibilities of actual actions and our politico-legal imaginary while at the same time rendering the traces of what-has-been readable. The fact that the past enters into legibility and can be redeemed by the work of historians refutes the idea of a past understood as a closed system of signification or as resolved experience. What this view brings to the fore is that the past is a trace inside the very texture of the present which is readable precisely because it intellectually and materially influences our historical situation. As such, "the past can be seized only as an image which flashes up at the instant when it can be recognized"[28].

Such a dialectical relation between now and 'what has been' exposes the limits of both present historiographical and memorial discursive practices inasmuch as it challenges the possibility of consigning the experience of the past to a harmonious narrative legitimising the present. In this sense, an insistence on the material and discursive experience of the legal past is able to critically appraise the ways in which our present posits itself as a historical necessary outcome of old registers of

---

26 Max Pensky, "Method and Time: Benjamin's Dialectical Images" in David S. Ferris (ed.) *The Cambridge Companion to Walter Benjamin*, Cambridge: Cambridge University Press, p. 180.

27 Walter Benjamin, 'Theses on the Concept of History', in *Id.*, *Illuminations*, transl. Harry Zohn, ed. by Hannah Arendt, New York: Shocken Books, 1969, p. 254 (TII) [1940].

28 *Ibid.*, p. 255 (TV).

legality which are held for being outdated and obsolete. Accordingly, "the materialist presentation of history leads the past to bring the present into a critical state"[29].

This retreat of the communist past in the realm of the symbolic is highly ambivalent. A discrete object of the study of past political ideologies and regimes, a case of legal evaluation, a display in a museum of horrors or a nostalgic reminiscence, communism, both understood as a trajectory of an ideology or as material experience inscribed in cultural and institutional practices, has lost its critical thrust. It has become part of the background of assumptions about our present. As such it is the disturbing Other who has to be silenced under the norm of the present. But it is also the spectre which the discourse seeking to close the past involuntarily conveys as the by-product of its own uncertainties. The communist past is thus the unconscious part of Eastern Europe's present, the material of the trauma which law and politics try to come to terms with by anchoring the subject in the present. In this way, the memory of communism is the guarantor of the closure of the potentialities of the present. It is the discursive evidence that the spectre's call is evil and any alternative from the calls of the present – any deviation from its injunctions – are inevitably leading to a temporal return of its framework and of what is portrayed as its criminal outcomes.

One should then resist to this present inasmuch as it obfuscates the problematic status of the communist trauma and of the intellectual devices it ushers in approaching the historical reality of dictatorial regimes. The departing point of our investigation at this stage aims to bring once again into a critical state the nature of really existing socialism. One should thus not shy away from addressing some fundamental questions which past research has either disregarded, or consciously avoided. Consequently, the question to be addressed is to which extent the communist past has been a moment of rupture in the historical becoming of Eastern European legal systems. Such an inquiry seeks to translate in to jurisprudential terms the overarching question over the inherent traits of what we can term wrongly or rightly Romanian communism.

Given its weight in constructing the representational framework of really existing socialism and its illocutionary force in defining the relation between law and politics in communist context, I propose a genealogical reading of totalitarianism as the first stage of an ongoing process of conceptual clarification. After a synoptical reading of the intellectual history of totalitarianism I defend a return to its critical thrust as presented in Hannah Arendt's work. Subsequently, I intend to set

29 Walter Benjamin, Arcades Project, Howard Eiland and Kevin McLaughlin trans. Cambridge, Ma.: Harvard University Press, 1999 [1940], p. 471; N7a, 5.

the basis for a theoretical refutation of the jurisprudential dogmatic assumption that totalitarianism necessarily excludes law and legal practice.

2. Totalitarianism: the genealogy of a concept

Totalitarianism as a descriptive denominator finds its roots in the Italian troubled times of the Fascist takeover. Coined as a critical concept by Giovanni Amendola as early as 1923, totalitarianism was intended to draw attention to what was perceived as a search for forced unity and cohesion under the aegis of the state-control that the Fascist movement pledged to obtain. According to Amendola, the Fascist takeover was aiming at nothing short of instituting a totalitarian system which would amount to an absolute domination of the political life of the country[30]. Adopted by Mussolini in his exhortations in favour of a strong state, it found its first theoretical application in the writings of the prominent theorist of Fascism Giovanni Gentile[31]. For Gentile, Fascism in its revolutionizing movement was a catalysing force which united entirely the body politic of the Nation. This enabled him to speak of the "totalitarian scope of the (Fascist) doctrine which concerns itself not only with political organization and political tendency but with the whole will and thought and feeling of the nation"[32].

The denotative sphere of the concept changes during the 1930s when the word is used to describe critically what was perceived as the oppressive political reality in polities such as Italy, Germany and USSR. To this era we owe also the semantic link between totalitarianism and a series of political trends and power technologies, such as mass propaganda, official ideology, militarism and social control. Bertrand Russell's political writings[33] of the late 1930s and Orwell's literary exploration of the dystopia of 1984, both stem up from the same representational drive attempting to catch the features of modern oppressive regimes. As such the new understanding of totalitarianism "laid a particular stress on how it had the will and the capacity to invade and to destroy hitherto unpolitical – 'unrationalised'

---

30 Giovanni Amendola, 'Maggioranza e minoranza' in *Id.*, *La democrazia italiana contro il fascismo 1922–1924*, Milano, Ricciardi, 1960, pp. 102.

31 On Gentile's relation to Fascism see Gabriele Turri, 'Giovanni Gentile: Oblivion Rememberance and Criticism', 1998, Vol. 70, No. 4, Journal of Modern History 913–933; Sergio Romano, 'Giovanni Gentile, philosophe du fascisme', Vingtième Siècle. Revue d'histoire, 1989, No. 21, pp. 71–82.

32 Giovanni Gentile, "The Philosophic Basis of Fascism", 1928, Vol. 6, No. 2, *Foreign Affairs*, p. 290.

33 Bertrand Russell, *Power [:] A New Social Analysis*, London: Routledge, 2004, pp. 145–65 [1938].

relationships: children's belief in their parents, close friendships, the love between a man and a woman"[34].

The geopolitics of the post-war era, marked by the Manichean antagonism between the presumably communist East and the presumably democratic West added another layer of political and intellectual complexity to the already ambiguous semiotic status of totalitarianism. Popper's distinction between open and closed societies[35] as well as his archaeological search for the philosophical roots of totalitarian thought, offer an exemplary addition to the intellectual history of the concept. Traced back to Plato's Republic, to Hegel's postulates of the State and to Marx's theory of revolution, totalitarianism is another word for a society which refuses dialogue, reason and, above all, any form of contestation[36]. Stemming from a long intellectual thread of historicism, totalitarianism is described as a historical project anchored in Western political thought that post-war democracies should have strongly opposed.

As such, the 1950s bear witness for a rather different use of the concept which is now devised to attest for a scission inside political thought and praxis within the Western tradition. On the basis of this new paradigmatic use, one would be able to sketch the limits of a rigid typology of political regimes, thus clearly delineating between democracy and its radical totalitarian other, or at least be able to draw the general lines of a nosological table of the misuses of governance. This intellectual trend, drawing on the fundaments of an essentialist paradigm attempts to provide an explanation of the deviations from the presupposed normality of liberal democracy.

It is in this epistemological framework that one could situate the work of Carl Friedrich and Zbigniew Brzezinski. Their reading of totalitarianism epitomizes in detail the tensions at work within the broader theoretical framework striving to establish a grammar of political evil. In this sense, driven by a quest of certainty, it posits the limits of a new political typology. It is by the use of new technologies of power that totalitarianism distinguishes itself from older forms of tyranny or authoritarianism. What totalitarianism brings on the stage of history is a refinement of social control through the monopoly over the armed force, over communication and violence in the benefit of the ideology of a single strictly hierarchical party composed of devoted members and guided by a charismatic

34 Abbott Gleason, "«Totalitarianism» in 1984", 1984, Vol. 43, No. 2, *Russian Review*, p. 148.

35 Karl R. Popper, *The Open Society and Its Enemies*, 5th ed., vol. I, Princeton: Princeton University Press, 1966, p. 176.

36 *Id.*, vol. II, p. 260.

leader[37]. Friedrich and Brzezinski's work marks the point where the concept of totalitarianism gains the traits of a syndrome specific to political pathology. From now on, the concept loses its critical undertones and shifts towards becoming an explicative model, which can be safely reduced to the interplay between a determined numbers of factors.

In other words, by recognising a specific distribution of political structural features, one could easily pin down totalitarianism on the panoply of political evils. Accordingly, "the basic features (…) commonly recognized to totalitarian dictatorship are six in number"[38]. These fundamental conditions of possibility of totalitarian rule can be safely described as forming a system of interaction between ideology and power structures. In Friedrich and Brezinski's words, "the pattern of interrelated traits of the totalitarian dictatorship consists of an ideology, a single party typically led by one man, a terroristic police state, a communications monopoly, a weapon monopoly and a central directed economy"[39]. This definition of the totalitarian system along with the image it conceals, that of an all-powerful, uniform and closed state, functioning like an inhuman mechanism, shall constitute itself as the official narrative that the emerging political scientific discourse assigns to the concept.

This process of rationalisation of the concept of totalitarianism, its shift from a critical category to a philosophical apology of Fascism, its return as a critical denunciation of non-democratic ruling and finally its reconstruction as a scientific category, is not estranged from the historical context and its political inflexions. As Marxist readings of the genealogy of totalitarianism point out, in the post-war context "the theory of totalitarianism has become less subtle and more rigid and positive"[40]. Indeed, in this manner, it seems that totalitarianism "adapted itself to the exigencies of the Cold War"[41]. Following this line of argument, totalitarianism is perceived as "stemming from the organicism and holism of right of left and being deductible (…) from this empoisoned ideological source"[42]. One can also suspect the discourse on totalitarianism of insidiously attempting to offer a global

---

37 Carl Friedrich and Zbigniew Brzezinski, *Totalitarian Dictatorship and Autocracy*, New York, Praeger, 1966.

38 Ibidem, p. 21.

39 Ibidem, p. 21.

40 Domenico Losurdo, "Pour une critique de la catégorie de totalitarisme", *Actuel Marx*, 2004, n° 35, p. 127.

41 Ibidem, p. 127.

42 Ibidem, p. 127.

theory of political modernity by reading the "entire horror of 20th century"[43] from a partisan standpoint.

The contextual reading of the concept of totalitarianism also exposes the inconsistences and the internal intellectual tensions inside the discourse producing it. By the end of the 1960s, once '"he moral Cold War consensus eroding"[44], totalitarianism is questioned "by those who had to use it not in the context of ideological struggle, or missionary efforts, but as putatively objective social scientists"[45]. Here one may find one of the paradoxes entailed by the positive rationalisation of totalitarianism, as the concept is compelled to show its vacuity before the empirical evidence of the multitude of real techniques of exercising power. As early as 1967 a new form of scepticism emerged in the field of soviet studies: "today a model which incorporates personal dictatorship and mass terror as essential features is grossly out of touch with the reality of several communist countries"[46]. Caught in the incongruity between the rigid totalitarian model and the more refined analyses of the Soviet world attesting distinct interests and power struggles inside the communist single party system, clientelist power networks traversing society[47], totalitarianism lost its efficiency as a framework for understanding contemporary political systems.

Along these historical developments, the question of totalitarianism as a historical reality itself starts to be radically challenged towards the middle of the 1980s. In this context a historian such as Walter Laqueur overtly asks whether "is it there now or has there ever been such a thing as totalitarianim"[48]. From another standpoint, not estranged from the ethical concerns raised by the memory of the Shoah, a series of debates burst around the legitimacy of positing a structural connection between communism and Nazism such as the concept of totalitarianism seemed to convey. What is already hinted at by this historiographical debate is that a comparative endeavour of the horrors of Stalinism and the Nazi crimes could fuel negationist stands as well as an overall relativisation of the place occupied by

---

43 Ibidem, p. 127.

44 A. Gleason, "«Totalitarianism» in 1984", *op. cit.*, p. 152.

45 Ibidem, p. 152.

46 John Armstrong, "Conclusion", 1967, Vol. 26, No. 1, *Slavic Review*, p. 27.

47 Robert Sharlet, "Systematic Political Science and Communist Systems", 1967, Vol. 26, No. 1, *Slavic Review*, pp. 22–26.

48 Walter Laqueur, "Is There Now or Has There Ever Been Such a Thing As Totalitarianism?", *Commentary*, 1985, No. 80, p. 29.

the Shoah in Western memory[49]. The German *Historikerstreit* of the 1980s following Ernst Nolte's controversial thesis of Nazism being primarily a reaction to the violent excesses of Bolshevism was only a starting point in an ongoing clash between memories of Western political violence. Indeed, not only did the debate cross the cultural boundaries of German historiography but it resonated with the growing intellectual concerns raised by the legacy of communism elsewhere in Europe and beyond.

Robert Conquest's concomitant publication of the *Harvest of Sorrow*[50] reopened the debate around the nature and the scope of communist terror in the English speaking world and pitched one against other traditional historians subscribing to a certain version of the totalitarian thesis and revisionists focused on the social aspects of the real communism. For its part, the collapse of the communist bloc and the explosion of literature in the field of Eastern European studies revived the classical use of the concept of totalitarianism. An iconic example of this shift is marked by the publication of French historian Stéphane Courtois's edited collection proposing nothing short of a moral condemnation of crimes perpetrated by communist regimes[51]. Under the logic informing this project, the nexus between Communism and Nazism is to be found in the scale of the recourse to terror and the systemic character of violence which has become a regular state's instrument. The thesis espoused by Courtois moved close to supporting a moral equivalence between the Nazi and communist crimes founded on "an 'equality' of the suffering of their victims"[52]. In the same line of intellectual engagements with totalitarianism one could also rank the work of intellectuals in former communist countries which were aiming to deconstruct the image of a radical break between communism and Nazism by fully embracing the classical concept of totalitarianism.

Already present in the cultural background informing the *Historikerstreit*, totalitarianism casted its shadow over the reading of the extremes and political violence exerted in European context along the 20s century. It enabled a focus on the purely functional similarities between the two regimes and was at the roots

49 Michael Halberstam, "Totalitarianism As a Problem for the Modern Conception of Politics", 1998, Vol. 26, No. 4, *Political Theory* 459, pp. 459–88.

50 Robert Conquest, *The Harvest of Sorrow: Soviet Collectivization and the Terror Famine*, Oxford: Oxford University Press, 1986.

51 Stéphane Courtois *et al.* (eds.), *Le livre noir du communisme*, Paris, Robert Laffont, 1997.

52 Richard Shorten, 'Hannah Arendt on Totalitarianism: Moral Equivalence and Degrees of Evil in Modern Political Violence', in Richard H. King and Dan Stone (eds.), *Hannah Arendt and the Uses of History*, New York: Berghahn Books, 2007, p. 176.

of steering historiography around themes such as violence, control and political agency. Moreover, its mostly implicit presence, at least during the 1980s, conflated historiographical discourse with moral concerns and added an undeniable political dimension to the writing of the past. By the end of the 20th century, the 'totalitarian' paradigm did not fail to mix in an uneasy tension between history, ethics and politics by postulating in a problematic moral equivalence the horrors of a past which was allegedly overcome by the post-historical sensitivity of the time.

On the other side of the political spectrum the critique of the concept becomes itself more radical. From now on, criticism will be levelled not only against rigid or essentialist readings of totalitarianism, but against the very concept. This criticism aims at exposing the fundamental ideological choice concealed by the use of this concept. In Žižek's words: "is not the notion of totalitarianism one of the main ideological antioxidants whose function throughout its career was to tame free radicals and thus to help the social body to maintain its politico-ideological good health?"[53]. What such a question implies is that behind the (mis)uses of totalitarianism lies hidden a univocal consensus over the reading of the meaning of democracy which is to be interpreted only accordingly to the explicit or implicit norms of the (neo)liberal paradigm.

Totalitarianism thus appears to be "an ideological notion that sustained the complex operation of (…) guaranteeing the liberal-democratic hegemony dismissing the Leftist critique of liberal democracy as the obverse, the 'twin', of the Rightist Fascist dictatorship"[54]. A strange standard of measuring democracy by which one could decide between political health and political pathology, totalitarianism presents itself as "far from being an effective theoretical concept"[55], rather as a "kind of *stopgap*"[56]. According to Žižek's critique this conceptual strategy "instead of enabling us to think, forcing us to acquire a new insight into the historical reality it describes it relieves us of the duty to think or even actively *prevents* us from thinking"[57]. Totalitarianism appears to be an obstacle to "all serious radical engagement"[58], be it in theoretical or even more persistently at the level of political praxis. It is as if through an ironic twist of the history of ideas, the concept of

53 Slavoj Žižek, *Did Somebody Say Totalitarianism?: Four Interventions in the (Mis)Use of a Notion*, London: Verso, p. 1.
54 Ibidem, p. 3.
55 Ibidem, p. 3.
56 Ibidem, p. 3 [original emphasis].
57 Ibidem, p. 3 [original emphasis].
58 Ibidem, p. 3.

totalitarianism would turn into the very instrument of what it used to be critical of, that is, dominant, totalising thought.

However, the Žižekian dismissal of the concept of totalitarianism rather than being a pure rebuttal of the historical reality of the totalitarian phenomenon is mostly levelled against the theoretical deadlock that totalitarianism entails for contemporary political thought. Read through the lenses of lacanian psychoanalysis, Nazism and communism, or at least Stalinism, are forms of political engagement which cannot account for the persistence of the Real otherwise than in a *perverse* manner. The framework informing the psychoanalytical reading of historical totalitarianism departs from the basic assumption that totalitarianism illegitimately confuses the symbolic structure of reality with the Real. As de Kesel points out: "Lacanian theory claims that reality always consists of signifiers that are, as such completely empty, senseless and without any truth"[59]. Accordingly, "every truth claim is built on a kind of of primordial lie, (a proton pseudos) that keeps unsaid that truth rests upon the signifiers' meaningless materiality"[60]. Consubstantial to all human activity, this precariousness of meaning haunts from within any truth-claim. It is neither characteristic of democracy nor of totalitarian orders. What marks the difference is the way one would relate to this foundational incongruity between the signifier and the signified. In this sense, democracy favours repression, that is the constant negotiation between the self-referential meaning construction of the Real as it is represented to the subject by means of the Symbolic and the formless Real, a field outside of reach whose structure stays impossible to the human subject[61].

Repression is thus the 'neutral' state which precedes any meaning-related subjective activity. It is the function through which the subject grounds its identity in the symbolic social structures. On its side, totalitarianism is a *negation* of the contingent, constructed, re-presented trait constitutive of reality[62]. Negation, in this sense, represents a phenomenon characteristic of *perversion*[63], that is of a suspension of the symbolic mediation with the Real. Negation is a structural confusion between the symbolic order sustained by the Big Other and the Real. Totalitarian

59 Marc de Kesel, "Act Without Denial: Slavoj Žižek on Totalitarianism, Revolution and Political Act", 2004, Vol. 56, No. 4, *Studies in East European Thought*, p. 304.

60 Ibidem, p. 304.

61 Jacques Lacan, *Le séminaire, vol. VII [:] L'éthique de la psychanalyse, 1959–1960*, ed. by Jacques-Alain Miller, Paris, Le Seuil, 1987, pp. 55–86 [1960].

62 Kesel, "Act Without Denial: Slavoj Žižek on Totalitarianism, Revolution and Political Act", *op. cit.*, p. 304.

63 Jacques Lacan, *Le séminaire, vol. X [:] l'angoisse, 1962–1963*, ed. by Jacques-Alain MILLER, Paris, Le Seuil, 2004, pp. 135–54 [1963].

perversion can thus be synthesised as follows: it takes truth as having some real foundation, as being the non-mediate expression of a structure with which any relation is discursively impossible.

Such an understanding of totalitarianism points towards the existence of a kernel of ideas that the historical deployment of the concept conveyed and which resists a complete identification with any of its genealogical expressions. The theory of totalitarianism exposes through its tortuous development not only a series of historical problematic associations and confused assertions, but also the tenets of a possible radical critique of the relation between state, violence and ideology. It is precisely this theoretical core that seems obscured by its historical becoming and which under the light of our present seems urgent to reclaim as a terrain for critical analysis of the past.

3. Re-reading totalitarianism: law, state of exception and the uncanny

It may as well be said that the concept of totalitarianism has lost today its path inasmuch as the heterogeneity of its uses is confusing and opens it to illegitimate appropriations and political reification. What strikes the historian in a genealogical reading of totalitarianism is precisely the continual loss of critical thrust which befell the uses of the concept. Indeed, "from a mostly critical concept, totalitarianism will become slowly [...] a device legitimising the existent social order and the advancing neoliberalism"[64]. It would therefore seem that totalitarianism has little to offer to a critical engagement with the communist historical experience of law in Central Europe. The question to be asked is to which extent at the beginning of the 21st century such an old and hollow notion could be used without reproducing the orthodoxy of an academic thought which did nothing short of "elevating it to the rank of ontological confusion" and which steered its shift to "an inevitable transcendental illusion which manifests itself each time a positive political order is directly identified, through an illegitimate shortcut, with the impossible Other of Justice"[65]. Otherwise said, what does remain from the concept of totalitarianism for the theorist searching an intellectual device which would enable countering the narrative espoused by dominant ideology oversimplifying the protean reality of the communist system?

---

64 Alain Caillé, «Démocratie, totalitarisme, parcellitarisme», 2005, No. 25, Revue du MAUSS, p. 102.

65 Slavoj Žižek, *Did Somebody Say Totalitarianism?...*, *op. cit.*, p. 6.

The answer I intend to advance here takes as a starting point the initial critical thrust the concept of totalitarianism concealed at the time of its first instantiations, inasmuch as "[i]mplicit in the idea of totalitarianism is a critique of modernity"[66]. According to Halberstam,

> [totalitarianism] haunts the modern ideal of political emancipation. It conjures up the image of the sorcerer's apprentice, of social and political forces spinning out of control, of a world gone awry, just when it was thought that humanity had made a great stride toward political maturity and intellectual independence, had begun finally to liberate itself from the idols of the past, and was ready to assume responsibility for its own destiny[67]

Even understood in this way, the concept of totalitarianism implies an undeniable notion of nihilism and participates in reinforcing the *status quo* as it stresses the limits of political potentialities. At the same time it also entails a dissolving critical thrust which acts as a reminder of the finitude concealed by any political project. Moreover, totalitarianism marks the limits of the tradition of the Enlightenment as a discourse centred on a metaphysical closure. In Caillé's words, "the interest entailed by the concept of totalitarianism [...] stays with the fact that it marks a limit point beyond which, departing from an exigency of democracy and even of radical democracy, one finds themselves in a reality which doesn't have any relation with democracy"[68].

Hannah Arendt's writings on the totalitarian system appear as a central moment in the analysis of the material history as she tries to take into account precisely the historical tensions and movements which determined its emergence whilst not avoiding the intellectual difficulties and the paradoxes raised by this experience. What Arendt brings to the fore is the sketch of a moving event, of which one is not able to perceive something else than confused traits of an eerie appearance on a background already filled with danger. Totalitarianism is for Arendt the sign or the symptom of an age where the absolute power to mould human condition according to ideology unveils its unsettling reverse. Arendt's radical claim can be grasped clearly when transposed in politico-theological terms.

According to Bernauer "[t]otalitarian horror emerges as a retribution for the sin or hubris of a culture which claimed an absolute power to transform human

66 Halberstam, "Totalitarianism As a Problem for the Modern Conception of Politics", *op. cit.*, p. 462.

67 Ibidem, p. 462.

68 Caillé, « Démocratie, totalitarisme, parcellitarisme », *op. cit.*, p. 102.

condition in accordance with ideological fictions"[69]. Developed at the wake of World War 2, Arendt's investigation seeks to understand the inner logic of the totalitarian event under its double guise, that of Nazism and communism. Her essay in political theory brings to the fore the idea of totalitarianism as *another world* which retreats in front of traditional theories and which challenges common logic. Totalitarian movements and their extreme violence which makes impossible becomes possible demand an innovative exercise in the field of theory. Arendt's reading is thus not a moral condemnation, though her approach is moved by an ethical call of refusal of totalitarianism, but an exemplary exercise in understanding the historical mechanisms of the emergence of totalitarianism. Read against the background of the advent of mass politics, of the call for progress and revolution, of the heydays of colonialism and counter-revolutions, of the rise of nationalism and the surge of anti-Semitism, totalitarianism appears as the excess of a modernity already gone awry.

Under this light, totalitarian systems are to be understood as the expression of a new political anthropology inasmuch as for Arendt, "totalitarianism illustrated the human capacity to begin, that power to think and to act in ways that are new, contingent and unpredictable"[70]. Accordingly, what is underlined is the novelty of totalitarianism, the event that it marks on the stage of history as well as the rift it produces on the scale of Western political thought. In front of the amorphous state violence, theory needs new concepts in order to overcome the paradoxes and the *aporias* entailed by traditional theory. As such, the main reason for which totalitarianism is considered as a break within the continuum of political praxis is its ability of questioning tradition and subverting determinism. For as long as it makes the un-thought possible by its channelling of social forces, it also creates a new object of inquiry for philosophical investigation. What Arendt exposes at the core of totalitarian political praxis, is an "an assault in the very ability to act and to think as a unique individual"[71].

One can note a tension at work between the impossibility of tracing a stable genealogy of totalitarianism, its inner and structural unpredictability according to the frameworks of the philosophy of history, which makes it the expression of a freedom to act beyond any limit posited by tradition and its functioning as

---

69 James Bernauer, "On Reading and Mis-reading Hannah Arendt", 1985, Vol. 11, No. 1 *Philosophy and Social Criticism*, p. 25.

70 Margaret Canovan, "Arendt's Theory of Totalitarianism: A Reassessment", in Dana Villa (ed.), *The Cambridge Companion to Hannah Arendt*, Cambridge: Cambridge University Press, 2000, p. 27.

71 Ibidem, p. 27.

a negation of individual autonomy. In this sense, totalitarianism would express at the same time an unsettling freedom and the end of any individual freedom. Notwithstanding Arendt's quest for understanding totalitarianism, her stand is unequivocal in respect to the political outcomes of its unfolding. As such, "total domination is the only form of government with which coexistence is not possible"[72]. Totalitarianism is hence understood as a limit-case questioning the very core of human political agency. A political evil and political enemy to the political itself, total domination stands for a typology which requires prudence and parsimony in its uses, as it is intimately connected to a specific historical context and a specific technique of exercising power as well as to a particular institutional setting. Therefore, totalitarianism is an eccentric and unstable movement, a singular phenomenon which condones little extrapolation.

What strikes the reader in this account of total domination is primarily its "strangeness", as "the phenomenon she pictures is not only terrifying, but weird and senseless, much less comprehensible than that presented in the dominant model"[73]. Indeed, we can notice a refusal of a general theory of totalitarianism as long as one is far from being "an abstract weberian ideal type used simply to aid research in particular cases"[74]. As such, the first step in the critical reconstruction of the concept of totalitarianism consists in reclaiming its rejection of essentialism as well as its grounding in the sphere of philosophy of history rather than in social sciences. That is so because totalitarianism in Arendt's account is a phenomenon which emerges in the Western tradition of politics at the crossroads between the projects of imperialism and the production of superfluous people.

Totalitarianism is thus the extimate of political modernity, a movement which is guided by a logic of flight, of a perpetual movement towards an aim which is never to be achieved, which is ever to be reached. At the core of totalitarianism lies a "perpetual motion mania"[75]. This continuous flight positively sustained by an apparent precariousness of domination inasmuch as it is personalised, localisable and identifiable contributes to the internal coherence of the movement. In Arendt's words, "if there is such a thing as a totalitarian personality or mentality, this extraordinary adaptability and the absence of continuity are no doubt its outstanding characteristics"[76].

---

72 Hannah Arendt, *Origins of Totalitarianism*, New York: Harcourt Brace, 1975, p. xvii [1958].

73 Canovan, 'Arendt's Theory of Totalitarianism: A Reassessment', *op. cit.*, p. 33.

74 *Id.*, 37.

75 Arendt, *Origins of Totalitarianism*, *op. cit.*, p. 306.

76 *Ibid.*

According to this account, the totalitarian movement reveals itself as a "purely destructive and futile"[77] enterprise. In contrast to the traditional image of the omnipotent totalitarian state supported by coherent and unified institutional hierarchy, Arendt's reading offers the image of a "a shapeless hectic maelstrom of permanent revolution and endless expansion"[78]. The central paradigm underlying totalitarian drive is undoubtedly that of "permanent revolution"[79], totalitarian leadership finding itself under the contradictory burden of a dual task which appears absurd inasmuch as "he must establish the fictitious world of the movement as a tangible working reality for everyday life, and he must, on the other hand, prevent this new world from developing a new stability, for a stabilization of its laws and institutions would surely liquidate the movement itself"[80]. From this standpoint, it would appear at a first glance that any form of normative logic would be an obstacle that total domination would either exclude or circumvent in its deployment. The normative fascinates and irritates at the same time totalitarian motion, as it steers the movement towards achieving its utopian goal by precisely constraining it. Herein lays the paradox of law in totalitarian settings. Owing to its normative nature, law appears as a limit which defends the status quo, but can be as well the condition of the radical change driven by totalitarianism, the means through which a new regime of normality is imposed over the realm of the past.

Law in the totalitarian context described by Arendt is also the bearer of values superior to bourgeois legal facticity. Within the framework of the total state it becomes the avatar of a hyperlegality which goes beyond the limited horizon of positive justice. Law is not called to protect civil rights anymore, but nothing short of the presupposed laws of Nature and History. The weberian bureaucratical model of the Nation state, with its rigid structure and its legal double constructed as a closed system devoid of gaps and lacunae is thus a relic of the past which the totalitarian motion necessarily has to undermine inasmuch as it limits its unfolding. Under this light, it becomes apparent the totalitarian disdain for inner structures and classical normativity "[a] hierarchically organized chain of command means that the commander's power is dependent on the whole hierarchic system in which it operates"[81]. Consequently, "every hierarchy, no matter how authoritarian in its direction, and every chain of command, no matter how arbitrary or dictatorial his

77 Canovan, 'Arendt's Theory of Totalitarianism: A Reassessment', *op. cit.*, p. 35.

78 Ibidem., p. 29.

79 Arendt, *Origins of Totalitarianism*, *op. cit.*, p. 389.

80 Ibidem, p. 391.

81 Ibidem, p. 391.

orders, tends to stabilize and would have restricted the total power of the leader of a totalitarian movement"[82].

According to this reading, the law cannot continue its autonomous and serene life: under the strains of totalitarian movements, it is reduced to being a peripheral phenomenon in the life of the new polities, to a state of 'pure decision'. It is forced to renounce its nature and to submit to a process of transmutation at the end of which it is going to be a simple act of political power. As Arendt writes, "[o]n the language of the Nazis, the never-resting, dynamic 'will of the Fuehrer' – and not its orders, a phrase that might imply a fixed and circumscribed authority – becomes the 'supreme law' in a totalitarian state"[83]. Consequently, what one might witness at a first glance in the presence of the organization of a totalitarian state, is a de-institutionalisation, a form of de-juridicisation of the social structure, a rejection and a refusal of law which spring from the inherent totalitarian tendency towards continual movement – a constant change and becoming which the norms could hardly seize and sustain.

Considering the heterogeneous structure of organs of power with overlapping competences devised to occult the centre of power, the institutional edifice of the totalitarian state reveals as an idiosyncratic construction. Thus the form of the totalitarian state is less that of a political community as it is that of a "secret society established in broad daylight"[84]. At this juncture, Arendt stresses the destitution of the law as a core feature of totalitarian rule, by offering perhaps one of the most compelling reading of evil law in modern setting: "if lawfulness is the essence of non-tyrannical government and lawlessness is the essence of tyranny, then terror is the essence of totalitarian domination"[85]. One should be careful when addressing this construal of totalitarian law, for to be sure, Arendt is pointing towards the novelty and ambiguity of totalitarian rule.

Indeed, for much too long the Western legal thought had a certain difficulty in coming to terms or even to acknowledge the possibility of evil law. As it has been stated with regards to the philosophical underpinnings of such a stand, "[t]he Western tradition has continually affirmed that no one is wicked voluntarily, that Being and Good are the same, and that evil comes from nothingness, that it is nothing but impotence of being"[86]. Comforted by the classical jurisprudential

---

82 Ibidem, pp. 364–365.
83 Ibidem, p. 365.
84 Ibidem, p. 376.
85 Ibidem, p. 464.
86 Jacob Rogozinski, "Hell on Earth: Hannah Arendt in the Face of Hitler" in Ari Hirvonen and Janne Porttikivi (eds.), *Law and Evil: Philosophy, Politics, Psychoanalysis*, London: Routledge, 2010, p. 101.

tradition of natural law as well as by the pure formalism of modern positivism, jurisprudence stood under the Kantian spell of the impossibility of radical evil. In Kant's words: "[m]an (even the most wicked) does not, under any maxim whatsoever, repudiate the moral law in the manner of a rebel (renouncing obedience to it)"[87]. Law, understood either as an instantiation of some form of objective morality, or as a pure formal, content-neutral form, cannot find itself in connivance with totalitarian rule. The (in)famous Hart-Fuller debate over the Grudge Informer case in Nazi law[88], Kelsen's dismissal of totalitarian law as law[89] as well as Fuller's reading of the Stalinist legal order[90], they all point towards the same conclusion. Law, if it is to be called as such, cannot be complicit to illegality or its own transgression.

Yet one has somehow to live and tackle at least with the historical reality of, say, Nuremberg laws or that of the Stalinist Criminal Code, with the reality of lawful deportation orders and that of the construction of the New Man in Berlin and Bucharest alike, one which was an ideological process of interpellation involving legal categories inasmuch as it involved public festivities and mobilisation of the masses. It is against this background that Arendt's destitution of the law should be read. Rather than being pure lawlessness, totalitarianism opens the space for a new form of domination which is unprecedented and certainly bears only a face-value resemblance with traditional category such as despotism and tyranny. Totalitarian terror is to be understood as being precisely "the realization of the

---

87 Immanuel Kant, *Religion within the Boundaries of Mere Reason*, transl. and ed. by Allen Wood and George Di Giovanni, Cambridge: Cambridge University Press, 1998, p. 31 [1793].

88 HLA Hart, "Positivism and the Separation of Law and Morals", 1958, Vol. 71, No. 4, Harvard Law Review, pp. 593–629; Lon Fuller, "Positivism and Fidelity to Law — A Reply to Professor Hart" 1958 Vol. 71, No. 4, Harvard Law Review, pp. 630–642.

89 Although made from a positivist standpoint, Kelsen's dismissal of totalitarian law is twofold, first as a forgetting in his *Theory of law and state*, where in a work of 446 he dedicates only two pages to what he coins as the "party dictatorship", secondly as a misrecognition, where he analysis totalitarian law through the category of "autocracy": Hans Kelsen, *The General Theory of Law and State*, New York, Transaction Publishers, 2006, pp. 301–302 [1945]; Hans Kelsen, "Foundations of Democracy", 1955, Vol. 66 No. 1, Ethics, pp. 1–101.

90 Lon L. Fuller, "Pashukanis and Vyshinsky: a Study in The Development of Marxist Legal Theory", 1949, Vol. 47, No. 8, Michigan Law Review, pp. 1165, where the author stresses that Stalinist law is after all mere law, by stating that "in the process of attempting to operate a great governmental machine, the Soviet leaders have rediscovered some ancient truth. They have learned that state without justice is impossible legality (…) and that some respect must be paid, sooner or later, to the principle of legality".

law of movement; its chief aim is to make it possible for the force of nature or history to race freely through mankind, unhindered by any spontaneous human action"[91]. The unlawful law of this edifice is thus a crucial point in the deployment of the modern totalitarian drive: "the rulers themselves do not claim to be just or wise, but only to execute historical or natural laws"[92]. With the unfolding of totalitarian domination, law is no longer applied, but simply executed inasmuch as it responds to the inner call of the movement. Thus, "terror is lawfulness"[93].

Arendt's paradigmatic reading finds its continuation in the contemporary investigation brought by Giorgio Agamben in the field of legal and political philosophy. Indeed, his reading of the state of exception and of the changes befalling sovereignty in modernity, not only owes much to the Arendtian understanding of the modern undoing of the liberal project[94], but furthers the understanding of the status of law in the context of the unparalleled dissolution of classical concepts of legality and politics that totalitarianism has brought to light. As he writes,

> The totalitarianism of our century has its ground in this dynamic identity of life and politics, without which it remains incomprehensible. If Nazism still appears to us as an enigma, and if its affinity with Stalinism (on which Hannah Arendt so much insisted) is still unexplained, this is because we have failed to situate the totalitarian phenomenon in its entirety in the horizon of biopolitics[95].

The question to be addressed when faced with totalitarianism is not one of raising symbolic and historiographical defences comforting our present *nomos*, not one of asking rhetorically and "hypocritically"[96] how such horrors were possible, rather it is "to investigate carefully the juridical procedures and deployments of power"[97] which rendered possible the advent of totalitarian structures and their laws. It would perhaps be the question analysing "modern democracy's decadence and gradual convergence with totalitarian states"[98].

91 H. Arendt, *Origins of Totalitarianism*, *op. cit.*, p. 465.
92 Ibidem, p. 465.
93 Ibidem, p. 465.
94 Giorgio Agamben, *Homo Sacer [:] Sovereign Power and Bare Life*, transl. Daniel Heller-Roazen, Stanford: Stanford University Press, 1998, p. 10 [1995].
95 Ibidem, p. 85.
96 Ibidem, p. 97.
97 Ibidem, p. 97.
98 Ibidem, p. 10.

In his salient re-reading of the Schmittian concept of *Ausnahmezustand*[99], Agamben points out to the paradox of the state of exception which signals an area in the body of the law where the traditional distinction between law, understood as a normative category and fact, as a descriptive one, becomes inoperative. As he argues, "exceptional measures (...) find themselves in the paradoxical position of being juridical measures which cannot be understood in legal terms"[100]. Far from being a marginal category of constitutional law pertaining to which under the strain of necessity or military threat, the constitutional guarantees have to be suspended in order for the body of the law to be defended by precisely a-legal measures, the state of exception epitomizes the paradoxes at the core of modern legality. According to Agamben, "[t]he particular 'force' of law consists in this capacity of law to maintain itself in relation to an exteriority"[101]. It should be noted here that the state of exception is not the case of a lacuna in the law, but the status of law under the conditions of late modernity, or that of the law as such in the Western legal tradition: "[l]aw is made of nothing but what it manages to capture inside itself through the inclusive exclusion of the *exceptio*: it nourishes itself on this exception and is a dead letter without it"[102]. It is by and through the creation of this zone of indistinction between fact and norm and between an inside-of-the-law and an outside-of-the-law, the application of the law is possible. In this manner the law presents itself precisely "as if the juridical order [*il diritto*] contained an essential fracture between the position of the norm and its application, which (...) can be filled only (...) by creating a zone in which application is suspended but the law [*la legge*], as such, remains in force"[103].

This symbolic crack at the core of the legal system renders it open to appropriations and connivance with politics. It is the space where history, violence and legal discourse come together in rendering the new form of the sovereign which embodies the law through its transgression. Read through these lenses totalitarianism appears thus as the limit point through which the outside of lawlessness and violence become part of the body of the law. To further understand the totalitarian status of the law, a recollection of the Lacanian theory of the Real might appear

99 Literally, "state of exception". As Schmitt notes, "[i]n the exception the power of real life breaks through the crust of a mechanism that became torpid by repetition": Carl Schmitt, *Political Theology*, Cambridge, Ma.: MIT Press, 1985, p. 15 [1922].

100 Giorgio Agamben, *State of exception*, transl. Kevin Attell, Chicago: University of Chicago Press, 2005, p. 7 [2003].

101 G Agamben, *Homo Sacer: Sovereign Power and Bare Life, op. cit.*, p. 18.

102 G Agamben, *State of exception, op. cit.*, p. 27.

103 Ibidem., p. 31.

necessary. In purely semiotic terms the Real is an amorphous structure which resides outside the sphere of the subject and precedes[104] the symbolic structuring of discourse: "without zones, subdivisions, organized highs and lows, or gaps and plenitudes: the real is a sort of unrent, undifferentiated fabric woven in such a way to be fully everywhere"[105]. In this sense, the Real can be understood as "a realm of 'immediate being' that is never accessible in itself, but only appears through the mediation of imaginary and symbolic representation"[106]. In other words nothing meaningful can be said by and of the Real inasmuch as its existence is purely extra-discursive, if not pre-discursive. However, under special circumstances, such as psychosis, traumas or different affects, the Real becomes enmeshed in the structure of the Symbolic, disturbing its consistency. The feeling of uncanny or anxiety are read precisely as a threatening overpresence of the Object of the Real unsettling the overall symbolic structure which renders reality a meaningful constituted narrative. As Lacan notes, in anxiety the "lack lacks'[107], suggesting that "anxiety indicates not a lack to be overcome, but a lack that has not been fully established and requires elaboration in order to be secured"[108].

Thus the nervousness connected to anxiety is to be traced back to a disappearance of the '*loss that made it possible to deal with a coherent reality*'[109], the distance that opens the possibility for the subject to create itself as a distinct entity and to structure the surrounding movement of the Real. It is perhaps not a surprise that the feeling of the uncanny is historically traceable to the romantic reaction to the French revolution[110] and certainly doubles the Hegelian reading of the Revolutionary terror. As Dolar notes, "[t]here is a specific dimension of the uncanny that

104 This concept of the Real would be questioned in Lacan's later work. After *Seminar XI*, we witness the emergence of another version of the Real, one which is posited by the very process of symbolization: Jacques Lacan, *The Seminar. Book XI: The Four Fundamental Concepts of Psychoanalysis*, ed. by Jacques-Alain Miller, transl. Alan Sheridan, New York: Norton and Company, 1978.

105 Bruce Fink, *The Lacanian Subject: Between Language and Jouissance*, Princeton: Princeton University Press, 1995, p. 24.

106 Charles Shepherdson, *Lacan and the Limits of Language*, New York: Fordham University Press, 2008, p. 27.

107 Jacques Lacan, *Le Séminaire. Vol. X. L'angoisse*, Paris: Le Seuil, 2004, p. 53 (1963).

108 Charles Shepherdson, "Foreword", in Roberto Harrari, *Lacan's Seminar on 'Anxiety'*, ed. by Rico Franses, transl. Jane C. Lamb-Ruiz, New York: Other, 2001, p. xlviii.

109 Mladen Dolar, "I Shall Be with You on Your Wedding-Night: Lacan and the Uncanny", 1991, No. 58 October, p. 13.

110 Freud's work on the uncanny (*das Unheimliche*) builds up mainly on ETA Hoffmann's *The Sandman*: Sigmund Freud, "The Uncanny" in *The Standard Edition of the Complete*

emerges with modernity that is closely linked with the advent of modernity and which constantly haunts it from the inside"[111]. Totalitarian law is thus apparent to the psychoanalytical structure of anxiety inasmuch as it describes a point where the unformalized and presupposed laws of history and nature are included at the core of the legal system. It is the place where the otherwise formless exercise of mere violence is rendered lawful.

To sum up, what this psychoanalytical reading traces back to is the possibility of a rendering of the Real inside the framework of the Symbolic. Whether it takes the form of a *rendu* or that of a grimace[112], it formalises semiotically the relation between law and "force of law" or violence as apparent in the structure of the state of exception as a relation between a structured discourse and a disturbing outside irrupting and thwarting the production of meaning. The state of exception in itself thoroughly captures the displacement of law in modernity under the pressure of totalitarian politics. It is perhaps the closest reading of the destitution of the law to Arendt's paradigmatic understanding of totalitarianism as a space in which the law is subjected to change rather than disappearance.

Such a construal of law and totalitarianism is certainly disturbing inasmuch as it points towards the unfamiliar which nests at the core of our familiar image of law as a crucial presence in democratic settings. It blurs, of course, the symbolic boundaries we have joyfully erected in order to sanitize the past, but perhaps does more justice to the historical evidence archived by the body of laws enacted during our communist and authoritarian past, some of which still surviving today. It perhaps reminds us the basic fact that law was a part of the structure of the dictatorships – of the left or of the right alike – not only as a repressive obscure force, but openly, as a constitutive part of the polity. Its traces are still around us, part of our "tainted"[113] legal present, inside our legal dogmatic, our legal principles and legal practices. The past is concealed by the mere fact of being present.

Psychological Works of Sigmund Freud, Volume XVII (1917–1919): *An Infantile Neurosis and Other Works*, ed. by James Starchey, London, Hogarth, 1955, pp. 217–256 [1919].

111 M. Dolar, "I Shall Be with You on Your Wedding-Night…", *op. cit.*, p. 7.

112 Slavoj Žižek, "Grimaces of the Real, or When the Phallus Appears", 1991, No. 58, *October*, p. 48.

113 "Tainted law" is precisely "law that appears to have been produced, or absorbed and "sanitised", by a democratic order but which is connected, explicitly or implicitly, with the anti-democratic past.": Stephen Skinner, "'Tainted Law'? The Italian Penal Code, Fascism and Democracy", 2011, Vol. 7, No. 4, International Journal of Law in Context, p. 440.

David Marrani

Institute of Law, Jersey, United Kingdom

9. Postmodern Evolution of Places of Justice: The Use and Abuse of Transparency

Introduction

A postmodern approach to places of justice has seen judicial architecture moving away from more traditional designs, which has had the effect of 'deconstructing' these palaces of justice. The key question would seem to be: does this affect the importance of the concept of justice and, in particular, the idea that justice has to be 'seen to be done'. As Krier notes, 'All great human institutions are to this day symbolised by classical monuments: St Peter's in Rome, the Capitol in Washington, Westminster in London',[1] and we should add to this list all the great palaces of justice. In fact, 'The dignity, authority and self-respect of such bodies [including the palaces of justice][2] are made visible in the majesty of their architecture'.[3] The risk with postmodern courthouse design, however, is that there is no recognition of such aspects: the new Civil Justice Centre in Manchester provides a useful example here. As observed by Mulcahy in her account of an exchange about the building between Stephen Quinlan and an architectural historian, 'the new Manchester centre [is] not recognisable as a courthouse'.[4] This statement mirrors the results of interviews conducted on the other side of the Channel by Lecourtois about the new Caen courthouse in Normandy. Lecourtois notes that the design triggered a range of public reaction: 'From the exterior it is not as representative of justice as the old courthouse', or 'In the former one, there were the columns, and that is more Roman … Viewed from the exterior one cannot know that it is a courthouse'.[5] Furthermore, in relation to the issue of recognition of a building, we

---

1 Leon Krier, *Architecture: Choice or Fate* (Papadakis Publisher 2007) esp. 177.

2 My emphasis.

3 Krier (n 2) 177.

4 Linda Mulcahy, *Legal Architecture: Justice, Due Process and the Place of Law* (Routledge 2011) 14.

5 Caroline Lecourtois, 'Perception architecturale et image urbaine, le cas de CAEN' *Colloque international « images et citadinité »* (Algers, novembre 2005) 1–10, esp. 5.

need to assess carefully the perceptions, or lack of perceptions, that derive from a building that is unrecognisable.

For centuries, 'traditional' courthouse architecture has clearly 'shown' its judicial authority.[6] Postmodern designs seem to remove clarity from this message conveyed by the buildings, however. Classical judicial architecture has always shown a certain transcendence, something vertical in the design features that express, make visible, the links between God–Monarch–Judge; traditional design suggests something 'sacred', then, that perhaps conflicts with the immanence, the horizontality, of contemporary democracy. If we assume that the signified 'justice' is immutable and the signifier 'place of justice' is not, we must look carefully at the representation of justice in a postmodern democratic environment in which 'horizontality' rather than 'verticality' is supposed to be the defining trait, and in which courthouses have left the sacred in order to enter the capitalist market. As stressed by Resnik and Curtis, 'Most of the new courthouses, often clad in glass to make justice's transparency, celebrate courts without reflecting on the problem of access, injustice, opacity, and the complexity of rendering a judgement.'[7]

Some philological remarks

We may have forgotten in the contemporary era that to apply the law is to exercise a power – the power to decide on the meaning of words. From this perspective, we are all like Humpty Dumpty, who pretended to be a master of this game[8] Thus, I will open this enquiry by looking at the words 'palace' and 'justice', which are connected in the English phrase 'palace of justice' (as it is used in the *Oxford English Dictionary*) or in French, '*palais de justice*'.

'Palace'

The dictionary definition of a palace of justice is as follows: 'In France and French-speaking countries: a building housing a court of law; a law court'.[9] But courts of law, law courts, or courts of justice are, rather, an assembly of judges or other

---

6 Thomas A. Markus, *Buildings and Power, freedom and control in the origin of modern building types*(Routledge 1993) 34–35.

7 Judith Resnik and Dennis Curtis, *Representing Justice: Invention, Controversy, and Rights in City-States and Democratic Courtrooms* (Yale Law Library Series in Legal History and Reference, Yale University Press 2011) esp. xv.

8 Pierre Brunet, 'Humpty Dumpty a Babel? Les juges et le vocabulaire juridique' (2008) 17 *Chronique de Droit Européen et Comparé* (Les Petites Affiches) 1–9, esp. 2.

9 *Oxford English Dictionary* (2011).

persons legally appointed and acting as a tribunal to hear and determine any cause – civil, ecclesiastical, military, or naval. The palace of justice is a law court, a place where law has, or founds, its space, similar to the 'vast and luxurious residence belonging to or having belonged to an important person, a royal residence'. The word palace or *palais* comes etymologically from the classical Latin word *Palatium*, which was the name of one of the seven hills of Rome (also called *Mons Palatinus*).[10] It refers to the imperial residence or temple located on the Palatine Hill, imperial or royal residences in general, and in post-classical Latin, it also refers to (*palatium*) the emperor (4th century), royal officials (7th century), the bishop's palace (9th century), the prince's manor (11th century), and a town hall (12th century). Justice is so intangible, so noble, so sacred, that it needs a strong signifier: it needs to be hosted in a place similar to one devoted to other incarnations of power (emperors, kings and bishops).

'Justice'

According to the *Oxford English Dictionary*, there are three definitions of justice.[11] It is primarily the quality of being just. It also means the administration of the law (linked to the idea of the court and the king) and, finally, it refers to the person administering justice (which is also linked to the court and the king). If these three definitions appear *prima facie* to be naturally connected, the connection occurs, in my opinion, at different levels. If we respect moral values, or divine laws, as 'just' (in the first definition) then there is no need to go further, and no need for the other two definitions. We may reasonably assume that this form of justice can only exist in some sort of ideal society. The organisation of a 'normal' society requires a system that implements respect for the rules of that society, perhaps by way of sanctions, as it is generally agreed that there is a distance between the theoretical vision of contractarian theories and their application. Moving from a state of nature to a state of civilisation should be something that is desired by those involved, so that the rules they give themselves should be automatically respected. The place of justice that is the palace of justice becomes such an important space, such a central element of the 'real' existence of the law, that this is where it takes its full signification: it is a social dimension in which the administration, and the administrator, of the law are positioned. It illustrates perfectly the idea that the

10 Ibid; Although it is likely that palaces were a Greek 'invention'; See, for example, Colin F. Macdonald, 'The Palaces of Minos at Knossos' (2003) *Athena Review*, vol. 3, no 3 <http://www.athenapub.com/11knoss.htm> accessed 11 June 2015.

11 Ibid.

function of a building and the look of the building are intertwined, and in the case of palaces of justice, the perception of the building conditions the process of justice. Justice, Derrida notes, is the impossible. Indeed, 'La justice en elle-même, si quelque chose de tel existe, hors ou au-delà du droit n'est pas deconstructible'.[12] The signified 'justice' is not subject to any deconstruction and is therefore immutable; however, its representation – the signifier 'justice' – is.

This hypothesis, which mixes Derrida's definition and semiotics, leaves us with a signified (justice) and a signifier (the place of justice): the signified cannot be deconstructed and is immutable, but the signifier, a representation of this concept through buildings, is subject to evolution, fashion and trends. The following section will discuss the evolution in courthouse design, from a traditional architecture used in the main representatives of common and civil law legal traditions (in England and France) to a postmodern architecture that claims to be 'transparent'. I will then consider the dilemmas posed by such postmodern courthouse design, and the differences between notions of opacity and theories of transparency.

1. Evolution of places of justice: From traditional (opaque) to postmodern (transparent) law courts

In matters of law court design, according to Lecourtois,

> Trois principes programmatiques paraissent inviter à la mise en œuvre d'une échelle symbolique formelle. Ces principes se présentent sous forme de propositions par lesquelles les architectes sont invités à penser de manière spécifique certains éléments d'architecture. Ces éléments sont: 1) la monumentalité qui doit passer par un vocabulaire architectural spécifique (colonnes, frontons, emmarchement, statuaire); 2) l'ouverture à penser relativement à un traitement de la transparence et 3) la théâtralité ou pédagogie qui doit être mise en scène relativement aux temporalités de la justice.[13]

Justice has to be 'seen to be done': thus its signifier, the place of justice, combines monumentality, a particular use of transparency and theatricality. The place where this occurs plays an important role in the administration of the signified (justice) and for its administrator. Traditional courthouse architecture is an example of the secularisation of the religious architecture of England and France, which I will compare here; it has been questioned recently in discussions among architects about the necessary transparency of postmodern design.

---

12 Jacques Derrida, *Force de Loi, Le 'fondement mystique de l'autorité'* (Galilée 1994) 35.

13 Caroline Lecourtois, '„Espace de la conception" d'architectures judiciaires: les nouveaux palais de justice (Caen, Melun, Nantes, Grenoble et Pontoise)' (2010) *Diagonale Phi.* no. 4, Université Lyon 3, 31–52, esp. 38.

1.1 Comparing the traditional architecture of places of justice in France and England

For traditional architects, the place of justice was a palace of justice in which a complex system of values and ritual(s) were connected to the *architecture parlante*, (speaking or talking architecture). The monumental building opens up the mind through its theatricality, imposing upon the viewer the solemnity of the state and of authority.

The typical architecture of judicial buildings relates to sacred places – temples or churches; in this way, the link to holiness appears to link justice to god(s). In a truly Augustinian way, the temple of the god(s) has here become the temple of the mortal, which imposes a sensational image. Interestingly, the Greek temple 'was always set apart from the town, not only being put in a sacred enclosure, but usually also upon a headland, a citadel or acropolis',[14] while '[t]he Roman temple, like some Baroque church, was a feature in the street; it had a façade with a great flight of steps leading to a richly carved Corinthian portico' (Furneaux Jordan 1993, 46–47).[15] It is no surprise, then, that an architect such as Krier notes that the kinds of buildings discussed here are classical in origin:

> Classical: from Latin classical, of highest class ... make[s] [with the vernacular] distinctions of rank at different levels, between private and public, between individual and collective, between urban fabric and monument, between house and palace ... It is concerned with symbolic language, with the construction and decoration of public structures, with buildings, (...), and monumental features in general.[16]

For neoclassical architects, the place of justice was a palace, 'speaking through allegorical and metaphorical forms', which played with the natural movement of the Earth and the Sun, days and nights, life and death, light and darkness, contrasting the 'temple illuminated by justice' and the 'dark places devoted to crime'.[17] We might sense here the idea of a separation, of a dichotomy, a black and white vision of life and of the world.[18] The place where justice must be rendered is a sacred place because it is illuminated by justice and the light of the truth, which

14 Jordan R Furneaux, *Western architecture: a concise history* (Thames & Hudson 1993) 28.

15 Ibid, 46–47.

16 Krier, (n 2) 53.

17 Thomas Markus, *Buildings and Power, freedom and control in the origin of modern building types* (Routledge 1993) esp. 34–35.

18 We find this in the ritual of the trial itself, which is, in fact, the act of separating the good from the bad, the *triage*.

contrasts with the dark places devoted to crime.[19] We may, like Derrida, think that 'questioning … the very idea of building is aligned with a questioning of institutional authority'.[20] All the apparatus involved in the 'creation' of authority is therefore fundamental. In the case of judicial architecture, what is interesting is the presence of specific judicial ritual(s) that mix with the architecture.

Rather than the neoclassical, architects in England have traditionally used a different type of signifier: the gothic revival. This term (sometimes referred to as Victorian gothic or secular gothic) usually refers to the period of architecture practised in the second half of the nineteenth century (around 1830 to 1870). Eastlake observes,

> The renewal … of a taste for Mediaeval architecture, and the reapplication of those principles which regulate its design, represent one of the most remarkable phases in the history of art.'[21]

Eastlake traces the gothic to the sixteenth and seventeenth centuries, while also examining its re-appropriation in the Victorian era. It is another type of sacred design, as demonstrated by the 'Monasticon Anglicanum'.[22] The 1818 Church Building Act emphasized that Gothic was to be the ecclesiastical style. The commissioners responsible for the financial side of things essentially discovered that a Gothic church cost less to build than a neoclassical one. However, Eastlake notes that the design was adopted for civic buildings when the government decided that the new Houses of Parliament should be gothic.[23] This was reinforced by an acknowledgment of the versatility of the style and its obvious possible secularisation: 'the revival of the Gothic as a versatile style with secular application was the reconstruction of the Palace of Westminster'.[24] Pugin and Barry's design, which won the 1835 competition to redesign the Palace of Westminster after its destruction in a fire in 1834, employs the perpendicular Gothic style both inside and out.

The Royal Courts of Justice (the Law Courts) was probably the most successful Gothic public building after the St Pancras railway station. A restricted competition involving major architects of the day, including Barry, Waterhouse, Scott and

---

19 We may agree with Lacan that 'Truth begins to be established only once language exists'; Jacques Lacan, *My Teaching* (Verso 2008) 29; Hence, the notion of jurisdiction, *juris diction*, the place where the law is said.

20 Mark Wigley, *The Architecture of Deconstruction: Derrida's haunt* (MIT Press 1995) 47.

21 Charles L. Eastlake, *A History of the Gothic Revival* (Longmans, Green and Co 1872) 1.

22 Ibid, 2.

23 Ibid, 187.

24 Anthony Sutcliffe, *Architectural History of London* (Yale University Press 2006) 100.

Street (among 11 entries) was held in 1866 (Port 1968). The judges made no award at first but after much confusion selected Barry's plan and Street's elevation. In 1868, however, the contract was given to Street alone.[25,26] The main frontage was a multi-element stone design in a thirteenth century French style. The Gothic hall leading from the entrance was supposed to be similar to that found in the ritual of justice in France, a *salle des pas perdus*, with dimensions of 70m by 15m by 25m, like Lincoln Cathedral – another demonstration of the connection with the sacred.[27]

The Gothic Revival seemed to give a form to a particular feeling for the spiritual and for tradition, which were already associated with the monarchy and traditional English conservatism; neoclassical style, on the other hand, seems to voice the rational and the radical that is associated with the republicanism of France and the USA. It was therefore a nationalist or even a dogmatic nationalist discourse of 'speaking architecture' that developed in the nineteenth century. We should add that for Krier,

> In traditional cultures, invention, innovation and discovery are the means to modernise time-honoured and practical systems of thinking, planning, building, representing, communicating in the arts, philosophy, architecture, language, the sciences, industry and agriculture ... They are the means to an end ... Fundamental aesthetic and ethical principles are deemed to have universal values which transcend time and space, climate and civilisation. In modernist cultures, invention, innovation and discovery are ends in themselves ... There are no longer any universal ethical and aesthetic categories.[28]

1.2 Questioning what is here

The design of law courts matters. It matters particularly because recent years have seen the construction of radically different designs of courthouse buildings. I believe this should be questioned, and that we need to analyse how this new trend in courthouse design affects public understanding of the places and spaces where justice is done. One of the problems encountered in the representation of justice is that palaces of justice have imitated temples and churches, which has connected them

25 In appendix 283, he explains that St Pancras was a Venetian Gothic design, the 'first instance of the adaptation of medieval design for such a purpose in London'.

26 Eastlake (n 22) 128.

27 Sutcliffe, (n 25) 106–107; Pugin was strongly influenced by Lincoln Cathedral. See for illustration 'Pugin: God's Own Architect' <http://www.bbc.co.uk/programmes/p00n58pm> accessed 15 March 2015.

28 Krier (n 2) 51.

with the religious and the spiritual.[29] According to Latour, 'Now that the modernity of our world is coming to a close, we understand that it was no more secular than any other'.[30] The divide between the religious/the secular seems to vanish, or to have vanished. As a space where the ritual of justice develops, the place of justice is a microcosm that evidences the vanishing of this divide. As Duncan notes, 'A ritual site of any kind is a place programmed for the enactment of something. It is a place designed for some kind of performance', where 'participants perform or witness a drama – enacting a real or symbolic sacrifice'.[31] Could we apply this statement to 'postmodern' courthouses? For centuries, the traditional architecture of courts has clearly demonstrated authority[32]; modernism seemed to follow the same trend, but postmodern designs seem to be removing the clarity from the message conveyed by the buildings. For Jencks, 'Modern architecture died in 1972'[33]; postmodern architecture emerged as a critique of modernism. It is 'committed to pluralism, the heterogeneity of our cities and global culture, and acknowledge[s] the variety of tastes, cultures and visual codes of the users';[34] it employs 'curves, blobs, folds, crinkles, twits or scattered patterns', and 'sends complex messages, ones that often carry ironic, dissenting or critical meaning, those that challenge the status quo'.[35] This statement goes to the heart of the main issue: the function of the building and its design are connected, linking the appearance and the institution. For Heidegger, 'to appear' is what is in front of us; what 'appears', as in ancient Greek 'what is instituted', always meant what was left in front of us[36]. It could therefore be the case that as the signified justice is immutable, its signifier should not depart too much from the traditional way of representing it, otherwise the meaning of the complex messages

29 This has also been the case for museums, as explained by Duncan; See Carol Duncan, 'The Art Museum as Ritual' In Carol Duncan *Civilising Rituals, inside public art museum* (Routledge 1995) 7–20, esp. 7.

30 Bruno Latour, 'Visualisation and Social Reproduction: opening one eye while closing the other… a note on some religious paintings' In Gordon Fyfe and John Law (eds) *Picturing Power: Visual Depiction and Social Relations* (Sociological Review Monograph 35, Routledge 1988) 15–38, esp. 34.

31 Carol Duncan, 'The Art Museum as Ritual' In Carol Duncan *Civilising Rituals, inside public art museum* (Routledge 1995) 7–20, esp. 12.

32 Thomas Markus, *Buildings and Power, freedom and control in the origin of modern building types* (Routledge 1993), 34–35.

33 Charles Jencks, *The New Paradigm in Architecture: The Language of Postmodernism* (Yale University Press 2008) 9.

34 Ibid, 2.

35 Ibid.

36 Martin Heidegger, *Qu'appele t'On Penser?* (3rd. edn, PUF 1959) 189.

given out could be lost. In other words, we cannot play with the architecture of the courts of justice as we may play with other types of buildings, even those of other political institutions, without facing the risk of justice losing meaning.

We must question judicial architecture because, as explained by Derrida, 'the questioning of the very idea of building is aligned with a questioning of institutional authority'[37]. It is indeed the case that the design of public buildings resounds throughout the society of which they are supposed to be a part. Primarily, as previously mentioned, they represent a huge and long-term investment.[38] In fact, 'institutions are understood as buildings that can be displaced only by rethinking architecture'.[39] For Derrida, therefore, the rethinking of institutional politics turns out to be architectural.[40] What we see, what is put in front of us, what appears, is thus of significance. What is re-*presented* becomes a necessity in the buildings of political institutions, as 'we have delegated to hundreds of non-human lieutenants the task of disciplining, making, and moving other humans or other non-humans'; we thus have 'instruments [that] bring faraway places, objects and times to us which are thus represented – this is presented again – for our inspection'.[41] These public buildings are in fact the only proof, the sole evidence, of political power, its main and only representation, its main and only signifier: they give *soul* to the political through the eyes of whoever looks at them. Let us not forget that there is a crucial difference in law between the natural person and the legal person (artificial): in the case of a natural person, we have a real person; in the case of a legal person, we have a fiction. In consequence, one 'exists' while the other does not; one is 'alive', the other is not. Krier considers this issue when he writes, 'the value of ancient monuments does not reside in their material age but essentially in the quality of the ideas that they embody'.[42] These buildings are the signifier of signified ideas: they give them a

37 Mark Wigley, *The Architecture of Deconstruction: Derrida's haun* (MIT Press 1995) 47.

38 See HM Treasury (n 1); Also <http://www.ogc.gov.uk/documents/CP0067AEGuide7.pdf> accessed 11 June 2015; In addition, 'The long lifespan of the existing building stock means the majority of it will still be in use between 50 and 100 years' time' see Bullen P.A, 'Assessing Sustainable Adaptation of Existing Buildings to Climate Change' (COBRA 2004: The international construction research conference of the Royal Institution of Chartered Surveyors, 7–8 September 2004, Leeds Metropolitan University. London: The Royal Institution of Chartered Surveyors Foundation) 5 <http://www.rics.org/site/download_feed.aspx?fileID=2162&fileExtension=PDF> accessed 11 June 2015.

39 Wigley (n 38).

40 Ibid, 48.

41 Latour (n 31) 15.

42 Krier (n 2) 73.

'body'. This is particularly true for ideas such as justice and the law. Legal persons, including public persons, like corporations or states, need something, perhaps like a magician's trick, to give us the feeling that they are what they are, because '[t]he language of institution is that of buildings'[43] and, of course, because 'there is no institution without representation'.[44] An institution is supposed to create the presence of a fiction (a legal person) that is absent. Representation is the presence of the absent. In this sense, representation gives life to the institution, and 'institutionalises' it.

We could apply here, by analogy, Derrida's considerations on representation in his comments on Rousseau. He states that the signified 'sovereign people' are represented by 'the assembly', and therefore they are the representative signifier.[45] The institution will rule for, and on the behalf of, the sovereign. The representation follows a primitive presence and brings a final presence, and occurs when the signified is absent – as in the present case of justice. Derrida goes on to demonstrate that the representative is not the represented (the signifier is not the signified) but is only the representative of the represented (only the signifier, in fact). As representative, it is not simply the other of the represented.[46] This re-presentation brings the absent into the moment. It focuses on the signifier by giving it the function of representing the absent signified. Justice, our signified, is represented by the palaces of justice – its signifier. It brings us the impossible, the absent, and of course, the design that is adopted matters: depending on the radical nature or even the brutality of the design, it will give different representations of what justice is (or is supposed to be). From those designs, we may feel or perceive the authority of political power, what it wants to say about itself and about us, about individuals and society. It seems significant then that in our contemporary world all is being done to 'dismantle' traditional representation. While 'in democracy popular taste continues to have easier access to aristocratic than democratic high art',[47] signifiers of the places of justice are becoming transparent and architects claim to be in a process of opening up the old opaque courthouses.

1.3 Discourses of transparency

It seems extraordinary to witness the almost constant use of (the argument of) transparency by architects involved in the design of new courts. It seems obvious

43 Wigley ((n 38) 51.
44 Ibid, 51.
45 Jacques Derrida, *De la Grammatologie* (Editions de Minuit 1994) 418.
46 Ibid, 419.
47 Krier (n 2) 21.

for contemporary designs to be using glass and steel or aluminium. But if these are used for private dwellings and commercial buildings, does it mean we should or could use these materials everywhere, in all cases? We know that a legal person needs representation, and that a legal person encompasses public and private entities. But does applying the same treatment to the design of a commercial office block and to a public building make sense? What about in courthouses? To illustrate this point, I will use the case of the new Bronx courthouse designed by Uruguayan architect Viñoly. Viñoly is well known for designing commercial buildings that use a lot of glass. His design was a typical example of a postmodern courthouse, which opened in 2007. The façade of the courthouse is a great example of the use and abuse of glass and aluminium. But there is something more interesting here than the use of specific materials: the discourse supporting this use. Given the frequent use of glass, it is perhaps unsurprising that we find a systematic use by the architect of 'transparency' in the justifications for, and explanations of, his design:

> Rafael Viñoly, architect of the Bronx courthouse, sought a design that would give the judicial system an image of openness and transparency, rather than the opaque, closed feeling of the traditional courthouse. 'What interested me was transforming the public's perception that the building … represented an institution that was seen as closed and in need of protection from the community' … The [new] building speaks to the participatory and the democratic nature of the judicial system and its fundamental and constructive mission in our society.[48]

Womack-Weidner go on to note,

> The feeling of transparency and openness permeates the building. The courtrooms, jury deliberation rooms and robing rooms, all of which are in the interior of the building, have natural light from clerestory windows that 'borrow' daylight from the corridors between the courtrooms.

A non-exhaustive selection of articles in specialist and non-specialist publications brings further clarity to the argument, in which transparency is everywhere:

> This is achieved [transparency][49] by not concealing the building functions behind a representational face, but by allowing the buildings' program, structure and circulation to be viewed, providing a literal and metaphoric transparency of the judicial process.[50]

---

48 Anita Womack-Weidner, 'New York Opens Second Mega-Courthouse' (fall 2006) Benchmark, Journal of the New York State Unified Court System 2, no. 3, 1–2.

49 The author emphasis.

50 'Bronx County Hall of Justice' (2011) <http://architypesource.com/projects/61-bronx-county-hall-of-justice/description> accessed 15 March 2015.

The Bronx Criminal Court Complex, through its form and transparency, will redefine the relationship of the courthouse with the surrounding community. Glass is used to convey a sense of openness that stands in sharp contrast to traditional courthouse design.[51]

> 'The architects believe that this facades system gives the building an open and unintimidating appearance –all of its functions remain on public view, providing literal and metaphoric transparency to the judicial process.[52]
>
> Its project director, Fred Wilmers, called the courthouse 'a metaphor for the transparency of the judicial system, the openness of government.'.[53]

Located on 161st and 162nd Streets between Sherman and Morris Avenues, the Hall of Justice is a visually dynamic glass building where judicial transparency is not only a metaphor but also quite literal. With forty-seven courtrooms, seven grand jury rooms, the Department of Corrections, the Department of Probation, and the Bronx District Attorney's office, it is one of the largest courthouses in the country.[54]

Sometimes, a critical but rather isolated view is expressed:

But just as we recognize the protective value of transparency in government, and in the justice system, literal transparency can be a security feature, too. In the eighteenth century, the philosopher Jeremy Bentham envisioned a prison – the Panopticon – in which inmates could be under constant, surreptitious observation. Viñoly's courthouse is a compassionate Panopticon: It allows everyone to observe everyone else. This doesn't obviate the need for cameras or guards, but it limits the possibility of nasty surprises.'[55]

It is perhaps logical to have such a glass building and the many resulting statements about transparency in this context, but we should carefully consider this discourse about the use of glass/transparency because it collides with notions of openness and democratic processes. In fact, 'an equation of glass and access to

---

51 'The Bronx Criminal Court Complex' (2001) <http://wirednewyork.com/forum/showthread.php?t=3685&page=1> accessed 15 March 2015.

52 'Open curtain wall gives transparency to the judicial process' (2011) <http://archrecord.construction.com/projects/bts/archives/civic/07_bronxhall/default.asp> accessed 15 March 2015.

53 Robert Hilferty 'Jury Beauty' (*New York the Sun*, 26 February 2008) <http://www.nysun.com/arts/jury-beauty/71877/> accessed 15 March 2015.

54 "Viñoly in the Bronx' Opens in Art Gallery' (*Lehman College E News*. Vol. 3. 2009).

55 Justin Davidson, 'Bronx Clear, How a courthouse polices us through the glass' (*New York*, 4 February 2008) <http://nymag.com/news/intelligencer/43599/> accessed 15 March 2015.

justice is simplistic (...)'.[56] Transparency has been used by architects to push certain postmodern designs, certain representations of buildings, of legal persons, and they have not differentiated between public and private functions in so doing. It does not mean the design is actively wanted by the decision makers, as a true choice, but rather that the decision makers have followed the statements made by those who are supposed to know about buildings – the experts – the architects.[57]

According to Supreme Court Justice Felix Frankfurter, 'Justice must satisfy the appearance of justice'(Offutt v. United States 1954).[58] We could interpret this idea of the appearance of justice in many ways. Notably, I could drag this idea to the extreme end of the spectrum of 'appearance'. Here, the notion that justice has to be 'seen' to be done is fully translated by a glass building – a building so transparent that anyone can see inside it. For Mulcahy, 'Transparency is seen as undermining mystique and inviting public participation by rendering surprises less likely.'[59] The place where justice is (or is supposed to be) done should be 'opened' through the use of glass in postmodern court buildings. A new myth, a new great narrative, seems to emerge and to be based on a new paradigm: transparency. It is as if we were taking the affirmation that justice must be seen to be done a step further. Indeed, what is better than a transparent process, delivered in a transparent building? We are facing a new dilemma of postmodernity, of postmodern architecture: we want a transparent process in a transparent building, but are we certain that a transparent building is the way forward for conveying this new transparent process?

2. The dilemma of postmodern courthouse design: Transparency v. Opacity / Opacity v. Transparency

This section will further develop the discussion of transparency put forward by the architects. As mentioned, courthouse architects should operate on a symbolic scale. They should implement elements such as monumentality to demonstrate power and authority, together with a certain amount of transparency to open

56 Resnik, Curtis (n 8) 341.

57 We should keep in mind the lacanian 'subject supposed to know', the analyst, who is thought by the 'subject supposed to believe', the patient, to know everything, including his secret; Slavoj Zizek, *How to Read Lacan* (Grant Books 2006) 28–29.

58 Jerome S. Bruner, 'Foreword' in Oscar G. Chase *Law, Culture and Ritual: Disputing systems in cross-cultural context* (NYU Press 2005) xi.

59 Mulcahy (n 5) 152.

minds and theatricality for pedagogical purposes.[60] Lecourtois refers here to a certain level of transparency, not to full transparency, and she also notes that it merely concerns any demonstration of democratic values.

Transparency is fashionable in general architecture. We can walk the streets of many cities around the world and see clear examples of 'transparent' architecture, where buildings have a considerable amount of glass on their façades. But if perhaps it seems unimportant to question transparency in commercial buildings, this 'fashion' in architecture overspills into public building design and, more crucially, to the design of courthouses. To question this, we will next consider transparency in architecture and in psychoanalysis, and analyse how opacity is in fact the true transparency: the use of 'transparency' is more concerned with power. Finally, the next section will 'gaze', with Lacan, at (or through) a transparent building.

2.1 Transparency: Architecture and Psychoanalysis

If, using transparency, I deconstruct completely the opaque and old fashioned court of justice (or rather what we are told is an opaque, old fashioned design), I would not really 'see' the place of justice as a palace anymore, because it does not seem to suit the historical and human context of the 'liberal democratic/capitalist' era. The word transparent comes from Medieval Latin, *transpārēnt-em*, and is a present participle of *transpārēre*, composed of the prefix *trans* and the verb *pārēre*, to appear, to be visible. It also relates to *transpicio*, to see through. In addition, transparency relates to parenting: trans-parent. We therefore have a word that tells us the story of something that moves from one side to another and opens something. 'Trans' comes to us with the sense of coming 'across, through, over, to or on the other side of, beyond, outside of, from one place, person, thing, or state to another', but also 'across, crossing', or 'beyond, on the other side of', and finally, 'beyond, surpassing, transcending'. The trans-parent is, accordingly, something that goes beyond, or on the other side of the parents (both parents), and that gives access to the parents. What more is needed to convince us that transparency is about hierarchy and verticality. It is about power and control, rather than about openness and democracy?

It should be noted that there are many discussion of parenting in psychoanalysis, and we find the notion of transparency in psychoanalysis, particularly its loss; indeed, 'while Freud preached the loss of transparency, the Enlightenment

60 Caroline Lecourtois, '„Espace de la conception" d'architectures judiciaires: les nouveaux palais de justice (Caen, Melun, Nantes, Grenoble et Pontoise)' (2010) Diagonale Phi. no 4, Université Lyon 3, 31–52, esp. 38.

philosophers emphasized the gain of transparency'.[61] If transparency appears important, it is through its loss that psychoanalysis considers it. Transparency is not new. Resnik notes its political roots in the philosophy of Rousseau. (Judith Resnik 2011, 342)[62] For Bessire, transparency has been around since at least the nineteenth century, moving from the aesthetic into every field of study[63]; it is therefore not surprising to see transparency in fields such as architecture and law. However, we should consider the relationship between the two, in light of new court design as it relates to 'justice', and should keep in mind that psychoanalysis could provide some useful insights here. But first we should return to architecture, and to do so I will refer to Rowe and Slutzky's 1963 article on transparency both literal and phenomenal.[64] Rowe and Slutzky demonstrate the polysemy of the word transparency as follows:

> According to the dictionary definition, the quality, or state, of being transparent is both a material condition – that of being pervious to light and air – and the result of an intellectual imperative, of our inherent demand for that which should be easily detected, perfectly evident, and free of dissimulation. Thus the adjective transparent, by defining a purely physical significance, by functioning as a critical honorific, and in being dignified with far from disagreeable moral overtones, becomes a word which from the first is richly loaded with the possibilities of both meaning and misunderstanding.[65]

This striking statement shows *prima facie* the difficulties we face: the many possible meanings of the term and, of course, the potential for misunderstanding. It is also critical, I believe, to any study on court buildings. If the possibilities for diverse meanings and misunderstandings are vast, then the use of 'transparency' in court buildings carries these diverse meanings and misunderstandings, although the signified 'justice' remains unchanged. For Rowe and Slutzky, 'Transparency means a simultaneous perception of different spatial locations'[66]. Transparency not only abolishes distance but also produces immediacy: there is nothing to mediate, no

---

61 Weinert Friedel, 'Sigmund Freud: the loss of transparency' in Weinert Friedel *Copernicus, Darwin and Freud: Revolutions in the History and Philosophy of Science* (Wiley-Blackwell 2008, 185–270) 188.

62 Resnik, Curtis (n 8) 342.

63 Dominique Bessire, 'Transparency: a two-way mirror?' In Barrie Pettman (ed) *30 years of IJSE: Festschrift in honour of Professor John O'Brien* (Emerald Group Publishing 2005, 424–438) 424–438, esp. 425.

64 Colin Rowe and Robert Slutzky, 'Transparency: Literal and phenomenal' (1963) Perspecta 8, 45–54.

65 Loc. cit.

66 Loc. cit.

'protection'. Rowe and Slutzky open their enquiry by defining transparency in relation to painting, then move to architecture, in a process reminiscent of what Lacan did when he introduced architecture to the discussion of 'anamorphism … in a discussion of the role and function of projection' again emphasising the connection between architecture and psychoanalysis.[67] Rowe and Slutzky consider two types of transparency: 'Transparency may be an inherent quality of substance, as in a glass curtain wall; or it may be an inherent quality of organization. One can, for this reason, distinguish between a literal and a phenomenal transparency'.[68] Literal transparency here means the use of materials that make a building transparent (the glass walls and open floor plates of Gropius's Dessau Bauhaus, for example, while phenomenal transparency refers to an effect, a perception of what is created by a particular organisation of 'things' (the facades and interior spaces of Le Corbusier's Villa Stein at Garches, for instance).[69] Rowe and Slutzky observe:

> Literal transparency … tends to be associated with the *trompe l'oeil* effect of a translucent object in a deep, naturalistic space; while phenomenal transparency seems to be found when a painter seeks the articulated presentation of frontally displayed objects in a shallow, abstracted space.[70]

They add:

> Provided with the reality rather than the counterfeit of three dimensions, in architecture literal transparency can become a physical fact. However, phenomenal transparency will, for this reason, be more difficult to achieve; and it is indeed so difficult to discuss that generally critics have been willing to associate transparency in architecture exclusively with a transparency of materials.[71]

As summarised by Holm, 'Colin Rowe and Robert Slutzky define phenomenal transparency as a conceptual effect of modern spatial configurations, to be distinguished from properties of glass and other materials that allow for the penetration of the vision'.[72] Phenomenal and literal transparency are related to architectural *trompe l'oeuil*, one being the opposite of *trompe l'oeil*, while the other is linked to

67 Lorens Holm, 'What Lacan said re: architecture' (2000) Critical Quarterly vol. 42, 29–64, esp. 31.

68 Loc. cit, esp. 46.

69 Loc. cit.

70 Colin Rowe and Robert Slutzky, 'Transparency: Literal and phenomenal' (1963) Perspecta 8, 48.

71 Loc. cit. 49.

72 Lorens Holm, 'The New Yorkers' (2007) Architectural Theory Review vol. 12 no. 2, 104–120, esp. 115.

trompe l'oeil,[73] creating a (literal) transparency that has as its corollary a (phenomenal) opacity.[74]

'Transparency' is therefore not as simple as it seems, and we can, therefore, understand why decision makers might rely too much on 'those in the know': architects are supposed to know how complex these issues are. Another issue it seems relevant to question is the reason for using transparency, or the reason for using opacity. What are we hiding, and what do we want to show? Looking at (primitive) architecture, Holm observes that it is 'organised around emptiness', and 'enters the symbolic order by a process of "primitive sublimation"';[75] it thus relates to Freud's *Das Ding* 'the Freudian Thing'.[76] This emptiness appears as 'the presence of a hollow, a void, which can be occupied by any object and whose agency we know only on the form of the lost object, the *petit a*.' *Petit a* in lacanian theory is that which is lacking; as Zizek states,[77] it is something that will never be, 'except by circumnavigating the eternally lacking object'.[78] Architecture therefore both encloses emptiness and circulates around the lost object: the transparent quality of a building might correspond to the search for what is lacking. The opacity of traditional court buildings shows something that is present, while transparency shows us something absent that *should be* present: transparent court houses show us the entrance to the void. However, 'the signifier (symbolic order) screens us from the real'[79] and the opacity of the building appears to be crucial in the mechanism of mediation, creating distance and authority. That said, Holm goes on to state, 'Architecture is an empty temple awaiting the entry of God in a "lightning -flash of individuality"'.[80] This is a clear statement on the quality of the signifier, the building, and the link between the 'temple' (the sacred signifier) and individuality, or even subjectivity, which is instrumental in the perception of courthouses. To paraphrase Holm, architecture evolves and becomes not only something that encloses emptiness, but that represents it: it represents the absence of what is represented.[81,82] We

---

73 Lorens Holm, 'What Lacan said re: architecture' (2000) Critical Quarterly vol. 42, 47.
74 Lorens Holm, 'The New Yorkers' (2007) Architectural Theory Review vol. 12 no. 2, 15.
75 Lorens Holm, 'What Lacan said re: architecture' (2000) Critical Quarterly vol. 42, 29.
76 Loc. cit.
77 Slavoj Zizek, *The Fragile Absolute: Or, why is the christian legacy worth fighting for?* (Verso 2000) 145–146.
78 Lorens Holm, 'What Lacan said re: architecture' (2000) Critical Quarterly vol. 42, 33.
79 Loc. cit, 34.
80 Loc. cit. 36.
81 See also Jacques Derrida, *De la Grammatologie* (Editions de Minuit 1994) 418.
82 Lorens Holm, 'What Lacan said re: architecture' (2000) Critical Quarterly vol. 42, 43.

arrive at the postulate that 'an architecture which represents itself ... might appear behind its representation. [this would be an architecture] that 'signif[ies] the presence of an absence'. In the case of postmodern design, we do have the feeling of a complete absence. The signifier has 'opened' its facade in order to 'show' what is inside but there is nothing there – nothing but the 'objet a, the absent object which is the cause of desire, but which never satisfies desire'.[83] The void is authority, in my opinion, and the interaction between opacity and transparency highlights the true misrepresentation designed by the expert architects.

2.2 Transparency as the true opacity, opacity as the real transparency

Because I am analysing buildings, and perhaps because of the pertinence of psychoanalytic theory to this analysis, this section looks at the setting of the first psychoanalytic place: Freud's office. Freud's study in Vienna creates a space that is specifically organised for the then-new technique of analysis. In his papers on technique, Freud indicates that 'the doctor should be opaque for his patients and, like a mirror, should show them nothing but what is shown to him'.[84] What is important is the specific space created, which will foster the dynamic between the analyst and the analysand; the positions of the actors are, to Freud, adequate for the purpose. The location of the patient at initial contact is the classical doctor-patient face-to-face situation. The patient faces the doctor, but with a twist. He is central, but is facing a mirror placed on a window. The patient sits and faces his own image. What he sees is his reflection in the mirror. When Freud sits, he blocks the view of the mirror.[85] The mirror functions simultaneously as a window, as do the mirrors in Etruscan tombs, assisting the passage to the other world. Lacan's analysis of the mirror instructs us to 'think of the mirror as a pane of glass. You'll see yourself in the glass and you'll see objects beyond it'.[86] He dislocates the opposition between transparency/reflexivity, as with the position of the mirror on the window in Freud's study. The relationship between opacity and transparency in psychoanalytic theory is, therefore, as in architecture theory, not as straightforward as we might think. In the building, the bricks or concrete block the view from outside to the inside. They elaborate a psychic image of what is inside, because the facade (face), and hence the importance of its design, creates a specific feeling

83 Loc. cit. 44.

84 Diana Fuss and Joel Sanders, 'Berggasse 19: Inside Freud's Office' in Joel Sanders (ed) *Stud: architectures of masculinity* (Princeton Architectural Press 1998) 112–139, esp. 120.

85 Ibid, 120–121.

86 Ibid, 121.

when ‘it appears’; it is put in front of us, as Heidegger observes.[87] In a building made mostly from glass, there is no separation, no distance, because of its transparency. There could be an elaboration of an image but this image would be of another type of building: a shopping mall, an office block. The brick or concrete wall operates like the mirror that reflects an image of authority while a transparent glass wall cannot foster that psychic image.

1.

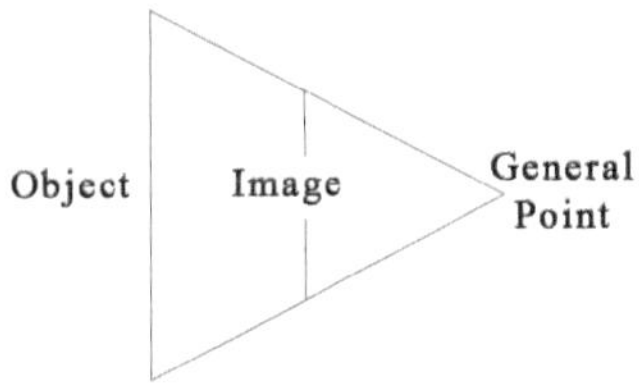

2.

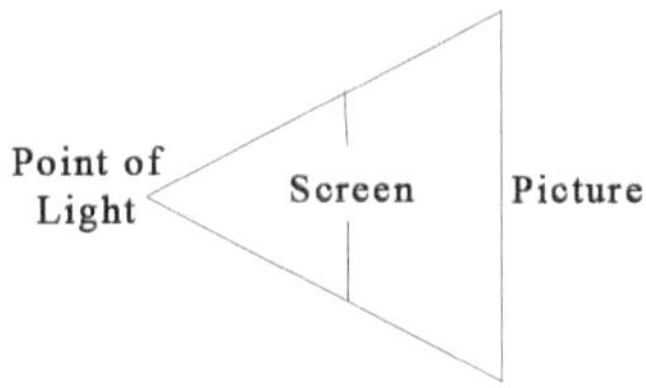

3.

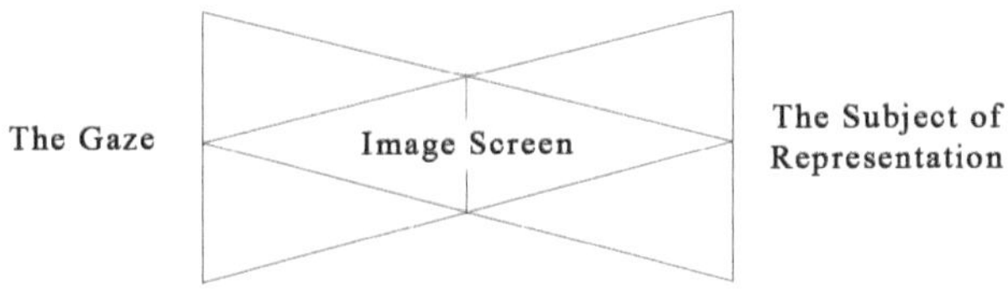

The image|screen of the linear perspective found in Lacan’s diagram is ‘both transparent (image) and opaque (screen). Any image is both a transparent window onto the world (Alberti the perspectivist’s metaphor) and a solid surface that reflects light’.[88] It is ‘the negotiated locus of identity and desire’[89] but also, and more importantly for our case, it provides a view of the world.[90] However, the view of the world appears to be different for a subject facing one type of court and a subject facing another type. The notion of the view of the world is therefore primordial to this essay as it refers to an additional process, that follows vision, the one of

87 Heidegger, *Qu’appele t’On Penser?* (3rd. edn, PUF 1959) 189.
88 Lorens Holm, ‘The New Yorkers’ (2007) Architectural Theory Review vol. 12 no. 2, 109.
89 Loc. cit.
90 Loc. cit, 110.

interpretation, which connects with the symbolic order found in lacanian theory. According to Holm, 'A plane reminded us that a twin tower is a symbol',[91] and if we transpose this point to courthouses, we find that a building that hosts the process of justice may be a 'real' building but it hosts one of the fundamental institutions – justice (and is therefore also 'symbolic').

In order to look further at the transparency of the building, we need to return to our earlier questions: transparency – to what end? Opacity – for what purpose? What are we hiding and what do we want to show? The function of the building and its face/façade are connected. According to Lacan, the interior is present in the exterior. In addition, Miller notes, 'the most interior – this is how the dictionary defines "intimate" (*l'intime*) has, in the analytic experience, a quality of exteriority'.[92] Thus, the façade of a building explains the inside. What appears in front of us tells us what is behind. The term interior is connected to the term *intimus*. It helps us to reach the deepest point in the interior: 'the most intimate is at the same time the most hidden'.[93] The point made by Miller about Lacan's work in this regard is that 'the most intimate is not a point of transparency but rather a point of opacity'.[94] The argument many architects make about transparency can therefore be read through lacanian theory: the idea that being able to see through a building will tell us the story of the process of justice being done inside, according to a democratic ideal, may make the design of a transparent building seem obvious. However, the notion that one may show the interior of the building through use of literal transparency (glass, windows) as a means to show its intimate mechanisms, to reach deep inside the process of justice, is false; one has to be able *not* to see through, even though this may seem prima facie to be contradictory. These things have to be hidden, as it is through opacity rather than through transparency that the most intimate level is reached. Psychoanalytic theory tells us that transparency does not give us access to the inside. A transparent palace of justice does not bring so much as a glimpse of the democratic process inside, for instance, or show that a fair trial has taken place.

---

91 Loc. cit, 114.

92 Jacques-Allain Miller, 'Extimité' In Mark Bracher, Francoise Massardier-Kennedy, Marshall W. Alcorn and Ronald J. Corthell (eds) *Lacanian Theory of Discourse: Subject, structure, and society* (NYU press 1997) 74–87, esp. 76.

93 Ibid; Miller also describes the notion of extimacy, a lacanian neologism created to explain that what is intimate is something or somewhere else. Interestingly, Lacan considers that extimacy is (p. 78) related to the Other of the Other of the signifier, the Other of the law, the Other that lays down the law to the Other, the Law as absolute, a metalanguage; see Ibid, 78.

94 Ibid.

For Holm, 'It is a dual paradox of the transparency of vision and the opacity of representation that seeing them *as if* they get smaller is to see them *as* the same size'.[95] Indeed, the 'visual field is composed not only of what I see, but what you see – this latter is usually more important – in so far as what you see is communicated to me by words, pictures, and other media, all of which constitutes what Lacan calls the field of the Other'.[96] What becomes important, then, is what you see: 'I do not see your view, but I frequently know what you see, especially if I am in it'.[97] The gaze becomes another key variable here. It is the presence of the Other: the subject is viewed not only as subject but also as the internalised presence of significant others.[98]

2.3 I gaze at a transparent building…

Allow me to look at this point at gaze.[99] After all, the building I consider, like any building, is positioned or located in front of me; it appears to me, as Heidegger puts it. I need to recognise it, to perceive it. It is a normal activity for me to look at it, and I gaze at it. I refer to Lacan here and his essay 'What is a picture?' in *The Four Fundamental Concepts of Psycho-Analysis*.[100] Of course, a building is not a picture; however, two observations are useful here. Firstly, with the increase of web browsing and digital photography, what we have most of the time is a series of (2D) pictures of (3D) buildings.[101] Furthermore, architects start with a 2D representation of future 3D buildings, so they conceptualise the building on plan before its construction. Secondly, the process of representation and the ways in which it is instituted – through pictures of a façade, or through the façade itself – is similar enough to art for us to use what Lacan describes in this essay on the picture. I suspect that postmodern buildings operate as what Lacan calls *trompe l'œil*. Lacan narrates the story of a competition between two ancient painters,

95 Lorens Holm, 'The New Yorkers' (2007) Architectural Theory Review vol. 12 no. 2, 106.

96 Loc. cit 108.

97 Loc. cit.

98 Loc. cit.

99 Some readers may consider that I am biased here, using only Lacan to analyse the notion of the gaze; For more, see Henry Krips, 'The Politics of the Gaze: Foucault, Lacan and Zizek' (2010) Culture Unbound 2, 91–102.

100 Jacque Lacan in Jacques-Allain Miller (ed) *The Four Fundamental Concepts of Psychoanalysis* (Vintage 1998) 105–123.

101 This might change of course. Technology will allow for 3D presentations. But they will remain presentation on a 2D screen.

Zeuxis and Parrhasios.[102] Zeuxis receives acclaim for painting grapes so life-like that even the birds that try to peck at them are fooled. In his pride, Zeuxis then goes to look at the work of Parrhasios. But Zeuxis sees only a veil, and so he asks to see the painting that Parrhasios has hidden behind the veil. Well, Parrhasios' painting *was* the veil, so well done that it fooled even the master of deceptive painting. Lacan points out, 'it is clear that if one wishes to deceive a man, what one presents to him is a painting of a veil, that is to say, something that incites him to ask what is behind it'.[103] This is the purpose of the *trompe-l'oeuil*:

> What is it that attracts and satisfies us in *trompe-l'oeuil*? When is it that it captures our attention and delights us? At the moment when, by a mere shift of our gaze, we are able to realize that the representation does not move with the gaze and that it is merely a *trompe-l'oeuil*. For it appears at that moment as something other than it seemed, or rather it now seems to be that something else.[104]

In a way, like Lacan, I consider that palaces of justice (like icons, or Holms' symbols) hold us under their gaze. But what makes evident the 'value' of the building is that whomever/whatever it represents (again, like icons), it has to do with God, and with the fact that God is also looking at it. Behind the building stands the social pact, articulated by the Names-of-the-Father.[105] Freud, says Lacan, was led irresistibly 'to link the appearance of the signifier of the Father, as the author of the Law, to death, even to the murder of the Father, thus showing that although this murder is the fruitful moment of the debt through which the subject binds himself for life to the Law, the symbolic Father, in so far as he signifies this Law, is certainly the dead Father'.[106] We know that the building is the signifier but we also know that it must always relate to a signified. Indeed, 'the peculiarity of the signifier [is] the fact that it is unable to signify itself.[107] When I gaze at the building hosting the courts of law, then, where the work of justice takes place, I should immediately interpret

102 Jacque Lacan in Jacques-Allain Miller (ed) The Four Fundamental Concepts of Psycho-analysis (Vintage 1998) 11–112.

103 Ibid, 112.

104 Ibid.

105 'Parce que Lacan rapproche le non-du-Père au nom-du-Père, la position symbolique du « père-régulateur » est un lieu de 'l'autorité'. See the connection made by Lacan between the 'no of the father' and the 'name of the father'. David Marrani, *Rituel (s) de Justice? Essai Anthropologique sur la Relation du Temps et de l'Espace dans le Procès* (EME 2011) 28.

106 Jacque Lacan, *Ecrits: A Selection* (trans. A. Sheridan, Routledge, 2005) 152.

107 Jacque Lacan in Jacques-Allain Miller (ed) The Four Fundamental Concepts of Psycho-analysis (Vintage 1998) 249.

(recognise) that it is a place where justice is going to be done. Subjectivity plays a strong part here: multiple subjectivities, of course. I understand immediately what I face, what I gaze at, when a *Palais de Justice* looks like a *Palais de Justice*. I realise that this is a partisan assumption because if I consider a 'vertical' building, showing and expressing the transcendence of God/King/Judge, I refer to a certain type of society. But when I consider a postmodern 'transparent' building, it brings another type of society to mind, because it is merely a *trompe-l'oeuil*.[108]

Perhaps, then, we need to turn to Benjamin here, and consider what is actually socially at stake with the use of glass. In Benjamin's work, the role of glass in architecture is aligned with the exposure of bourgeois hypocrisy and the negation of commodity fetishism.[109] Glass lacks aura and is the enemy of the secret: 'Like the camera, the function of glass is to liquidate cultural tradition, reshaping the entrenched social relations of domestic space'.[110] There is a feeling of revolution behind Benjamin's consideration/observation: he advocates the use of glass not in order to create a 'wall of windows', like the modernist architecture of Le Corbusier,[111] but to destroy the established order, not to open the interior onto the exterior, but to make the interior permanently available to the exterior. As 'opened', transparency equates here to openness:

> Faith in openness and transparency forms one of the pillars of architectural modernism. While a close connection does exists between 'the aesthetic' of the new architecture and the emergence of a more general 'openness' in society.[112]

What we arrive at is the replacement of one signifier by another. According to Lacan, this replacement takes place 'along the vertical substitutive axis of language'.[113] The signifier 'justice' thus moves from one type to another. The glass building becomes a metaphoric interpretation of Justice that builds its meaning in accordance with a new ideology for which the architect acts as the voice.

What society seems to want (we are told) is accountability, feedback, self-reflexivity. This trend towards the self-reflective seems to be pro-active (again, we are told). If I want to be certain of what is going on somewhere, I need to be able to see, to *see through*. And it seems obvious that I may gaze better if the wall

108 On another level, it could well be the case that as a legal academic, I am 'educated' to understand what is in front of me, while this is perhaps not the case for everyone.

109 Scott McQuire, 'From Glass architecture to Big Brother: Scenes from a cultural history of transparency' (2003) Cultural Studies Review vol. 9, no. 2, 103–123, esp. 106.

110 Loc. cit.

111 Loc. cit, 107.

112 Loc. cit 107.

113 Lorens Holm, 'What Lacan said re: architecture' (2000) Critical Quarterly vol. 42, 56.

I face is not a brick wall but a glass wall.[114] As such, transparency has become the true deconstructed architecture. Its physical expression is the use of glass in buildings, creating clear constructions that have an affinity with other contemporary products – such as the cosmetics of Neutrogena: transparent products are equated with a 'guaranteed purity'.[115] 'Purity guaranteed' underlay the design of Foster and Partners, the firm that won the 1992 commission to transform the Reichstag as the new home for the unified Germany's parliament. Foster's team focused on making the processes of government more transparent: 'not every part of the Reichstag can be open to the public but we have ensured that where possible it is transparent and its activities are on view'.[116] Here, too, definitions across disciplines collapse and end up blurring the meaning of words.

Conclusion

Transparent public buildings are seen as buildings without secrets. Foucault believes that transparency gives power: 'If Bentham's project [the Panopticon] aroused interest, this was because it provided a formula applicable to many domains, the formula of "power through transparency"'.[117] What lies beneath transparency, then, is an insidious capturing of power: power through transparency. We know by the observations made in relation to courts that transparency has now replaced opacity in court design. The old opacity was not the result of secrecy, however, but had a purpose: it was intended to contribute to the process of justice, which – via a specific ritual ('the hearing') taking place behind the wall, inside the building, including the use of light and shadow – symbolised the 'truth'.

One of the main problems of transparency is the abolition of distance, which is an essential element of the ritual of justice, so necessary to create authority and to render justice 'correctly'. The concern of transparency is immediacy: as

114 I am still considering something that separates – some kind of wall, but one that is transparent; I imagine an open space, like an open-plan contemporary office space.

115 Dominique Bessire, 'Transparency: a two-way mirror?' In Barrie Pettman (ed) 30 years of IJSE: Festschrift in honour of Professor John O'Brien (Emerald Group Publishing 2005, 424–438), 425.

116 Ascher Barntones, D., *The Transparent State: architecture and politics in postwar germany* (Routledge 2005) 201. Glass was also used in the German Federal Constitutional Court to 'create actual and metaphorical transparency in the aftermath of the horrors of the Third Reich; Linda Mulcahy, Legal Architecture: Justice, Due Process and the Place of Law (Routledge 2011), 152.

117 Michael Foucault, 'The Eye of Power' in Colin Gordon (ed) *Power/Knowledge: Selected Interviews and Other Writings, 1972–1977* (Pantheon books 1980) 146–165, esp. 156.

in capitalism, what is important is immediate profit. But im-mediate also means the abolition of the mediating process, in a situation where there is nothing in between – without mediation. According to Bud on Silverstone, a medium such as television may be described as a 'mythic phenomenon'. Silverstone's point is that 'we of the profane world have access to something which in its unmediated state and by its very distance is sacred'. Bud, by analogy, recognises 'the mythic role of the museum in providing a specially authentic, intense, or direct contact with the "sacred" subject', which 'acts to reduce fear and provide "understanding" of the special phenomenon'.[118] I will, in turn, apply this idea to court buildings, for this is, in essence, what happens in postmodern designs of places of justice: the mediation is removed (transparency), and we end up in contact with the 'sacred'. The *Palais de Justice* has become a glass palace. Contemporary office buildings are made of steel and glass that can easily be seen through. Transparent office buildings signify something of the transparency of capitalism and democracy, and something of the emptiness of the ideas that surround them.[119] But behind this permanent opening is concealed a permanent facilitation of surveillance and control.[120,121] The gaze is everywhere, on everything. There is a totalitarian aspect to this transparency that leaves the signifier 'justice' empty. We seem to be moving towards what is presented to us as democratic: a transparent democracy. However, we should remember that '[d]emocracy is defined by the insurmountable boundary that prevents the political subject from becoming consubstantial with power',[122] and that this particularity 'means that [in the language of psychoanalysis] the place of authority is "a purely symbolic construction" that cannot be occupied by any "real" political official'.[123] In other words, immediacy is not consistent with democracy.

We should not forget that transparency points to a generalised surveillance, which has always constituted the favourite means of dictatorships. Zizek explains that in a democratic society, the monarch (and I extend this to any figure of

118 R. Bud, 'On the Social Production of Visual Difference, the myth and the machine: seing science through museum eye' vol. 35, in Gordon Fyfe and John Law (ed) *Picturing Power: Visual Depiction and Social Relations* (Routledge 1988) 134.

119 Even the use of glass in stadium seems to voice the link between transparency and democracy. Resnik, Curtis (n 8) 341.

120 As noted here, transparency has invaded most discourses.

121 Dominique Bessire, 'Transparency: a two-way mirror?' In Barrie Pettman (ed) 30 years of IJSE: Festschrift in honour of Professor John O'Brien (Emerald Group Publishing 2005, 424–438) 426.

122 Claudia Breger, 'The Leader's Two Bodies, Slavoj Zizek's postmodern political theology' (2001) Diacritics vol. 31, no. 1, 73–90, esp. 78–79.

123 Loc. cit, 79.

authority, such as heads of state or judges) guarantees the non-closure of the social.[124] Medieval jurists were aware of this when they designed fictions to help the 'uninterrupted line of royal bodies natural, with the permanency of the body politic represented by the head together with the members, and with immortality of the office, that is of the head alone'.[125] While the medieval monarchy found a solution to the problem of interrex, the permanence of inter regnum in democratic society takes as its source the fact that the throne is empty: a general sense of emptiness is very present in democracy. This is perhaps why Laclau believes that the logic of totalitarianism has the same source as democracy.[126] Here, emptiness and full transparency are interrelated, and I assume that they are similar things. As a major *trompe-l'oeuil* or fascinating *tromperie*, the glass city of the *Wizard of Oz* reaffirms the sweet and subtle feeling of both *tromperie* and totalitarism. Dorothy feels safe in the Emerald City that is also a glass city: 'I am sure we are in no danger',[127] she says, as 'The houses of the city were all made of glass, so clear and transparent that one could look through the walls as easily as through a window'.[128] I have a feeling that the new myth built on the contemporary paradigm of transparency aims to suppress everything that is of the neoclassical era, or part of the Gothic revival – such as the temple design– which signified 'be careful when you enter here'; the intention has been to replace it with a postmodern office design that signals 'don't worry'. In conclusion, we could simply apply here what we learnt from the Wizard of Oz: the city may be transparent and may feel safe, but the powerful wizard turns out to be a fraud – an ordinary man hiding behind a curtain operating a giant console of buttons and levers, manipulating people and things.[129] Even in the glass city, then, great danger can be revealed. The glass walls, the transparent houses, did not prevent the *trompe-l'oeuil* of the fake wizard, and it seems likely that transparency in courthouse design will result in little more than some version of Orwell's vision: Big Brother will watch us here, too.

124 Loc. cit.

125 Ernst H. Kantorowicz, *The King's Two Bodies, a study in mediaeval political theology* (PUP 1997) 316.

126 Ernesto Laclau and Chantal Mouffe, *Hegemony and Socialist Strategy: Towards a radical democratic politics* (Verso 2001) 186.

127 Louise F. Baum, *Dorothy and the Wizard of Oz* (first published 1908, MobileReference 2008) 10.

128 Ibid, 11.

129 See Daniel Willis, 'The Emerald City: A study of Substance and Place' in Daniel Willis, *The Emerald City and Other Essays on the Architectural Imagination* (Princeton architectural press 1999) 87–98, esp. 96–97.

PART IV Empirical Perspectives

Vito Breda,

University of Southern Queensland, Toowoomba Australia

10. The Concept of Objectivity in the UK Supreme Court through a Comparative Looking Glass

1. Introduction

During a public lecture on astronomy, the speaker is interrupted by an old lady sitting at the back of the room: 'What you told us is nonsense! The world is flat and it is supported by a giant turtle. The lecturer quickly responded: 'What is the turtle standing on?'. To which the lady rebutted: 'You are a very clever young man, but it's turtle all the way down!'[1] The lecturer, who according to Hawking might be Bertrand Russell, had allowed the opportunity for the assumptions of the given argument to be questioned (that the world is flat and that it is held up by a giant turtle). Yet, he chose, showing perhaps a glimpse of arrogance, to question the internal logic of the old lady's argument. The decision was indeed unwise and his attempt to discredit the 'turtle argument' was quickly repelled.

The anecdote is a powerful reminder to all public speakers of the dangers of belittling an audience, but that is a trivial point. The message that Hawking wants to deliver in the opening lines of his book is twofold. Firstly, 'I will not make the same mistake'. *A Brief History of Time* will be focused squarely on a representation of reality that can be, within the margins of error of any scientific analysis, objectively verified. Secondly (and perhaps as a corollary of the first point), the book will not be about the interpretation of the semantic structure of a theory.

The anecdote, I think, is also quite useful in understanding the difficulty of developing an objective legal reasoning in common law systems. In common law, judges often have to marry factual analysis with an interpretative activity of legal norms, which might be extracted from a common understanding of a narrative. For instance, murder is defined in England and Wales by the judicial interpretation of a section of a seventeenth-century textbook (Edward Coke's *Institutes of the*

---

1 Stephen. Hawking, *A Brief History of Time: The Updated and Expanded Tenth Anniversary Edition* (Random House Publishing Group, 1998) 1.

Laws of England).[2] The facts of the murder might include a historical narrative of events (e.g. Mrs Smith was killed by a bullet), which might be objectively tested. It is up to the parties to show that a factual narrative might be engaged by the facts of the case. In the case of our example, the death of Mrs Smith will require an interpretation of Coke's book. The process is elegantly described by MacCormick:

> In these situations, the private complainer or public rule enforcer must bring forward some assertions about the state of facts in the world, and attempt to show how that state of facts would call for intervention on the ground of some rule that applies to the asserted facts. Accordingly, the logic of rule-application is the central logic of the law within the modern paradigm of legal rationality under the 'rule of law'.[3]

A judge, by way of comparison to a scientist such as Hawking, cannot avoid evaluating objectively 'hard' evidence that describes reality and, at the same time, s/he has to assess the plausibility of the 'soft' legal arguments that describe the semantic interpretation of the text. Even if the normative aspect of the idea of objectivity is normally excluded from the court's daily activity,[4] it appears that judges are asked to do what would appear to be two dissimilar activities: the evaluation of the scientific explanation of reality and the assessment of the parties' legal argument. Both activities demand, respectively, an evaluation of arguments based on pre-set criteria.

Let me dwell on this point. On a general level, the criteria of evaluation of factual and legal narratives might be different, since they are retrieved from different branches of science. For instance, the laws of physics might help with the ballistic trajectory of a bullet and philological assumptions might explain the significance of the term 'murder' in Coke's book. However, in both instances, the judge makes a legal assessment based on criteria set by a community of legal practitioners and

---

2 Edward Coke, *Institutes of the Laws of England; Or a Commentary upon Littleton, Not the Name of the Author Only, But of the Law Itself*, (London: E. Brooke R. Brooke, 1798), chap. 4:7.

3 Neil MacCormick, *Legal Reasoning and Legal Theory* (New Ed, Clarendon Press 1994) ix–x. Note that the paradigm that describes factual and semantic reasoning is, in MacCormick, a legal qualification process.

4 The debate over legal objectivity includes a normative debate that seeks to anchor it to an external criterion/criteria of evaluation. However, it is outside of the remit of this essay – and indeed of the research – to discuss the concept of objectivity in absolute terms. For a succinct analysis of the normative debate see, for instance, Brian Leiter, 'Law and Objectivity' in Jules L Coleman, Scott Shapiro and KE Himma (eds), *The Oxford handbook of jurisprudence and philosophy of law* (Oxford University Press 2004) 969–990.

also scientific experts. In describing the similarities between hard and soft sciences, Rorty, I think, delivers this point in clear narrative: 'They [hard and soft representation of reality] offer an account of enquiry which recognizes sociological, but not epistemological, differences between such disciplinary matrices as theoretical physics and literary criticism'. In short, having a shared idea of what is an objective analysis is an axiomatic aspect of any scientific endeavour. For instance, a basic mathematic formula requires abstracting, synthesis as well as an agreement in principle on what numbers mean.[5] Developing his argument, Rorty suggests that objectivity cannot be constructed in universal terms (neither in pure science, nor in the humanities) and the sooner we accept such a limitation, the more fruitful our understanding of the idea of objectivity will be.

The point I would like to make here is that judges can, and following Rorty, must adopt different criteria of objectivity in relation to the subject of their analysis.[6] In other words, an examination of the use of the concept of objectivity in the UK legal discourse should retrieve a cluster of criteria for both a scientific and interpretative perception of objectivity. An analysis of 98 cases did indeed confirm Rorty's analysis, and both the factual and interpretative ideas of objectivity. However, a second group of significances for the term objectivity (which is linked to a semantic interpretation of text) is, by way of comparison with the interpretation that associated it with factual narrative, far less common.

2. Research Methodology

The previous section discussed, albeit quite succinctly, the theoretical debates over the concept of objectivity. In judicial discourses, objectivity is assumed as an essential element of the evaluation of facts and of the interpretation of law. However, it remains unclear whether judicial objectivity might include a series of specifics for law criteria to assess 'hard' evidence and 'soft' semantic analyses. For instance, it is uncertain whether an objective assessment of a UK statute might include a specific grammatical analysis by the court, such as the one suggested in Langacker's *Foundation of Cognitive Grammar*.[7] There is anecdotal evidence,

5 Alfred N. Whitehead, *Science and Philosophy*, (Patterson: Littlefield, Adams and Co., 1964) 103.

6 Note that this point is speculative and there are theories of legal interpretation (for instance, of Genoa School) are based on the assumption that objective meaning of legal texts does not exist; so, objectivity is surely not so essential for legal interpretation. This reasoning is, however, not confirmed by this empirical analysis.

7 Ronald Langacker, *The Foundations of Cognitive Grammar: Volume I: Theoretical Prerequisites*, (Stanford: Stanford University Press, 1999).

retrieved from case law analyses,[8] which suggests a distinctive legal understanding of the concept of objectivity. However, Objectivity in the UK Judicial Discourse is one of the first analyses that seek to map out how UK judges use the concept in their decisions.

The study focused on a relatively large sample of reported decisions (98 cases) by the English and Welsh final appellate jurisdiction.[9] There are a number of reasons for focusing on the jurisprudence of a final appellate court. The number of cases for a ten-year analysis is reduced to a manageable 98 (rather than an unworkable 1000 reported decisions that referred to the term objectivity). In addition, it was assumed that the 'doctrine of the biding precedent' would enable the significance of a concept to trickle downwards to the lower courts. The doctrine of the precedent allows the research investigator to assume that a UK Supreme Court qualification for the term objectivity will be replicated within similar cases in the lower courts. It was also assumed that the seniority of the court should increase the quality of the reasoning behind the qualification of the concept of objectivity.

In addition, the project's methodology had to be standardised to allow for a comparative analysis of its results with other similar studies carried out in other legal systems. The research is part of a large comparative study that involved several European states (e.g. Italy, Germany and Poland) as well as an analysis of the use of the concept in Turkey and Brazil.[10]

To allow a 'like for like' comparison of the project results with similar activities carried out across Europe and beyond, the Objectivity in the UK Judicial Discourse study was divided into two distinct phases. The first hermeneutical phase focused exclusively on the textual meaning of the concept of objectivity. This stage of the research aimed at retrieving the effective (e.g. cognitive) significance of the term objectivity and, thus, reducing false positives. The test was based on Langacker's studies on semantics,[11] and excluded the number of references to objectivity from the project results that were inserted in the judicial discourse for rhetorical effect.

---

8 Neil MacCormick, "Reasonableness and Objectivity" in Notre Dame Law Review 74, 1998–1997, 1575.

9 On 1st October 2009, the UK Supreme Court substituted the House of Lords as the highest appeal jurisdiction in the UK in all legal disputes.

10 Adam Czarnota and Lidka Rodak, 'Epistemologia, aktywizm sędziowski i dwie tradycje prawa' in Wieslaw Staskiewicz (ed), *Dyskrecjonalnosc w prawie : materialy XVIII Ogólnopolskiego Zjazdu Katedr Teorii i Filozofii Prawa, Miedzeszyn k. Warszawy 22–24 wrzesnia 2008 r.* (LexisNexis 2010).

11 Ronald Langacker, *The Foundations of Cognitive Grammar: Volume I: Theoretical Prerequisites,* (Stanford: Stanford University Press, 1999).

In our sample, there were 12 rhetorical references that were discharged from the project.

The functional phase of the research sought to qualify the arguments that were derived from the reference to the concept of objectivity. This part of the study sought to retrieve arguments and criteria that were directly linked to the concept of objectivity. For instance, in the first phase of the study, the script *Helow v Secretary of State for the Home Department* included a reference to objectivity that could have been relevant to the project.

> My Lords, the *fair-minded* and informed observer is a relative newcomer among the select group of personalities who inhabit our legal village and are available to be called upon when a problem arises that needs to be solved objectively. Like the *reasonable man* whose attributes have been explored so often in the context of the law of negligence, the fair-minded observer is a creature of fiction.[12]

The functional analysis of *Helow v Secretary of State for the Home Department* retrieved two arguments from objectivity. The first derived argument from objectivity is a reference to a detached expert analysis. The second functional usage of the concept of objectivity is, instead, associated with the idea of reasonableness.

In short, the functional aspect of the case analysis sought to increase the depth of the project by retrieving second-level meanings for the concept of objectivity. In addition to the combination of hermeneutical and functional methodology, a series of adjustments were necessary to ensure the compatibility of the results between civil law and common law systems. Firstly, the term 'objectivity' was not appropriate to the aims of the research. For instance, the search for 'objectivity' in the Lexix database of All England Law Reports retrieved only 18 cases. That was insufficient for the project. The research focused, instead, on equivalent terms (such as objectively and objective assessment) that inferred a process of judicial evaluation.

Secondly, results were retrieved from the Lexis@Library database. It is one of the two most popular legal databases available in common law countries. So that civil law lawyers are not left out in the cold here, it is worth mentioning that there is not an official collection of case law in England and Wales. The task of summarising cases and reporting them is in the hands, so to speak, of private publishing houses. The All England Law Reports is one of the many commercial firms dealing with such activity. Even if it might not be the most authoritative, for instance, the Law Reports series is checked by a judge before publication, The All England Law

---

12 *Helow v Secretary of State for the Home Department* – [2009] 2 All ER 103, para. 1.

Reports has the advantage of only reporting the court's decisions (excluding the party arguments), which were the principle focus of the study.

Thirdly, the Objectivity in the UK Judicial Discourse project divided the results into sections: public law and private law cases. In contrast with other European legal systems, the debate over the concept of objectivity has been widely influenced by established analyses such as that of MacCormick.[13] The standards of an objective assessment, MacCormick argues, vary according to the area of law. Even if the project did not intend (at least at its conception) to assess MacCormick's argument, there was the possibility of testing its veracity. In the next section, the project results are discussed at length, but it can be anticipated that a separation between law areas will enable a sharp distinction to be made in terms of the perception of the concept of objectivity in the public and private law subjects.

3. Project Results

The Objectivity in the UK Judicial Discourse project was designed to map out the different meanings of the concept of objectivity in the jurisprudence of the House of Lords and in UK Supreme Court decisions. The previous section explained the different steps undertaken during the studies. An evaluation of the use of the concept of objectivity requires a hermeneutical analysis of court decisions that includes figurative narratives (such as the reference to a reasonable person) and objective assessment (e.g. to affirm a scientific evaluation of facts through an expert witness). In this part of the essay, I will present the results of the study.

During the ten-year period considered by the research (which starts on the 1st of January 2000), the concept of objectivity was referred to in 98 different cases (out of 800 circa) by the House of Lords and its successor, the UK Supreme Court. The hermeneutical phase of the project revealed that within the sample, on 12 occasions the reference to objectivity was inserted in the script of the case for rhetorical effect or to reproduce one of the parties' arguments. For instance, in *Joseph v Spiller* a semantic analysis of the case script shows a textual reference to the concept of objectivity, but it is reported as one of the party's submissions.

> Counsel for the plaintiff submitted that the defendant had to establish that: (i) the words complained of were comment; (ii) the <u>comment was on facts</u>; (iii) the facts commented on constituted a matter of public interest; (iv) the comment was <u>objectively 'fair'</u>; that is the comment was one that was capable of being honestly founded on the facts to which it related, albeit by someone who was prejudiced and obstinate; (v) the comment represented

13 Neil MacCormick, 'Reasonableness and Objectivity', Notre Dame Law Review 74, 1998–1997, 1575.

> the defendant's honest opinion. If he discharged all these burdens, the defence could none the less be defeated by proof of malice on the part of the defendant.[14]

The functional analysis of *Joseph v Spiller* showed two interpretations of the concept of objectivity. For instance, there is an attempt to associate a factual analysis with a requirement for the fair evaluation of the defendant's behaviour. The House of Lords, however, dismissed the plaintiff's narrative and the reference was not considered as part of the project's results.

As expected from Rorty's analysis, the Objectivity in the UK Judicial Discourse project retrieved eight functional usages of the concept. Usages are arguments derived from the concept. In the tables that follow, the first column reports the type of functional argument made from objectivity, the second reports the number of instances in which the argument has been used (within the 98 cases), and the third column shows the percentage of the arguments (in relation to the 90 arguments retrieved from the sample of cases).

Table 1: The UK Judicial Use of the Concept of Objectivity

Objectivity: The UK Judicial Use of the Concept of Objectivity: ALL Law Areas	**Arguments/ Usages**	**Percentage**
Factual Narrative	64	71%
Expert Witness	8	9%
Reasonableness	7	8%
Fairness	4	5%
Intention of Individuals	2	2%
Intention of Parliament	2	2%
Impartial Witness	2	2%
The Assessment of an Ordinary Man	1	1%

At first sight, we can note an imbalance in the use of arguments from objectivity. In over two-thirds of the instances in which the court referred to objectivity, it developed an argument based on a factual narrative. That is an evaluation of evidence that describes a series of events. For instance, in *Majorstake Ltd v Curtis*, Lord Hope associated the concept of objectivity with a survey of a property.

> The Leasehold Reform, Housing and Urban Development Act 1993 enables the landlord, unconstrained by their existing state, to identify the premises by drawing his own line around the tenant's flat in support of his counter-notice or whether it refers to the existing and objectively recognisable state of the premises [...] The context indicates that

14 Joseph and others v Spiller and another [2011] 1 All ER 947, para. 64.

> the extent of those premises does not depend on the intention of the landlord. On the contrary, it is something to be determined objectively by examining the existing state of the building within which the tenant's flat is situated.[15]

If narratives based on explaining 'hard evidence' were added to an expert witness evaluation, (such as an estimation by a surveyor in *Majorstake Ltd v Curtis*), 80% of the arguments from objectivity would be based on 'hard' scientific analyses.

One of the possible reasons for the small number of references to the objective interpretation of legal texts could be historical. In the second part of the twentieth century, a series of cases gave the opportunity to the House of Lords to clarify its role as the final appellate court in England and Wales. The concerns that arose from this debate were mainly focused on the constitutional limitations imposed on the judicial interpretations of legal texts. Lord Atkin, dissenting and obviously displeased, put the point across in a pungent narrative.

> I protest, even if I do it alone, [...] I know of only one authority which might justify the suggested method of construction: ""When I use a word,'" Humpty Dumpty said in rather a scornful tone, "it means just what I choose it to mean, neither more nor less". "The question is," said Alice, "whether you can make words mean so many different things". "The question is," said Humpty Dumpty, "which is to be master – that's all"." After all this long discussion the question is whether the words 'If a man has' can mean 'If a man thinks he has'. I am of opinion that they cannot, and that the case should be decided accordingly.[16]

In *Liverside v Anderson*, Lord Atkin is indeed concerned with the interpretation of his peers,[17] yet the reference to Carroll's Alice meeting with Humpty Dumpty has become the canonical narrative to describe an unreasonable judicial interpretation of a legal text.[18]

The rise of Humpty Dumpty as a fictitious canonical figure and his association with an unhinged wigged judge has not helped the perception – shared by civil law academics and practitioners – that common law practices allow for an unreasonable level of flexibility. In particular, there is concern that common law judges interpret concepts in a way that is reasonably accepted by their own community,

15 *Majorstake Ltd v Curtis* – [2008] 2 All ER 303, paras. 2–3.

16 *Liversidge Appellant v Sir John Anderson and Another Respondent*, A.C., 1941, CCVI, 206, p. 246.

17 Plasencia Madeleine, 'Who's Afraid of Humpty Dumpty: Deconstructionist References in Judicial Opinions' in Seattle University Law Review, 21, 1997, 215.

18 Jacco Bomhoff, 'ComparativeLawBlog: Humpty Dumpty and the Law' <http://comparativelawblog.blogspot.co.uk/2006/12/humpty-dumpty-and-law.html> accessed 4 August 2012.

perhaps belittling the law as an expression of democracy.[19] The idea of a 'common law made by the judges, for the judges' is also hinted at in Rorty's essays.[20]

However, since the *Liversdge v Anderson* case, a great deal has been done to reduce the interpretative scope of UK judges. The issue of the objective interpretation of statutes has been, for instance, directly engaged by Lord Diplock: 'Where the meaning of the statutory words is plain and unambiguous it is not for the judges to invent fancied ambiguities as an excuse for failing to give effect to its plain meaning because they themselves consider that the consequences of doing so would be inexpedient, or event unjust or immoral'.[21] Two points can be deduced from Diplock's argument. Firstly, English and Welsh judges must be aware of their constitutional mandate. To support his argument, Lord Diplock made an explicit reference to the UK Constitution:

> My Lords, at a time when more and more cases involve the application of legislation which gives effect to policies that are the subject of bitter public and parliamentary controversy, it cannot be too strongly emphasised that the British constitution, though largely unwritten, is firmly based upon the separation of powers; Parliament makes the laws, the judiciary interpret them [...] Under our constitution it is Parliament's opinion on these matters that is paramount.[22]

Secondly, Diplock recognises that clear rules, within the margins of error of any semantic activity, should lead judges to objective and unbiased interpretation. In short, Diplock argues that the dilemma as to whether a legal text is objective or not cannot be constructed as a debate over whom is entitled to make a clear interpretation of a legal text. Rather, the task of the judiciary is to set criteria that define an objective interpretation.

The narrative might appear only partially satisfying. Having criteria of an objective assessment set by a particular group is only relatively better than accepting a subjective analysis. However, the objection is unsound. Recall that even pure sciences (from mathematics to physics), that seek to explain 'hard phenomena', depend on pre-set criteria decided on and shared by a community of scientists. The margins of appreciation in a semantic interpretation might be larger, yet they are (as scientific standards) anchored to a set of agreed criteria by experts in that field.

The practice of associating objectivity with factual narratives is not significantly different in the public and private law areas. In 68% of the public law (Table 2)

19 Richard Rorty, *Objectivity, Relativism, and Truth* (Cambridge University Press 1991).
20 ibid 188.
21 *Duport Steels Ltd v Sirs* (1980) 162 ICR 162 (House of Lords) 177.
22 *Duport Steels Ltd v Sirs* (n 20) 177.

cases and 75% of private cases (Table 3), the concept of objectivity has been associated with a factual narrative.

Table 2: The UK Judicial Use of the Concept of Objectivity in Public Law Areas

Objectivity: The UK Judicial Use of the Concept of Objectivity in Public Law Areas	Arguments/ Usages	Percentage
Factual Narrative	32	68%
Reasonableness	6	13%
Intention of Individuals	2	4%
Impartial Witness	2	4%
Expert Witness	2	4%
Intention of Parliament	1	2%
The Assessment of an Ordinary Man	1	2%
Fair-minded Assessment	1	2%

Table 3: The UK Judicial Use of the Concept of Objectivity in Private law Areas

Objectivity: The UK Judicial Use of the Concept of Objectivity in Private Law Areas	Arguments/ Usages	Percentage
Factual Narrative	32	75%
Expert Witness (Independent Assessment)	6	14%
Fairness	3	7%
Reasonableness	1	2%
Intention of Parliament	1	2%

On a general level, the results of the Objectivity in the UK Judicial Discourse project show that the House of Lords and the UK Supreme Court judges tend to shy away from the use of objectivity in interpretive activities (the so-called soft textual analysis). It is worth noting that a limited number of uses of an argument from objectivity do not make the concept less important for its judicial qualification. For instance, in *R v G; R v J*, the House of Lords adopted the criterion of reasonableness to limit a legalistic interpretation of criminal norms.

> Of course, if accepted, the explanation would show that the accused's purpose was not to commit an act of terrorism. But that is not the issue under s 58. Under s 58(1), the mere fact that the defendant's purpose was not to commit an act of terrorism is neutral. What he has to show is that he had an objectively reasonable excuse for possessing something which Parliament has made it, prima facie, a crime for him to possess because of its potential utility to a terrorist. An intention to use information in connection with a bank robbery may well be an explanation of why the defendant had the information,

> but it cannot be a 'reasonable' excuse for having it. So the accused would be guilty of the s 58(1) offence.[23]

So whilst in the overwhelming number of instances, judges in the final appellate jurisdiction for England and Wales tend to associate the concept of objectivity with hard factual narratives, Law Lords and UK Justices might, in complex cases (such as *R v G*), adopt soft criteria of evaluation.

Before moving on to the analysis of the cases in private law, it is worth pursuing the analysis of the public law cases a step further. In particular, a grouping of significances of the term objectivity associated with a factual narrative across different families of law (criminal, human rights, public law, land, tax, immigration) again reveals an imbalance.

Table 4: The reference to facts of the case as objective in different areas of law

Factual Narratives: Breakdown of Results per Subject of Law	Arguments/ Usages	Percentage
Human Rights	14	44%
Criminal Law	11	34%
Public Law	4	13%
Land Law	1	3%
Tax Law	1	3%
Immigration	1	3%

From the reading of Table 4, human rights cases are far more likely to invoke the principle of objectivity, understood as a factual narrative, than are any other public law areas. The higher number as well as the typology of arguments from objectivity highlights, perhaps, one of the most intersecting results of the research. For instance, it might generate a series of speculative arguments over the process of the accommodation of human rights in a common law system, which previously did not experience them. Recall that it is only from 1998 that some of the rights that are protected by the European Convention on Human Rights were introduced into the UK legal systems.[24] Given the relative novelty, it is expected that common law judges will seek to qualify, in practice, the extent of the protection of the ECHR freedoms.

---

23 *R v G; R v J* – [2009] 2 All ER 409, para. 79.

24 Human Rights Act 1998, C. 42; Convention for the Protection of Human Rights and Fundamental Freedoms, 4 November 1950, T.S. 71(1953), Rome.

In addition, the lexical structure of the rights upheld in the ECHR is, by a way of comparison to other rights, more general. For instance, in the past few years, the House of Lords has been asked to qualify (in practice) what the remits are of Art 5 of the ECHR that protect individual freedoms in relation to UK police powers to stop and search UK legal residents. In *Gillan v Metropolitan Police*, Lord Bingham explained that Mr Gillan's wait while carrying out a routine police search did not amount to an arrest (that would have triggered the protection of the individual freedom ex Art 5 of the ECHR).

> The respondents for their part do not, I think, contend that compliance with the procedure is in any meaningful sense voluntary; but they submit that viewed objectively, and in the absence of special circumstances, the procedure involves a temporary restriction of movement and not anything which can sensibly be called a deprivation of liberty.[...] I do not think, that in the absence of special circumstances, such a person should be regarded as being detained in the sense of confined or kept in custody, but more properly of being detained in the sense of kept from proceeding or kept waiting. There is no deprivation of liberty [ex Art 5 ECHR].[25]

Again, a more articulated study might be needed in this area to flesh out a stronger analysis, but it is plausible to suggest that the higher number of arguments from objectivity in human rights cases (within the sample considered by the project) is related to the novelty of the area of law and to the intrinsic vagueness of human rights norms.

The analysis of the use of the concept of objectivity in private law areas (contract law and family law) was similar to other areas of law. Again, a large number of usages of the concept of objectivity (75%) were attached to a factual narrative with a limited space left to the other significances. Even if a breakdown of the data of the factual narrative in private law has not been carried out, anecdotal evidence suggests that contract law cases were more concerned with a qualification of the term objectivity than were those of family law.

4. Conclusion

Objectivity in legal discourse is important. It is essential that judicial narratives project a perception of fairness and independence from the parties and legal practitioners across the whole community. However, objectivity is a contested concept.

---

25 *R (on the application of Gillan and another) v Metropolitan Police Commissioner and another* [2006] 4 All ER 1041, paras. 22–25. The European Court of Human Rights rejected the House of Lord's interpretation of the case, albeit regarding Art 8 of the ECHR. *Gillan & Quinton v UK* [2010] 50 EHRR 45.

Even if we were to exclude *relativism* that refutes the theoretical existence of an objective analysis, the concept of objectivity changes its significance in relation to the context.

The research carried out in the Objectivity in the UK Judicial Discourse aimed at clarifying how final appellate judges (in the UK House of Lords and UK Supreme Court) interpreted the concept of objectivity. The research cases were decided on during the ten-year period that started on the first of January 2000 and ended on the first of January 2010. The project retrieved a sample of 98 cases in which the House of Lords (until 2009) and, after that, the UK Supreme Court have referred to the concept of objectivity. The sample of references was analysed using a lexical and functional methodology. The results of the analyses of the sample show a high level of consistency on the usages of the concept of objectivity. The majority of judicial interpretations of the term make a uniform use of the concept by linking its significance to a factual explanation linked to hard evidence. Specifically, 68% of the public law cases and 75% of the private law cases expressly linked the concept of objectivity with a factual narrative.

However, the most important aspect of the research is related to the eight arguments derived from the concept of objectivity. These arguments are legal narratives that judges derived from the concept of objectivity (reported in Table 1). For instance, the concept of objectivity was associated with the criterion of the assessment of a fair-minded individual. In public law subject areas (e.g. criminal law, administrative law), instead, the cluster of arguments from objectivity appears to contradict established assumptions (such as the one suggested by MacCormick). Reasonableness is not strongly associated, at least in the way described by MacCormick, with the concept of objectivity.

In conclusion, Objectivity in the UK Judicial Discourse shows a variety of interpretations of the concept of objectivity. For instance, it appears that judges adopt different standards of objectivity in factual and semantic analyses. At first sight, such a result might appear worrying. Are UK judges using subjective criteria to decide on cases? The brief answer to the query is negative in nature. Variations in standards (and on the typology of arguments derived from objectivity) are axiomatic of the type of analysis that judges are required to carry out.

Antal Szerletics

National University of Public Service, Budapest, Hungary

11. Paternalism and 'Objective' Best Interests

1. Introduction

It is possible to characterize the system of surrogate decision-making in the Mental Capacity Act (MCA 2005 England & Wales) as a structure that aims to ensure that decisions made on behalf of incapacitated people are limited to 'soft paternalistic' interventions. Soft paternalism, i.e. paternalism that interferes with substantially nonvoluntary actions, is generally considered to be morally uncontroversial[1] because it does not subordinate the agent's 'right' (i.e. the agent's right to autonomy in this case) to his or her 'good'. This paper contends that although the system of surrogate decision-making in the MCA seems to fit well within a liberal political framework, there are certain value-driven background assumptions that influence the way mentally incapacitated people are paternalised, both with respect to the construction of the concept of mental capacity (i.e. the statutory 'threshold' for paternalistic interventions) and the determination of best interests.

2. Mental capacity and voluntary choices

The system of surrogate decision-making in the MCA can be characterized as a legal construct that aims to ensure that surrogate decisions are limited to 'soft paternalistic' interventions with respect to those who fall under the scope of the Act. The distinction between soft and hard paternalism is a key distinction for those authors who gear the justifiability of paternalism to the principle of autonomy;[2] roughly put, soft paternalism is considered to respect personal autonomy because it interferes only with substantially nonvoluntary conducts,[3] while hard paternalism is said to be morally impermissible because it imposes external constraints on otherwise voluntary actions. For sure, it can be disputed whether voluntary choices are

1 Thaddeus Pope, 'Counting the Dragon's Teeth and Claws: The Definition of Hard Paternalism' (2004) 20 Georgia State University Law Review 659 <http://readingroom.law.gsu.edu/gsulr/vol20/iss3/6>.

2 Joel Feinberg, 'Legal Paternalism', Rights, Justice and the Bounds of Liberty (Princeton University Press 1980) 118.

3 ibid.

always autonomous and whether the notion of voluntariness precisely grasps the essence of an autonomous judgment. For now, let us presuppose that 'substantially' nonvoluntary choices are nonautonomous and examine whether the decisions of mentally incapacitated people can be considered as being nonvoluntary. Strictly speaking, a non-competent choice can be voluntary because this is what the person wants (*voluntas*) on the level of 'first order preferences'.[4] A more plausible interpretation of these concepts, I suspect, would reveal a relation of inclusion between the two categories. Mentally incapacitated people are generally considered to lack the cognitive capacities to make voluntary decisions,[5] while those deemed to have mental capacity may still make nonvoluntary decisions due to a multitude of other factors such as the lack of adequate information, undue external influence, manipulation and so on. In fact, many legal regulations considered as typical instances of paternalism are aimed at preventing or correcting the negative consequences of (predominantly) nonvoluntary self-regarding actions or omissions. The same soft paternalistic motive is recognizable in the protection afforded to the group of 'vulnerable adults' under the inherent jurisdiction of the High Court. Vulnerable adults, irrespective of their mental capacities, are considered unable to make 'substantially' voluntary decisions in certain situations due to undue influence, exploitation or coercion which they cannot resist because of their inherent or social vulnerability (e.g. physical or mental disabilities, social dependency, etc.).[6] These people, although they fall outside the scope of the MCA, can be subjected to similar best-interests decision-making as those who lack mental capacity.

The position that mentally incapacitated people can, or sometimes even need to be paternalistically treated is rarely questioned; there seems to be a general consensus here and even authors who can hardly be accused of pro-paternalistic 'inclinations' seem to subscribe to this view. J. S. Mill, for example, allows forcibly

4 See, e.g.: Gerald Dworkin, *The Theory and Practice of Autonomy* (Cambridge University Press 1988) 20.

5 Mitigated by the MCA's decision-specific understanding of mental capacity.

6 Munby LJ gives a description of the 'vulnerable adult' in *Re SA (Vulnerable Adult with Capacity: Marriage)* [2005] EWHC 2942 (Fam), [2006] Fam Law 268. In paragraph 82, he writes that '[i]n the context of the inherent jurisdiction I would treat as a vulnerable adult someone who, whether or not mentally incapacitated, and whether or not suffering from any mental illness, or mental disorder, is or may be unable to take care of him or herself, or unable to protect him or herself against significant harm or exploitation, or who is deaf, blind, or dumb, or who is substantially handicapped by illness, injury or congenital deformity'.

preventing people from exposing themselves to danger if they are in a state 'incompatible with the full use of the reflecting faculty'.[7] Although Mill's 'principled anti-paternalism' is often said to rest on consequentialist grounds, it can be argued that his willingness to accept soft paternalism in certain situations and his focus on the voluntariness of self-harming actions reflect a deontological concern for autonomy.[8] Arguably, such a deontological concern is also present in the MCA when it makes the lack of capacity a necessary threshold for 'best interests' interventions.[9] *However, it is unsure whether the idea of voluntary choice and the concept of mental capacity will 'bear the enormous weight' that autonomy-centred justifications of paternalism have to place on them.*[10]

A possible reason for this can be that voluntariness and mental capacity both seem to admit of different degrees. If this is so, then setting a fixed threshold for voluntariness or mental capacity will inevitably classify certain decisions that fall somewhere in the 'grey area' between clear instances of voluntariness and non-voluntariness as being 'fully' voluntary or involuntary (and mentally capacitous or incapacitous, respectively). This classification is somewhat arbitrary, insofar as the placement of the threshold often seems to depend on group consensus and, to a certain extent, evaluative decisions. For sure, determining whether someone has mental capacity is predominantly a medical issue; it is, nevertheless, possible to criticize the present procedure of capacity assessment in the MCA for focusing too much on individual cognitive skills (i.e. the ability to understand, retain and use or weigh the information relevant to the specific decision[11]) and neglecting factors such as the individual's (and his or her surrounding community's) social circumstances, relations and emotional dispositions. Thus, it can be argued that the MCA reflects a *certain* conception of mental capacity (and, arguably, a *certain* conception of autonomy in the background) that places emphasis on the process of unhindered preference formation from a predominantly internalist perspective. But on a different account of autonomy, mental capacity can be conceived as a concept that is *essentially* geared to social relations and the recognition of others. Here, I do not only refer to the presence of external enabling conditions that help to facilitate capacitous decision-making. Of course, the successful exercise of one's

7 John Stuart Mill, *On Liberty* (Norton 1975) 89.

8 This is a disputed issue. See, e.g.: Gerald Dworkin, 'Paternalism' (1972) 56 The Monist 64, 72.

9 See: Mental Capacity Act 2005 s 1(5).

10 Arneson paraphrased. Richard J Arneson, 'Joel Feinberg and the Justification of Hard Paternalism' (2005) 11 Legal Theory 259, 268.

11 See: Mental Capacity Act 2005 s 3 (1).

cognitive faculties depends on the external support he or she receives for understanding and processing the information relevant to the decision (e.g. the way in which questions are framed or information is presented to someone). However, it may be that the model of capacitous decision-making cannot be reduced to the presence of certain individual skills and strictly defined enabling conditions, but there is something 'more phenomenological' to the process of decision-making that invites mutual recognition and constant exchange between the subject and the surrounding 'others'.

The statutory separation between the categories of 'unwise' and 'mentally incapacitated' decisions also demonstrates the uncertainty of the incapacity threshold. The MCA explicitly states that 'a person is not to be treated as unable to make a decision merely because he makes an unwise decision'.[12] A seemingly foolish choice, however grave its consequences might be, shall not 'cloud' one's judgment on mental capacity since it might reflect a difference in values rather than an absence of competence.[13] As Henderson J pointed out, competent adults are generally free to make unwise decisions:

> Just as a testator has always had the freedom [...] to make testamentary dispositions which are unreasonable, foolish or contrary to generally accepted standards of morality, so too a person in his lifetime has the freedom to act in a manner which is (for example) unwise, capricious, or designed to spite his relations. The pages of English fiction and of the law reports alike bear ample testimony to the exercise of this basic human right, even if it is not one enshrined in so many words in the European Convention on Human Rights.[14]

Contrary to this approach, an unwise decision, if we accepted that an unwise decision would be at odds with best interests, will not be allowed in the case of a mentally incapacitated person. The reason for this differentiation is presumably that mental incapacity is usually associated with medical conditions that affect an autonomous preference formation. The MCA, for example, requires that there shall be 'an impairment of, or a disturbance in the functioning of, the mind or brain' in order to establish the lack of capacity.[15] There are, however, borderline cases when it is hard to separate an unwise decision from a pathological one, especially if we consider that the classification of mental disorders often seems to rely on the consensus of medical practitioners rather than on empirical evidence. The respect for

12 See: Section 1 (4) MCA.

13 *Ms B v An NHS Hospital Trust* [2002] EWHC 429 (Fam), [2002] 2 All ER 449 [100] (Butler-Sloss LJ).

14 *D v R (The Deputy of S) & Anor* [2010] EWCOP 2405, [2010] EWHC 2405 (COP) [39] (Henderson J).

15 See: Mental Capacity Act 2005 s 2 (1).

unwise decisions seems to be based on the presuppositions that values, in the case of mentally competent adults, are autonomously formed[16] and that the preference formation of mentally disordered people is entirely different from those with a 'sound' mind. Certain mental disorders, however, can be interpreted as reflecting unwise value choices rather than pathological ones (e.g. *anorexia nervosa*).

A sort of perfectionist tendency appears with respect to the unwise options of incapacitated people insofar as it seems that best interests decision-makers are inclined to make decisions that further the 'objective'[17] best interests of the protected person. Even if the person had capacity, he or she would have chosen an unwise option. Lewison J, for example, claims that an unwise decision can never be in someone's best interests once the decision-making power shifts to the surrogate decision maker due to the lack of capacity. He writes that 'I cannot see that it would be a proper exercise for a third party decision maker consciously to make an unwise decision merely because P would have done so. A consciously unwise decision will rarely if ever be made in P's best interests.'[18]

3. Beyond the capacity threshold: the elements of the best interests standard

3.1 Principles of surrogate decision-making

In the absence of a valid advance directive, decision-making on behalf of incapacitated people (often referred to as 'surrogate decision-making'[19]) can take place along two legal standards. The substituted judgment standard, based on the principle of respect for autonomy, requires the surrogate decision-maker to reconstruct what the incapacitated person would have wanted if he or she had capacity in the specific situation and to make a decision that corresponds to this hypothetical construct.[20] In US jurisprudence, the best interests standard is usually applied when evidence

---

16 The category of vulnerable adults is an immediate exception here.

17 Objectivity understood as all elements of the best interests standard except for 'subjective' past wishes and feelings.

18 *Re P* [2009] EWHC 163 (COP), [2009] EWCOP 163 [42] (Lewison J).

19 Sometimes the expression 'substituted decison-making' is also used to refer to decision-making on behalf of incapacitated people. This seems unfortunate because it can be confused with the substituted judgment standard.

20 Agnieszka Jaworska, 'Advance Directives and Substitute Decision-Making' in Edward N Zalta (ed), *The Stanford Encyclopedia of Philosophy* (Summer 2009, 2009) <http://plato.stanford.edu/archives/sum2009/entries/advance-directives/> accessed 5 March 2015.

of the patient's past values and preferences is ambiguous or nonexistent. It is often characterized as an 'objective' test (as opposed to the 'subjectivity' of substituted judgments) and it is said to rely on community norms or sometimes the perspective of 'a reasonable person,' choosing as most people would choose for themselves.[21]

The present situation in England is somewhat different from the United States. Best interests is neither a secondary, 'fallback' principle that complements the substituted judgment standard, nor it can be equated with a set of community norms or with the reasonableness standard. It integrates many diverse elements and this diversity is the result of a historical progress that gradually extended the meaning of the concept beyond 'mere' medical interests and started to incorporate broader welfare considerations into the best interests assessment scheme.[22]

3.2 Best interests and welfare

Paternalistic interventions are subject to two basic limitations under the MCA. The lack of mental capacity can be considered as a minimum threshold for surrogate decision-making which aims to ensure full respect for the (self-regarding) decisions of mentally competent adults. 'On top of this,' the MCA contains a consequentialist requirement when prescribing that surrogate decisions must further the best interests of the incapacitated person. Similarly to any consequentialist moral theory that must come up with a plausible theory of the 'good,' it seems essential that mental

---

21 Rebecca Dresser, 'Treatment Decisions for Dementia Patients: The Search for Normative Boundaries' <https://bioethicsarchive.georgetown.edu/pcbe/background/dresser.html> working paper accessed 7 July 2012.

22 The power to make medical welfare decisions in the best interests of an incapacitated adult was (re) established in *F v West Berkshire HA* [1991] UKHL 1, [1990] 2 AC 1 by applying the common law doctrine of necessity. The House of Lords, in the same judgment, adopted the *Bolam test* as the standard which should be applied in deciding whether a proposed operation is in the (medical) best interests of the incapacitated patient. The *Bolam* test was originally used to determine the standard of reasonable care for doctors and other medical professionals in cases of medical negligence. According to the classical formulation, 'a doctor is not guilty of negligence if he has acted in accordance with a practice accepted as proper by a responsible body of medical men skilled in that particular form of treatment; nor is he negligent merely because there is a body of opinion which would adopt a different technique'. *Bolam v Friern Hospital Management Committee* [1957] 1 WLR 582. Although opinions had already been divided about the appropriateness of the Bolam test as a standard of best interests in *Re F [1989]*, the test was subsequently applied in cases such as *Airedale NHS Trust v Bland* [1992] UKHL 5, [1993] AC 789 or *Re T (Adult: Refusal of Treatment)* [1992] EWCA Civ 18, [1993] Fam. 95.

capacity law provides a clear account of best interests which is able to give sufficient directions to practitioners and, at the same time, proves to be a reliable standard against which the legality of surrogate interventions can be tested.

Sadly, this does not seem to be the case. Best interests, in its present form, can be described as a complex legal notion that integrates diverse (and often conflicting) considerations and, arguably, reflects an unprincipled adoption of different value-theories that can be (at least partly) attributed to the permissive wording of the MCA and inconsistent judicial practice.

On the face of it, case law seems to endorse a predominantly *welfarist* approach. It has been repeatedly stated that the evaluation of best interests is 'akin to' a general welfare appraisal[23] that 'encompasses medical, emotional and *all other* welfare issues'.[24] Justice Hedley tells us:

> If one asks what has to be taken into account in considering the best interests of any human being [...] the answer is a very wide ranging one: his health, his care needs, his need for physical care and his needs for consistency. There is, of course, more to human life than that, there is fundamentally the emotional dimension, the importance of relationships, the importance of a sense of belonging in the place in which you are living, and the sense of belonging to a specific group in respect of which you are a particularly important person.[25]

The way in whichemotional well-being should be balanced against physical health and safety is a recurring theme of best interests assessments, especially in relation to placement decisions of elderly or vulnerable people. As it was argued in *Local Authority X v MM and KM*, '[p]hysical health and safety can sometimes be bought at too high a price in happiness and emotional welfare. [...] What good is it making someone safer, if it merely makes them miserable?'[26]

If one conceives best interests in terms of welfare, two basic factors will determine the outcome of a best interests assessment, i.e. (1) the way the concept of welfare is constructed and, somewhat relatedly, (2) the person who determines what serves the welfare of the incapacitated adult. Mental capacity law can be said to feature a whole palette of consequentialist value theories in this respect. The

---

23 See: *Re A (Medical Treatment: Male Sterilisation)* [2000] 1 FLR 549, [2000] 1 FCR 193 (Thorpe LJ). See also: *Re MB* [1997] EWCA Civ 3093, [1997] 2 FLR 426; *Re Y (Mental Patient: Bone Marrow Donation)* [1997] Fam 110; *Re GM; FP v GM and A Health Board* [2011] EWHC 2778 (COP).

24 *Re A (Medical Treatment: Male Sterilisation)* [2000] 1 FLR 549, [2000] 1 FCR 193 (Butler-Sloss LJ). Emphasis added.

25 *Re GM; FP v GM and A Health Board* [2011] EWHC 2778 (COP) [21] (Hedley J).

26 *Local Authority X v MM and KM* [2007] EWHC 2003 (Fam), [2008] Fam Law 213 [120] (Munby J).

MCA takes into account the 'actual preferences' of the incapacitated person when prescribing that the best interests assessor must consider, 'so far as is reasonably ascertainable', the 'present wishes and feelings' of the protected person.[27] Besides the epistemological difficulties that might arise with respect to ascertaining the present preferences of certain mentally disabled people,[28] a more fundamental issue is that people's actual desires do not always correspond to what are generally considered to be someone's 'objective' or 'long-term' welfare interests. Individual preferences are malleable[29] and they are even more malleable in the case of the mentally disordered who are considered more likely to make 'mistakes' when it comes to the determination of 'long-term' interests. Thus, present preferences are usually balanced against a set of other welfare considerations based on a fairly limited guidance provided by case law. Munby LJ in the *Re M* case states that the best interests assessor must, among other things, consider (1) P's degree of incapacity, because 'the nearer to the borderline the more weight must in principle be attached to P's wishes and feelings'; (2) 'the strength and consistency of the views expressed by P'; (3) 'the extent to which P's wishes and feelings are, or are not, *rational, sensible, responsible* and *pragmatically capable of sensible implementation* in the particular circumstances'.[30]

The next question is how a non-individualised notion of welfare interests is constructed. The starting point here is the presupposition that there are certain goods that promote the welfare of *any* human being irrespective of the individual's preferences or desires (typically e.g. physical health, emotional stability, adequate human relations, etc.). There have been various efforts in moral philosophy to come up with an account of objective welfare goods.[31,32] In practice, however, the

27 See: Mental Capacity Act 2005 s 4 (6).

28 E.g. autistic patients. Present preferences can be considered to be completely missing in other cases, e.g. in the cases of PVS (persistent vegetative state) patients.

29 Cf. the problem of adaptive preferences. See, e.g: Eyal Zamir, 'The Efficiency of Paternalism' (1998) 84 Virginia Law Review 229, 245.

30 *Re M (Statutory Will), ITW v Z and Others* [2009] EWHC 2525 (Fam), [2011] WLR 344 [35] (Munby J). Emphasis added.

31 Cf. the works of Martha Nussbaum. See, e.g: Martha Nussbaum, *Frontiers of Justice: Disability, Nationality, Species Membership*, Cambridge, MA: Harvard University Press, 2006; Martha Nussbaum, *Women and Human Development: The Capabilities Approach*, Cambridge: Cambridge University Press, 2000.

32 Cf. the works of Martha Nussbaum. See, e.g: Martha C Nussbaum, *Frontiers of Justice: Disability, Nationality, Species Membership* (Belknap Press 2007); Martha C Nussbaum, *Women and Human Development: The Capabilities Approach* (Cambridge University Press 2001).

choice of these seems to take place in a less 'principled' way. Judges usually appeal to welfare goods that are 'relatively undisputed'; some of these are probably best seen as being minimally or, 'at best', modestly objective.[33] Consider the following quote from a case in which the court had to decide whether the lack of pain and discomfort contributes to the welfare of patients in minimally conscious state:

> Able-bodied people frequently feel [...] that disability invariably restricts the enjoyment of life. With the growth in understanding about disability in recent years, however, has come an awareness that people with disability often experience profound enjoyment of life, within the limitations that their disability may impose. [Consequently] I do not accept the submission that the absence of pain or discomfort is not in itself a positive feature of life. Comfort and contentment can be, in my view, profoundly positive sensations.[34]

Even if one accepts that most welfare goods are construed in a minimally objective way, the balancing process seems to leave substantial space for the discretion of the best interests assessor. The MCA lays down no hierarchy between the elements of best interests and 'the weight to be attached to the various factors will, inevitably, differ depending upon the individual circumstances of the particular case'.[35] As mentioned before, there is some guidance with respect to present and past wishes and feelings but it seems that the weighing of the relevant best interests elements is often affected by the assessor's preferences, convictions and values. As Lewison J 'admits', 'having gone through these steps [i.e. the statutory checklist], the decision maker must then form a value judgment of his own giving effect to the paramount statutory instruction that any decision must be made in P's best interests'.[36]

The introduction of the so-called 'balance sheet' to the assessment procedure can be seen as an attempt to introduce a more formalized judicial approach. According to established practice, judges, when determining best interests, shall draw up a balance sheet indicating on each side of it the actual 'benefits' and 'disbenefits' associated with the proposed decision, together with the potential gains and losses

33 A modestly objective account of welfare goods would presumably come close to what is called an 'ideal preferences' theory. This approach focuses on the preferences one would hold under 'ideal epistemic conditions', i.e. in a calm and rational state of mind, paying heed to all the relevant information and without any external pressure or prejudice. Zamir (n 29) 235.

34 *W v M and others* [2011] EWHC 2443 (Fam), [2012] 1 All ER 1313 [235] (Baker J).

35 *Re M (Statutory Will), ITW v Z and Others* [2009] EWHC 2525 (Fam), [2011] WLR 344 [32] (Munby J).

36 *Re P* [2009] EWHC 163 (Ch), [2009] 2 All ER 1198 [39] (Lewison J).

and with the probabilities that the gain or loss might accrue.[37] Such an exercise can be seen as a useful tool to strike a 'fairer' (i.e. more elaborate, comprehensive and transparent) balance between competing interests but it still fails to give any specific guidance as to the balancing of the different factors.

3.3 Perfectionist elements

Although best interests assessment focuses mainly on welfare, there are certain elements that come closer to a 'perfectionist' ideal of the good.[38] A peculiar way to argue for the execution of a will or a gift on behalf of an incapacitated person is to refer to the person's 'abstract' interest in how he or she will be remembered after his or her death. As it was stated by Lewison J: '[…] what will live on after P's death is his memory; and for many people it is in their best interests that they be remembered with affection by their family and as having done "the right thing" by their will.'[39] Of course, it can be rightfully questioned whether a will or a gift executed by a surrogate decision-maker will be able to induce pleasant memories towards the incapacitated person.[40] It can also be disputed if 'being remembered in a certain way' is a valuable good as such, especially that the 'the having done

---

37 *Re A* [2000] 1 FLR 389 (Thorpe LJ) (no numbered paragraphs). See also, *Simms v An NHS Trust* [2002] EWHC 2734 (Fam), [2003] 2 WLR 1465; *Re S, London Borough of Newham v BS & Anor* [2003] EWHC 1909 (Fam), [2003] 2 FLR 1235; *Re S (Adult Patient: Family life), Sheffield City Council v S* [2002] EWHC 2278 (Fam); *Re GC* [2008] EWHC 3402 (Fam) (Hedley J); *Dorset CC v EH* [2009] EWHC 784 (Fam); *W, M and S v A NHS Primary Care Trust* [2011] EWHC 2443 (Fam). According to Lewison J in para. 44 of *Re P* [2009] EWHC 163 (Ch), [2009] 2 All ER 1198 the Parliament in the Mental Capacity Act actually endorsed the balance sheet approach which explains the continuing use of the concept. Obviously, there are certain situations where this approach cannot be applied; 'there is no balancing operation to be performed where a patient has a definite diagnosis of permanent vegetative state and where the futility of the treatment would justify its termination.' *Re CW, A Primary Care Trust v CW* [2010] EWHC 3448 (COP) [66] (Ryder J).

38 Where perfectionism is understood in the sense that certain states of affairs make a person's life good without necessarily increasing the person's welfare. *Cf.* Thomas Hurka, *Perfectionism* (Oxford University Press 1993) 17–8.

39 *Re P* [2009] EWHC 163 (Ch), [2009] 2 All ER 1198 [44] (Lewison J). This argument comes up in other Court of Protection cases as well. See *Re M (Statutory Will), ITW v Z and others* [2009] EWHC 2525 (Fam), [2011] WLR 344 [38] (Munby J); *Re D, VAC v JAD & Ors* [2010] EWHC 2159 (Ch), [2011] 1 All ER 859 (Hodge J).

40 Re *G (TJ)* [2010] EWHC 3005 (COP), [2010] EWCOP 3005 [63] (Morgan J).

the right thing' clause invites a moral judgment to which there may be more than one possible answer.

3.4 Autonomy and best interests

Patient autonomy is also a relevant factor in best interests assessments. It can acquire a welfarist interpretation, in the sense that leading an 'autonomous' life (i.e. a relatively independent life with adequate support) is often considered to bring along a positive change in the incapacitated person's well-being, such as a more stable emotional life, increased self-esteem and positive self-perception. Thus, freedom maximizing (enhancing) paternalism follows a welfare consequentialist reasoning in most best-interests decisions.[41]

Autonomy seems to acquire an 'inherent' value in the context of the substituted judgment standard. As it has been mentioned previously, the MCA integrates this standard into best interests when prescribing that the best interests assessor must consider the 'past wishes and feelings' and 'beliefs and values' that would influence the person's decision if he or she had capacity.[42] From a historical perspective, substituted judgments are not entirely alien to the English legal system; they had been used for a long time in relation to financial decision-making by chancery courts.[43] In these cases, the judge had to base his decision on the assumption 'that the patient becomes a sane man for a sufficient time to review the situation but knows that after a brief interval of sanity he will once more be as he was before'.[44] An 'objectified' version of this test also existed in relation to people who never had capacity. Here the court was to assume that the patient would have been 'a normal decent person, acting in accordance with contemporary standards of morality'.[45]

As things stand today, 'past wishes and feelings' can be overridden by welfare and perfectionist considerations subject to an almost uncontrolled process of

---

41 As opposed to a liberal perfectionist reasoning. See, e.g. *A Primary Care Trust v P and AH* [2009] EW Misc 10 (COP), [2011] 1 FLR 287 [64] (Hedley J). 'The advantages of independent living mean that at 24, it will open up experiences which other young people of his age are able to enjoy. It will protect his control of epilepsy through compliance with medication. It will enable him to develop a social and emotional independence of his own for after all, AH is most unlikely to outlive him. It will free him from the dominating effects of an obsessive and smothering relationship.'

42 See: Mental Capacity Act 2005 s 4 (6).

43 A landmark judgment here was *Re Hinde, ex parte Whitbread* [1816] 2 Mer 99 (Lord Eldon).

44 *Re L (WJG)* [1966] Ch 135 (Cross J).

45 *Re C (A Patient)* [1992] 1 FLR 51 (Hoffmann J).

judicial balancing.[46] This, arguably, opens the way to a kind of judicial 'hard paternalism' that might disrespect autonomous choices for the sake of promoting 'objective' welfare interests (if one accepts that the wishes and feelings of the autonomous past-self adequately represent the mentally incapacitated present-self).

3.5 Whose best interests?

In principle, the best interests test allows only for the consideration of the incapacitated person's interests – wider social issues and the interests of family members and carers are usually disregarded. Of course, in many situations the interests of others are inseparable from the interests of the protected person and judges come up with different solutions to take these into account. In the case of *Re Y*, for example, a mentally incapacitated woman was deemed to be the best suitable donor for her sister who suffered from pre-leukemic bone marrow disorder. The Court, when deciding about the permissibility of the donation, held that the bone marrow harvest was in Y's best interests as it would prolong her sister's life and Y would continue to receive emotional and psychological support from her sister 'in return'.[47] In the *Simms v Simms* case, Butler-Sloss LJ took a more straightforward approach. She attributed a decisive weight to the emotions and feelings of the patients' family members when making her decision in favour of an experimental medical treatment despite the fact that the experimental treatment was not expected to improve the conditions of the patients in *any* way.[48] In paragraph 64, she argues:

> The impact of refusal by this court of granting the declarations on each set of parents [...] would in my view be enormous and palpable. In a finely balanced case I should give the views of the parents and the effect upon them of refusal great weight in the wider considerations of the best interests test [...].

---

46 The same guidance applies as with present wishes and feelings. See *Re M (Statutory Will), ITW v Z and others* [2009] EWHC 2525 (Fam), [2011] WLR 344 [35] (Munby J). If the proposed surrogate decision does not affect the welfare interests of the protected person ('in the absence of any countervailing factors'), it is possible to base a best interests decision entirely on the substituted judgment standard. *Cf. Re G (TJ)* [2010] EWHC 3005 (COP), [2010] EWCOP 3005 [65] (Morgan J).

47 *Re Y (Mental Patient: Bone Marrow Donation)* [1997] Fam 110 p. 113, [1997] 2 WLR 556.

48 *Simms v An NHS Trust* [2002] EWHC 2734 (Fam), [2003] 2 WLR 1465. In the earlier *Re A* case, her wording was a bit more 'cautious' when stating that 'the question whether third party interests should ever be considered in a case concerned with the best interests of a patient ought to be left open'. *Re A (Mental Patient: Sterilisation)* [2000] 1 FLR 549, [2000] 1 FCR 193, 8.

Although these judgments show a tendency to move away from the individualistic approach of the MCA, the cases in which judges are willing to consider the interests of others seem to remain largely situation and 'judge'-specific.

3.6 The indeterminacy of best interests

Best interests decisions can be considered to be indeterminate in two ways. The specific situation that surrounds the decision-making procedure is factually 'given' in the sense that the surrogate decision-maker is bound to stay *within* the framework of facts when working out the actual formula of best interests. Evidence, however, is subject to evaluation and many best interests cases require the evaluation of complex evidentiary issues. Moreover, available options that can further an incapacitated person's interests are contingent on factors such as medical technology or financial resources. Strictly speaking, it might be in the best interests of a self-harming mentally ill patient to receive strong anti-psychotic medication if there are no sufficient resources and therefore no alternative treatment options to control his behavior. However, if such treatment methods are available, it can hardly be argued that strong anti-psychotic medication is in his or her best interests.

Best interests, as demonstrated previously, is also subject to the interpretation of the best interests assessor. The open texture of the concept can be explained with the need for a case sensitive approach when dealing with such complex issues as selecting the 'best' course of action for someone. Best interests will acquire different meanings in different situations and judicial arguments will often reflect an 'ad hoc' endorsement of values and moral principles that seem to underpin the 'desired' outcome of the case. The legislator's reluctance to give clear statutory guidance on best interests can also be explained with concerns of value neutrality, namely that any substantive guidance seems to *a priori* impose a certain conception of 'good' on the protected person. Thus, it is possible to understand the objectivity of best interests in a way that refers to the objectivity of the assessment procedure, for example to a procedure that is transparent, non-biased and, supposedly, free of any preliminary value judgments.

Against this backdrop, it is somewhat surprising to see judicial statements claiming that the 'best interests test ought, logically, to give only one answer' or that 'while a number of different courses might be lawful in any particular case, there could only logically be one best option.'[49] Obviously, much of this can be explained with a formalistic view of the legal system and with the common misperception

49 *SL v SL* [2000] EWCA Civ. 162, [2001] Fam. 15 (Butler-Sloss, Thorpe, Mance LJ) (no numbered paragraphs).

that personal value judgments can be removed from judicial (and, for that matter, moral) reasoning. In this sense, I see judicial appeals to the concept of 'objective' best interests as rhetorical tools to maintain two illusory presuppositions: (1) the belief in a legal system that can deliver one right answer even in the most complicated situations, and (2) the presupposition that it is possible to decide about issues that are deeply intertwined with personal values in a value-neutral way (*without* recourse to values).

Bibliography

Agamben G., Homo Sacer [:] Sovereign Power and Bare Life, transl. Daniel Heller-Roazen, Stanford: Stanford University Press (1998).
State of exception, transl. Kevin Attell, University of Chicago Press (2005).

Anscombe, G. Modern Moral Philosophy, the Journal of the Royal Institute of Philosophy (1958).

Althusser L., Balibar E. Czytanie Kapitału Wiktor Dłuski tr, 1st edn, Państwowy Insytut Wydawniczy (1975). Idéologie et appareils idéologiques d Etat, in Id., Positions (1964–1975) Editions Sociales (1976).

Amendola G., Maggioranza e Minoranza, La democrazia italiana contro il fascismo 1922–1924, Ricciardi (1960).

Arena F. J., La Identificación de la Acción Individual, Analisi e diritto, 1 (2008).

Arendt H., Origins of Totalitarianism, Harcourt Brace (1975).

Armstrong J., Conclusion, Slavic Review, 26 (1967).

Arneson R. J., Joel Feinberg and the Justification of Hard Paternalism, Legal Theory 11 (2005).

Barntones A. D., The Transparent State: Architecture and Politics in Postwar Germany, Routledge (2005).

Austin J., How to Do Things with Words, Harvard University Press (1975).

Alexy R., A Theory of Legal Argumentation: The Theory of Rational Discourse as Theory of Legal Justification, OUP (1989).
On the Concept and the Nature of Law, Ratio Juris, 21(2008).

Atienza M., Los Límites de la Interpretación Constitucional. De Nuevo Sobre los Casos Trágicos., Biblioteca Virtual Miguel de Cervantes (2005).

Badiou A., D un Désastre Obscur, Editions de l Aube (1998).

Baker Gordon P, Wittgenstein s Method. Neglected Aspects, Blackwell Publishing (2004) and PMS Hacker, Scepticism, Rules and Language, Basil Blackwell (1984).

Bańko M., ed, Wielki słownik wyrazów obcych, PWN (2003).

Baran, B. Przyczynek Do Krytyki Bieżących Badań Nad Racjonalnością, Studia Filozoficzne 2 (1980).

Barroso L., Interpretação e Aplicação da Constituição. Fundamentos de uma dogmática constitucional transformadora, Saraiva (2009).

Baum L. F., Dorothy and the Wizard of Oz, Mobile Reference (2008).

Benjamin W., Theses on the Concept of History, Llluminations, transl. Harry Zohn, ed. Arendt, H.,: Shocken Books, (1969).
Arcades Project, Eiland H., and McLaughlin K., trans. Harvard University Press (1999).

Berger P.L. and Luckmann T, The Social Construction of Reality: A Treatise in the Sociology of Knowledge, Anchor Books (1966).

Bernauer J., On Reading and Mis-reading Hannah Arendt, Philosophy and Social Criticism 11 (1985).

Bernstein R., Beyond Objectivism and Relativism: Science, Hermeneutics, and Praxis, University of Pennsylvania Press (1991).

Bessire D., Transparency: a two-way mirror? In Barrie Pettman ed. 30 years of IJSE: Festschrift in honour of Professor John O Brien, Emerald Group Publishing (2005).

Bix B., Cautions and Caveats for the Application of Wittgenstein to Legal Theory in Joseph K Campbell and Michael O Rourke and David Shier ed., Topics in Contemporary Philosophy MIT Press (2005).

Bobbitt Philip C, What it Means to Follow a Rule of Law? in Linda Meyer ed., Rules and Reasoning: Essays in Honor of Fred Schauer, Hart Publishing (1999).

Boyle J., The Politics of Reason: Critical Legal Theory and Local Social Thought, University of Pennsylvania Law Review (1985).

Breger C., The Leader s Two Bodies, Slavoj Zizek s postmodern political theology, Diacritics 31 (2001).

Bruner J. S., Foreword in Oscar G. Chase Law, Culture and Ritual: Disputing systems in cross-cultural context, NYU Press (2005).

Brunet P., Humpty Dumpty a Babel? Les juges et le vocabulaire juridique, 17 Chronique de Droit Européen et Comparé, Les Petites Affiches (2008).

Bud R., On the Social Production of Visual Difference, the Myth and the Machine: Seeing Science Through Museum Eye, in Fyfe G., and Law J. ed. Picturing Power: Visual Depiction and Social Relations, Routledge 36 (1988).

Burnett H., Introduction to Feminist Jurisprudence, Cavendish Publishing Limited (1998).

Butler J., Uwikłani w Płeć. Feminizm i Polityka Tożsamości, trans. Karolina Krasuska, Dobrzyńska T, Tekst. Próba Syntezy ed. Instytut Badań Literackich (1993).

Caillé A., Démocratie, Totalitarisme, Parcellitarisme, Revue du MAUSS 25 (2005).

Campbell T., The Legal Theory of Ethical Positivism, Dartmouth (1996).

Canovan M., Arendt s Theory of Totalitarianism: A Reassessment, in Dana Villa (ed.), The Cambridge Companion to Hannah Arendt, Cambridge: CUP (2000).

Clark H., Introduction: Depression and Narrative, Clark H., eds. Telling the Dark: Depression and Narrative, State University of New York Press (2008).

Coke E., Institutes of the Laws of England; Or a Commentary upon Littleton, Not the Name of the Author Only, But of the Law Itself, London: E. Brooke R. Brooke (1798).

Coleman J.L., and Leiter B., Determinacy, Objectivity and Authority, in Andrei Marmor ed., Law and Interpretation, Clarendon Press (1995).
Determinacy, Objectivity, and Authority in Andrei Marmor ed., Law and Interpretation: Essays in Legal Philosophy, OUP (1998).
Objectivity in Law and Morals, CUP (2001).

Collins H., Marxism and Law, OUP (1982).

Conquest R., The Great Terror: Stalin s Purge of the Thirties, Macmillan (1968).
The Harvest of Sorrow: Soviet Collectivization and the Terror Famine, OUP (1986).

Courtois S. et al. ed., Le livre noir du communisme, Paris, Robert Laffont (1997).

Crenshaw K., Race, Reform, and Retrenchment: Transformation and Legitimation in Anti-discrimination Law, Harvard Law Review 101 (1988).

Cyrul W., Legal Drafting: From Text to Hypertext in Law and Legal Cultures in the 21st Century: Diversity and Unity ed. M. Pieniążek, Oficyna Wydawnicza AFM, (2009).

Czarnota A. and Rodak L., Epistemologia, Aktywizm Sędziowski i Dwie Tradycje Prawa in Wieslaw Staśkiewicz ed., Dyskrecjonalność w Prawie: Materialy XVIII Ogólnopolskiego Zjazdu Katedr Teorii i Filozofii Prawa, Międzieszyn k. Warszawy 22–24 Wrzesnia 2008, LexisNexis (2010).

Danto C., Basic Actions, American Philosophical Quarterly (1965).

Delgado, R. The Inward Turn in Outsider Jurisprudence, Wm. & Mary Law Review, 34 (1993).
Jacques Derrida, De la Grammatologie, Editions de Minuit (1994).

D Arcy E., Human Acts, Clarendon Press, (1963).

Davidson D., Intention, Harvard University Press (1963).
Essays on Action and Events, Clarendon Press, (1980).

De Boeck A. and Van Hoecke M., The Interpretation of Standards clauses in European Contract Law in Standard Contract Terms in Hugh Collins ed. Europe: A Basis for and a Challenge to European Contract Law, Kluwer (2008).

de Kesel M., Act Without Denial: Slavoj Žižek on Totalitarianism, Revolution and Political Act, Vol. Studies in East European Thought, 56 (2004).

Derrida J., Force de Loi, Le Fondement Mystique de l Autorité, Galilée (1994).

Dewey J., Democracy and Education, Dover Publications (2004).

Dobrzyńska T, Tekst. Próba syntezy ed. Instytut Badań Literackich (1993).

Dolar M., I Shall Be with You on Your Wedding-Night: Lacan and the Uncanny, 58 (1991).

Dubisz S., Uniwersalny słownik języka polskiego PWN, Vol. K-Ó ed. S. Dubisz, Wydawnictwo Naukowe PWN, Warszawa (2008).

Durkheim E., The Rules of Sociological Method, Lukes S. ed., The Free Press (1982).

Duncan C., The Art Museum as Ritual In Carol Duncan Civilising Rituals, inside public art museum, Routledge (1995).

Dworkin R., Law s Empire, Belknap Press (1986).
The Theory and Practice of Autonomy, CUP (1988).

Eastlake C. L., A History of the Gothic Revival, Longmans, Green and Co (1872).

Feldman H., Objectivity In Legal Judgment, Michigan Law Review 92 (1994).

Feinberg J., Legal Paternalism, Rights, Justice and the Bounds of Liberty, Princeton University Press (1980).

Fink B., The Lacanian Subject: Between Language and Jouissance, Princeton University Press (1995).

Finnis J., Natural Law and Natural Rights. OUP (1979).

Fish S., Intention is All There is: a Critical Analysis of Aharon Barak s Purposive Interpretation in Law Vol. 28 Cardozo Law Review (2008).

Foot P., Hart and Honoré: Causation in the Law. The Philosophical Review (1963).

Foucault M., The Eye of Power in Colin Gordon ed. Power/Knowledge: Selected Interviews and Other Writings, 1972–1977, Pantheon books (1980).

Frankfurt H. G., The Problem of Action, American Philosophical Quarterly (1978).

Fraser D., Law after Auschwitz, Durham, NC: Carolina Academic Press (2005).

Frege G., Űber Sinn und Bedeutung, French translation; in Ecrits Logiques et Philosophiques, C. Imbert (1971).

Friedel W., Sigmund Freud: the loss of transparency in Weinert Friedel Copernicus, Darwin and Freud: Revolutions in the History and Philosophy of Science, Wiley-Blackwell (2008).

Friedrich C. and Brzeziński Z., Totalitarian Dictatorship and Autocracy, Praeger (1966).

Fuller L., Pashukanis and Vyshinsky: a Study in The Development of Marxist Legal Theory, Michigan Law Review, 47 (1949).
Positivism and Fidelity to Law — A Reply to Professor Hart, Harvard Law Review 71 (1958).

Fumerton R., and Kress K., Causation and the Law: Preemption, Lawful Sufficiency, and Causal Sufficiency Law and Contemporary Problems (2001).

Furet F., Le Passé d une Illusion, Calman Lévy (1995).

Furneaux J., Western Architecture: a Concise History, Thames & Hudson (1993).

Fuss D., Sanders J., Berggasse 19: Inside Freud s Office in Joel Sanders ed. Stud: Architectures of Masculinity, Princeton Architectural Press (1998).

Galdia M., Legal Linguistics, Peter Lang (2009).

Garapon A., O juiz e a Democracia – O Guardião das Promessas, Revan (2001).

Gardner J., Truth and Method, Continuum (1989).
Complicity and Causality Criminal Law and Philosophy (2007).

Gentile G., The Philosophic Basis of Fascism, Foreign Affairs, 6 (1928).

Giddens A., The Consequences of Modernity, Polity Press (1990).
Modernity and Self-Identity: Self and Society in the Late Modern Age, Stanford University Press (1991).

Gilligan C., In a Different Voice: Psychological Theory and Womens Development, Library of Congress Cataloguing in Publication (1993).

Girard R., The Scapegoat, transl. Freccero Y., Johns Hopkins University Press (1986).
Violence and Representation in the Mythical Text, Comparative Literature, 92 (1977).

Gizbert-Studnicki T., Język Prawny a Język Prawniczy, Zeszyty Naukowe Uniwersytetu Jagiellońskiego, Prace Prawnicze 55 (1972).
Konepcje natury rzeczy w zachodnioniemieckiej filozofii prawa, Etyka, 19 (1981).
Język Prawny z Perspektywy Socjolingwistycznej, Zeszyty Naukowe Uniwersytetu Jagiellońskiego, Prace z Nauk Politycznych 26 (1986).

Gleason A., Totalitarianism in 1984, Russian Review 43 (1984).

Glenn P., The Politics of Truth: Power in Nietzsche s Epistemology, Political Research Quarterly 57 (2004).

Goldman I., The Individuation of Action, The Journal of Philosophy (1971).
A Theory of Human Action (Princeton University Press (1976).

Gonzalez L., Las Paradojas de la Accion, Publicaciones de la Universidad de Alicante (2001).

Goodrich P., ed., Law and the Postmodern Mind: Essays on Psychoanalysis and Jurisprudence, University of Michigan Press (1998).

Habermas, J., Between Facts and Norms: Contributions to a Discourse Theory of Law and Democracy, MIT Press (1998).
The Structural Transformation of the Public Sphere: An Inquiry Into a Category of Bourgeois Society, Burger T. et Alii ed., MIT Press (1989).

Halberstam M., Totalitarianism As a Problem for the Modern Conception of Politics, Political Theory 26 (1998).

Halliwell S., Aristotle s Poetics ed. Stwphen Halliwell, Chicago University Press, Chicago (1986).

Halpin A., Reasoning with Law, Hart Publishing (2001).

Harding S., Rethinking Standpoint Epistemology: What is Strong Objectivity? in Cudd, A., et Alii ed. The Feminist Standpoint Theory Reader, Intellectual and Political Controversies, Routledge (2003).

Harris, J., The Marxist Conception of Violence, Philosophy and Public Affairs (1974).
Bad Samaritans Cause Harm, The Philosophical Quarterly (1984).

Hart H.L.A., Positivism and the Separation of Law and Morals, Harvard Law Review 71 (1958),
Postscript: Responsibility and Retribution in H.L.A. Hart, Punishment and Responsibility: Essays in the Philosophy of Law, Clarendon Press (1970),
The Concept of Law, Clarendon Press (1994).

Hart H.L.A., and Honoré T., Causation in the Law, OUP (1985).

Hartog F., and Revel J., Note de Conjoncture Historiographique ed., Les Usages Politiques du Passé,: Ecole des Hautes Études en Sciences Sociales (2001).

Hawking S., A Brief History of Time: The Updated and Expanded Tenth Anniversary Edition, Random House Publishing Group (1998).

Heidegger, M., Qu Appele t On Penser?, PUF (1959).

Herbert Z., The Collected Poems 1956–1998, Harper Collins (2007).

Holm L., What Lacan said re: architecture Critical Quarterly, 42 (2000).
The New Yorkers Architectural Theory Review, 12 (2007).

Honoré, T., Causation and the Remoteness of Damage, International Encyclopaedia of Comparative Law, 9 (1983).

Hunt, P., Ideology, Discourse, Ideology, Discourse, Ideology, British Journal of Sociology, 44 (1993).

Hurka T., Perfectionism, OUP (1993).

Jabłoński P. and Pichlak M., Miejsce Refleksji Krytycznej w Instytucjonalnej Wiedzy o Prawie LVII–LVIII Principia (2013).

Jackson B., Semiotics and Legal Theory, Deborah Charles Publications, Liverpool (1997), Linguistics and Poetics in Style in Language, Massachusetts Institute of Technology Press (1960).

Jacobson R., Jasińska – Kania A. ed. Współczesne teorie socjologiczne, Wydawnictwo Naukowe Scholar (2006).

Jasińska – Kania A. ed. Współczesne Teorie Socjologiczne, Wydawnictwo Naukowe Scholar (2006).

Jaworska A., Advance Directives and Substitute Decision-Making in Edward N Zalta ed., The Stanford Encyclopedia of Philosophy (2009).

Jencks C., The New Paradigm in Architecture: The Language of Postmodernism, Yale University Press (2008).

Joas H., Pragmatism and Social Theory, University of Chicago Press (1993).
The Creativity of Action, The University of Chicago Press (1996).

Kant I., Religion within the Boundaries of Mere Reason, Wood A. et Alii ed., CUP (1998).

Kantorowicz E. H., The King's Two Bodies, a Study in Mediaeval Political Theology, PUP (1997).

Kelsen H., Foundations of Democracy, Vol. 66 No. 1, Ethics (1955),
Causality and Accounting in Hans Kelsen, Essays in Legal and Moral Philosophy, Springer (1973),
Pure Theory of Law, Translation from the Second German Edition by Max Knight, University of California Press (1967).
The General Theory of Law and State, New York, Transaction Publishers (2006).

Kennedy D., Form and Substance in Private Law Adjudication, Harvard Law Review 89 (1976).

Kenneth K., Legal Reasoning and Coherence Theories: Dworkin s Rights Thesis, Retroactivity, and the Linear Order of Decisions, California Law Review, 72 (1984).

Kleinig J., Criminal Liability for Failures to Act Law and Contemporary Problems (1986).

Kłodawski M., Hipertekst a Technika Legislacyjna – o Możliwości Zmiany Paradygmatu Polskiego Prawodawstwa in A. Samonek ed. Teoria prawa. Między Nowoczesnością a Ponowoczesnością Wydawnictwo Uniwersytetu Jagiellońskiego, (2012).

Koczanowicz L., G.H. Mead, Wydawnictwo Uniwersytetu Wrocławskiego (1992).

Kopaliński W., Słownik Wyrazów Obcych i Zwrotów Obcojęzycznych z Almanachem, Oficyna Wydawnicza RYTM, (2006).

Kozak, A. Myślenie Analityczne w Nauce Prawa i Praktyce Prawniczej, Pichlak M. ed, Wydawnictwo Uniwersytetu Wrocławskiego (2010).

Kramer M., Objectivity and the Rule of Law, CUP (2007).

Krier L., Architecture: Choice or Fate, Papadakis Publisher (2007).

Kripke S. A., Wittgenstein on Rules and Private Language, Harvard University Press (1995).

Krips H., The Politics of the Gaze: Foucault, Lacan and Zizek, Culture Unbound, 2 (2010).

Kristeva, J., Woman Can Never Be Define, Marks E. et Alii ed., New French Feminism, Schocken Books (1984).
Women' s Time, Signs, 7 (1981).

Lacan J., Le seminaire, Encore, 1972–1973, ed. Miller J., Le Seuil (1975).
Ecrits: A Selection, Routledge (2005).

Laclau E. and Mouffe C., Hegemony and Socialist Strategy: Towards a Radical Democratic Politics, Verso (2001).

Langacker R., The Foundations of Cognitive Grammar: Volume I: Theoretical Prerequisites, Stanford: Stanford University Press (1999).

Laqueur W., Is There Now or Has There Ever Been Such a Thing As Totalitarianism?, Commentary, 80 (1985).

Latour B., Visualisation and Social Reproduction: Opening One Eye While Closing the Other… a Note on Some Religious Paintings, Fyfe G. et Alii ed. Picturing Power: Visual Depiction and Social Relations, Sociological Review Monograph, Routledge (1988).

Lecourtois C., Perception Architecturale et Image Urbaine, le Cas de CAEN Colloque International, Images et Citadinité, Algers (2005).
Espace de la Conception d' Architectures Judiciaires: les Nouveaux Palais de Justice, Diagonale Phi, Université du Lyon 4 (2010).

Legrand P., Comparative Legal Studies and the Matter of Authenticity, Leiter B. ed., Objectivity in Law and Moral, CUP (2001).

Leiter B., Law and Objectivity, Coleman. J. et Alii ed., The Oxford Handbook of Jurisprudence and Philosophy of Law, OUP (2004).

Losurdo D., Pour une Critique de la Catégorie de Totalitarisme, Actuel Marx, 35 (2004).

MacCormick, N. Legal Reasoning and Legal Theory, OUP, 1978.
Reasonableness and Objectivity, Notre Dame Law Review, 74 (1999).
Coherence in Legal Justification in Peczenik, A. et Alii ed. Theory of Legal Science, Theory of Legal Science: Proceedings of the Conference on Legal Theory and Philosophy of Science, Kluwer (1984).

Macdonald C. F., The Palaces of Minos at Knossos, Athena Review, 3 (2003).

Mack E., Bad Samaritanism and the Causation of Harm, Philosophy and Public Affairs (1980).

Mackie J. L., The Cement of the Universe: A study of Causation, Clarendon Press (1980),
Causes and Conditions Sosa A. et Alii. ed., Causation, OUP (1993).

MacKinnon C., Feminism, Marxism, Method and the State: An Agenda for Theory, Signs, 7 (1982).

Malinowski A., Redagowanie Tekstu Prawnego, Wybrane Wskazania Logiczno – Językowe Wyd. LexisNexis (2006).

Markham R., Rumania under the Soviet Yoke, Meador (1949).

Marmor A., No Easy Cases? in Andrei Marmor, Interpretation and Legal Theory, Clarendon Press (1992).

Markus T. A., Buildings and Power, Freedom and Control in the Origin of Modern Building Types, Routledge (1993).

Marrani D., Rituel (s) de Justice? Essay Anthropologique sur la Relation du Temps et de l' Espace dans le Procès, EME (2011).

Marx K. Thesis on Feuerbach Friedrich Engels, Ludwig Feuerbach and the End of Classical German Philosophy, Electric Book Co (2001).

McGuinness B., Approaches to Wittgenstein, Routledge (2002).

McQuire S., From Glass architecture to Big Brother: Scenes from a Cultural History of Transparency, Cultural Studies Review, 9 (2003).

Mill J. S., On Liberty, Norton (1975).

Miller J.-A., Extimité in Bracher, M., et Alii ed. Lacanian Theory of Discourse: Subject, Structure, and Society, NYU Press (1997).

Minow M., Justice Engendered, Harvard Law Review 10 (1986).

Moore M. S., Causation and Responsibility, Social Philosophy & Policy (1999).

Morawski L, Wstęp do Prawoznawstwa, Wyd. Dom Organizatora, Toruń (2006).

Mulcahy L., Legal Architecture: Justice, Due Process and the Place of Law, Routledge (2011).

Nalini J., Ética da Magistratura – Comentários ao Código de Ética da Magistratura Nacional – CNJ Revista dos Tribunais, (2009).

Nancy J., La Comparution/The Compearence: From the Existence of Communism to the Community of Existence, Political Theory, 20(1992).
La Communauté Désœuvrée, Christian Bourgois (1999).

Nino C. S., Introducción a la Filosofía de la Acción Humana, Editorial de la Universidad de Buenos Aires (1987).

Nussbaum M.C., Women and Human Development: The Capabilities Approach, CUP (2000).
Human Functioning and Social Justice: In Defence of Aristotelian Essentialism in Naffine N. ed., Gender and Justice, Ashgate Dartmouth (2002),
Frontiers of Justice: Disability, Nationality, Species Membership, Harvard University Press (2006).

O Neill O., Modern Moral Philosophy and the Problem of Relevant Descriptions, A. O Hear ed. Modern Moral Philosophy, Royal Institute of Philosophy Supplement, CUP 54 (2004).

Olivier K. Walsh L., ed. Contemporary French Feminism, OUP (2004).

Patterson D., Normativity and Objectivity in Law William and Mary Law Review, 43 (2001).

Pensky M., Method and Time: Benjamin s Dialectical Images in David S. Ferris (ed.) The Cambridge Companion to Walter Benjamin, CUP (2004).

Peregrin J., Wittgensteinstein a Pravidla Našich Jazykových her in R Kišoňová et Alii eds. Wittgensteinovské Skúmania, Schola Philosophica (2008).

Pichlak, M., Między Aksjologią a Ontologią Dyskursu Konstytucyjnego: Obiektywizacja Wartości w Prawie Przegląd Prawa i Administracji (2013).

Plasencia M., Who's Afraid of Humpty Dumpty: Deconstructionist References in Judicial Opinions in Seattle University Law Review, 21 (1997).

Poe E.A., The Purloined Letter in The Works of Edgar Allan Poe, Armstrong and Son 4 (1884).

Pope T., Counting the Dragon s Teeth and Claws: The Definition of Hard Paternalism, 20 Georgia State University Law Review (2004).

Popper K. R., The Open Society and Its Enemies, 5th ed., vol. I, Princeton: Princeton University Press (1966).

Postema G. J, Objectivity Fit for Law in Brian Leiter ed., Objectivity in Law and Morals, CUP (2007).

Procházka R., Dobrá Vôľa, Spravodlivý Rozum: Hodnoty a Princípy v Súdnej Praxi Kalligram (2005).

Raz J., The Authority of Law: Essays on Law and Morality, OUP (1979).

Resnik J. and Curtis D., Representing Justice: Invention, Controversy, and Rights in City-States and Democratic Courtrooms, Yale Law Library Series in Legal History and Reference, Yale University Press (2011).

Ricoeur P., From Existentialism to the Philosophy of Language 10, Criterion (1971).

Critique and Conviction: Conversations with François Azouvi and Marc de Launay, Columbia University Press (1998).

Soi-même comme un autre, L'Ordre Philosophique. Editions du Seuil, Paris (1990).

Speaking and Writing in Interpretation Theory: Discourse and the Surplus of Meaning, TCU Press (1976).

Task of Hermeneutics in Hermeneutics and the Human Sciences ed. J. B. Thompson, CUP (1981).

Refleksja Dokonana, Wydawnictwo Antyk, Kęty (2005).
The Hermeneutical Function of Distanciation in From Text to Action. Essays in Hermeneutics, Northwestern University Press, (2007).
Reflections on the Just, Chicago University Press (2007).
Explanation and Understanding in From Text to Action. Essays in Hermeneutics, Northwestern University Press, Evanston (2007).

Ricoeur P., Dauenhauer B., Ihde D, The Conflict of Interpretations, Ihde D. ed. Continuum, Northwestern University Press (2004).

Rodak, L. Objective Interpretation as Conforming Interpretation, Oñati Socio-Legal Series 1 (2011).

Rogozinski J., Hell on Earth: Hannah Arendt in the Face of Hitler Hirvonen A. et alii eds., Law and Evil: Philosophy, Politics, Psychoanalysis, London: Routledge (2010).

Romano S., Gentile G., Philosophe du Fascism, Vingtième Siècle, Revue d histoire, 21 (1989).

Rorty R., Objectivity, Relativism, and Truth, CUP (1991).

Rowe C. and Slutzky R., Transparency: Literal and phenomenal, Perspecta 8 (1963).

Russell B., Power A New Social Analysis, Routledge (2004).

Sarkowicz R., Stelmach J., Teoria prawa, Wydawnictwo UJ (1996).

Scales, A. The Emergence of Feminist Jurisprudence: An Essay, Yale Law Journal, 95 (1986).

Scalia A., Response in A Matter of Interpretation: Federal Courts and the Law, Princeton University Press (1997).

Schmitt C., Political Theology, MIT Press (1985).

Sen A. Positional Objectivity, Philosophy and Public Affairs, 22 (1993).

Sharlet R., Systematic Political Science and Communist Systems, Slavic Review, 26 (1967).

Shepherdson C., Foreword, Harrari, R., et Alii eds. Lacan s Seminar on Anxiety, Other (2001),
Lacan and the Limits of Language, Fordham University Press (2008).

Shorten R., Hannah Arendt on Totalitarianism: Moral Equivalence and Degrees of Evil in Modern Political Violence, King R., et Alii ed. Berghahn Books (2007).

Siemek, M. Idea Transcendentalizmu U Fichtego I Kanta: Studium Z Dziejów Filozoficznej Problematyki Wiedzy, Państwowe Wydawn Naukowe (1977).
Drogi Współczesnej Filozofii, 1st edn, Czytelnik, Filozofia, Dialektyka, Rzeczywistość Państwowy Insytut Wydawniczy (1982).

Simester P., Agency Law and Philosophy 16 (1996).

Singer J., The Player and the Cards: Nihilism and Legal Theory, Yale Law Journal, 94 (1984).

Skinner S., Tainted Law? The Italian Penal Code, Fascism and Democracy, International Journal of Law in Context, 7 (2011).

Sosa E., Normative Objectivity, in Ernest Garzón Valdés, Werner Krawietz, Georg Henrik von Wright, Ruth Zimmerling ed., Normative systems in Legal and Moral Theory, Duncker&Humbolt (1997).

Stelmach J., Brożek B., Methods of Legal Reasoning, Springer Science & Business Media (2006).

Sutcliffe A., Architectural History of London, Yale University Press (2006).

Taekema, S., Beyond Common Sense: Philosophical Pragmatism s Relevance to Law Nordisk Juridisk Tidsskrift (2006).

Tamas G. M., A Capitalism Pure and Simple, Left Curve, 32 (2008).

Taylor G. H., Ricoeur and Law: the Distinctiveness of Legal Hermeneutics ed. Davidson. S., ed. The Continuum International Publishing Group (2010).

Tismăneanu V., Stalinism for All Seasons, University of California Press (2003). Democracy and Memory: Romania Confronts Its Communist Past, Annals of the American Academy of Political and Social Science, 617 (2008).

The American Bar Association, Brief on Communism: Marxism, Leninism, its Aims, Purposes, Objectives and Practices, West Publishing (1951).

Thompson D., The Truth about Communism, Public Affairs Press (1948).

Tuori K., Critical Legal Positivism, Ashgate (2002).

Turri G., Gentile, G., Oblivion Rememberance and Criticism, Journal of Modern History, 70 (1998).

Van Hoecke M., Law as communication, Hart Publishing (2002).

von Wright G., On the Logic of Norms and Action in Risto Hilpinen ed., New Studies in Deontic Logic. Norms, Actions, and the Foundations of Ethics, Springer (1981).

Waldron, J., Normative (or Ethical) Positivism in Coleman J.L. ed., Hart s Postscript: Essays on the Postscript to The Concept of Law, OUP (2001).

Warat L., O Direito e sua Linguagem Cooperadora de Direito e Ciências Sociais (1976).
A Pureza do Poder (UFSC (1982),
Introdução Geral ao Direito – a Epistemologia Jurídica da Modernidade, Antonio S. Fabris (1995),
Territórios Desconhecidos – A Procura Surrealista Pelos Lugares do Abandono do Sentido e da Reconstrução da Subjetividade, Fundação Boiteux (2004),
A Rua Grita Dionísio! Lúmen Júris Editora (2010).

White A. R., Introduction in Alan R. White (ed.), The Philosophy of Action, OUP, (1968).

White H., The Value of Narrativity in the Representation of Reality, Critical Inquiry, 7 (1980).

Whitehead A. N., Science and Philosophy, Patterson: Littlefield, Adams and Co. (1964).

Wigley M., The Architecture of Deconstruction: Derrida's haunt, MIT Press (1995).

Willis D., The Emerald City: A study of Substance and Place in Daniel Willis, The Emerald City and Others, Essays on the Architectural Imagination, Princeton Architectural Press (1999).

Wilson G., and Shpall S., Action, The Stanford Encyclopaedia of Philosophy (2012).

Wimsatt W., Beardsley M. Intentional Fallacy in The Verbal Icon: Studies in the Meaning of Poetry University of Kentucky Press (1954).

Wittgenstein L., The Blue and Brown Books Harper Torchbooks (1965).
Philosophical Investigations, Blackwell Publishers (2001).
On Certainty, Basil Blackwell (1969).

Wolcher L. E., Ronald Dworkin's Right Answers Thesis Through the Lens of Wittgenstein Rutgers Law Journal 43(1997).

Wolff L., Inventing Eastern Europe, The Map of Civilization on the Mind of the Enlightenment, Stanford University Press (1994).

Wolska, D. Odzyskać Doświadczenie : Sporny Temat Humanistyki Współczesnej, Universitas (2012).

Womack-Weidner A., New York Opens Second Mega-Courthouse, Benchmark, Journal of the New York State Unified Court System 3 (2006).

Wronkowska S., The Rational Legislator as the Model for the Real Lawmaker in Polish Contributions to the Theory and Philosophy of Law Ziembiński, Z. ed., Editions Rodopi B. V. (1987).

Wróblewski J., Legal Language and Legal Interpretation, Law and Philosophy, 4 (1985).

Zajadło J., Łacińska Terminologia Prawnicza ed. Zajadło J., Oficyna a Wolters Kluwer business, (2009).

Zamir E., The Efficiency of Paternalism, Virginia Law Review 84 (1998).

Zapf C., and Moglen E., Linguistic Indeterminacy and the Rule of Law: On the Perils of Misunderstanding Wittgenstein Georgetown Law Journal 84 (1996).

Zieliński M., Interpretacja Jako Proces Dekodowania Tekstu Adam Mickiewicz University, Prace Wydziału Prawa, 54 (1972).

Ziembiński Z., Le Langauge du Droit et le Language Juridique. Les Criteres de Leur Discretement Archives de Philosophie du Droit, 19 (1974).

Zimmerman J., Administrative law, Oficyna a Wolters Kluwer Business (2014).

Žižek S., Grimaces of the Real, or When the Phallus Appears, No. 58, October (1991).

The Fragile Absolute: Or, why is the Christian legacy worth fighting for?, Verso (2000).

How to Read Lacan, Grant Books (2006).

Did Somebody Say Totalitarianism? Four Interventions in the (Mis)Use of a Notion, London: Verso (2011).

DIA-LOGOS
Schriften zu Philosophie und Sozialwissenschaften
Studies in Philosophy and Social Sciences

Herausgegeben von
Edited by
Tadeusz Buksiński & Piotr W. Juchacz

"*Dia-Logos. Studies in Philosophy and Social Sciences* is a peer-reviewed book series publishing valuable monographs and edited volumes on various aspects of philosophy and social sciences. The series is intended to be an interdisciplinary forum of deliberation according to our firm belief that challenges of the contemporary world require common and multilevel research. The *Dia-Logos* series does not represent a single ideology or school of thought, but it is open to different trends and various styles of reflection, trying to understand better the contemporary world. We invite the submission of manuscripts of monographs and edited volumes from academic philosophers and social scientists."

Bd. / Vol. 1 Piotr W. Juchacz / Roman Kozłowski (Hrsg.): Freiheit und Verantwortung. Moral, Recht und Politik. 2002.

Bd. / Vol. 2 Norbert Leśniewski / Ewa Nowak-Juchacz (Hrsg.): Die Zeit Heideggers. 2002.

Bd. / Vol. 3 Marek Kwiek (ed.): The University, Globalization, Central Europe. 2003.

Bd. / Vol. 4 Ewa Czerwińska-Schupp (Hrsg.): Philosophie an der Schwelle des 21. Jahrhunderts. Geschichte der Philosophie, Philosophische Anthropologie, Ethik, Wissenschaftstheorie, Politische Philosophie. 2003.

Bd. / Vol. 5 Danuta Sobczyńska / Pawel Zeidler / Ewa Zielonacka-Lis (eds.): Chemistry in the Philosophical Melting Pot. 2004.

Bd. / Vol. 6 Marek Kwiek: Intellectuals, Power, and Knowledge. Studies in the Philosophy of Culture and Education. 2004.

Bd. / Vol. 7 Marek Kwiek: The University and the State. A Study into Global Transformations. 2006.

Bd. / Vol. 8 Andrzej Przylebski (Hrsg.): Das Erbe Gadamers. 2006.

Bd. / Vol. 9 Ewa Czerwińska-Schupp (ed.): Values and Norms in the Age of Globalization. 2007.

Bd. / Vol. 10 Tadeusz Buksiński (ed.): Democracy in Western and Post-Communist Countries. Twenty Years after the Fall of Communism. 2009.

Bd. / Vol. 11 Marek Zirk-Sadowski / Mariusz Golecki / Bartosz Wojciechowski (eds.): Multicentrism as an Emerging Paradigm in Legal Theory. 2009.

Bd. / Vol. 12 Bartosz Wojciechowski: Philosophical Approach to the Interculturality of Criminal Law. 2010.

Bd. / Vol. 13 Marek Nowak / Michał Nowosielski (eds.): (Post)transformational Migration. Inequalities, Welfare State, and Horizontal Mobility. 2011.

Bd. / Vol. 14 Tadeusz Buksiński (ed.): Religions in the Public Spheres. 2011.

Bd. / Vol. 15 Bartosz Wojciechowski / Piotr W. Juchacz / Karolina M. Cern (eds.): Legal Rules, Moral Norms and Democratic Principles. 2013.

Bd. / Vol. 16 Ewa Nowak / Dawn E. Schrader / Boris Zizek (eds.): Educating Competencies for Democracy. 2013.

Bd. / Vol. 17 Tadeusz Buksiński (ed.): Identities and Modernizations. 2013.

Bd. / Vol. 18 Karolina M. Cern: The Counterfactual Yardstick. Normativity, Self-Constitutionalisation and the Public Sphere. 2014.

Bd. / Vol. 19 Vito Breda / Lidia Rodak (eds.). Diverse Narratives of Legal Objectivity. An Interdisciplinary Perspective. 2016.

Bd. / Vol. 20 Marek Woszczek: Platonic Wholes and Quantum Ontology. Translated by Katarzyna Kretkowska. 2015.

Bd./Vol. 21 Roman Hauser / Marek Zirk-Sadowski / Bartosz Wojciechowski (eds.): The Common European Constitutional Culture. Its Sources, Limits and Identity. 2016.

www.ingramcontent.com/pod-product-compliance
Ingram Content Group UK Ltd.
Pitfield, Milton Keynes, MK11 3LW, UK
UKHW041827100926
8556IPUK00002B/57